Graham Bartlett *with* Peter James

DEATH COMES KNOCKING

POLICING ROY GRACE'S BRIGHTON

PAN BOOKS

First published 2016 by Pan Books
an imprint of Pan Macmillan
20 New Wharf Road, London N1 9RR
Associated companies throughout the world
www.panmacmillan.com

ISBN 978-1-5098-1048-2

3 5 7 9 8 6 4 2

A CIP catalogue record for this book is available from the British Library.

Typeset by Ellipsis Digital Limited, Glasgow
Printed and bound by CPI Group (UK) Ltd, Croydon, CR0 4YY

With all my love for
Julie, Conall, Niamh and Deaglan
– my reasons for being

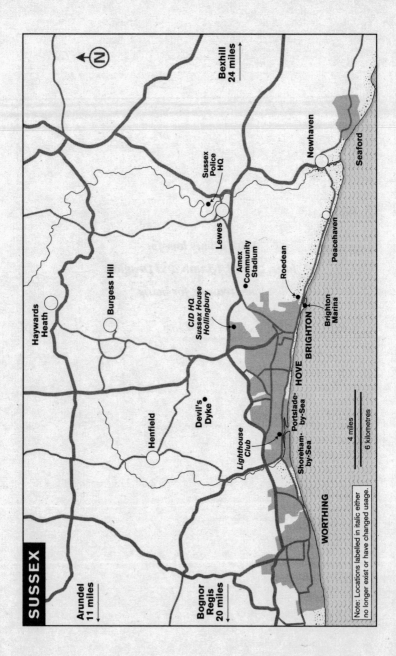

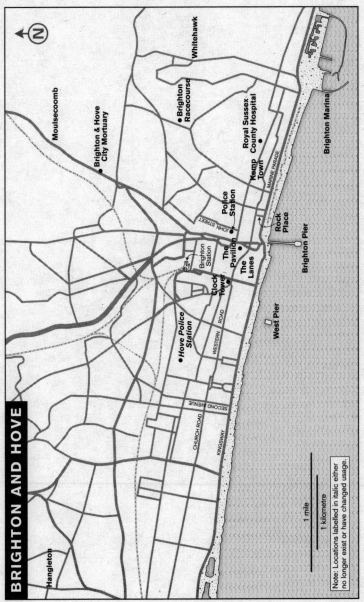

BRIGHTON AND HOVE

Hangleton

Moulsecoomb

Brighton & Hove City Mortuary

Whitehawk

Brighton Racecourse

Royal Sussex County Hospital

Kemp Town

MARINE PARADE

Police Station

JOHN STREET

Hove Police Station

Brighton Station

The Pavilion

Clock Tower

The Lanes

Rock Place

WESTERN ROAD

SECOND AVENUE

CHURCH ROAD

KINGSWAY

West Pier

Brighton Pier

Brighton Marina

1 mile

1 kilometre

Note: Locations labelled in italic either no longer exist or have changed usage.

Contents

Foreword

For many years my 'real life' Roy Grace, Detective Chief Superintendent David Gaylor, was my principal contact in Sussex
Police, working closely with me on the planning of my stories
and introducing me to any officers he felt would be helpful
to my research on each successive Roy Grace novel, to lend
my books the authenticity I try hard to maintain. When he
retired, I was immensely fortunate to have that baton taken on
by his good friend, Chief Superintendent Graham Bartlett,
himself a former senior homicide detective, who then became
Commander of Brighton and Hove Police.

Graham and I instantly hit it off and he was an invaluable
help to me for several years – also becoming a very good friend.
When he was coming up to retirement, at the almost ridicu-
lously young age of forty-eight, he again ensured that I had a
wide number of officers, at all levels, who would continue to
give me all the access and research help that I would need,
because he felt that the books gave the public an accurate and
informative insight into what is really involved in policing. He
also told me that he harboured ambitions to become a published author, and sent me examples of blogs he had written
over the years, for me to judge his penmanship skills.

I was very impressed by his writing style, which was clear,
lucid, very readable and, most importantly of all, highly engaging. He told me he would like to write a book in his retirement,
and asked if I would be willing to offer some guidance. I agreed
and arranged to meet up with him for a bite of lunch.

Then I had a true light bulb moment. Many people had been suggesting to me, over the years, that I should write a non-fiction book about my research with the police. As I neared the country pub where we were meeting, the idea crystalized in my head and I became increasingly excited. Throughout his thirty-year career, Graham had the unique experience of policing Brighton and Hove at every rank and had been involved in many of the cases that provided inspiration both for characters and for plots of my novels. He clearly had writing talent. Might he consider collaborating on a book with me about what it was really like to be a police officer in Roy Grace's Brighton? I felt I could work with him and steer him.

He agreed enthusiastically, so I pitched the idea to my agent and to my publishers who all loved it. I asked Graham to write the first chapter and send it to me.

When I read the opening lines, I groaned inwardly! Unlike in his blogs, he had fallen into the same trap of so many police officers who fancy themselves, after retirement, as authors. He had tried hard but still slipped into 'plod speak' from time to time, struggling to shake off his training that had taught him the detailed formality required in witness statements.

Graham needed direction, and if I could give him that, I knew he was capable of brilliance. I wondered how I was going to break it to him gently that his writing ambition was in danger of falling at the first hurdle unless he would accept my advice. Although he had been a very tough cop, afraid of no-one, he had a deeply sensitive side. I knew from those blogs that he was a genuinely capable writer, but would he take my criticism? And more importantly, what guidance could I give him?

I need not have worried. Graham happily absorbed the feedback, always eager to learn and improve. He knew he was a beginner but his passion and dedication drove him on. Together, we chose the stories, I coached him to find a new and more engaging writing style and the rest, as they say, is history. And often, quite a dark one ... but with more than a few light touches of true gallows humour.

Peter James
Sussex

PROLOGUE

Not long ago, some people would have urged you to buy just a one-way ticket to Brighton rather than bothering with a return – chances were you'd be dead before you could use the homeward part.

'Slaughterhouse of Europe', 'Crime Capital of Britain', 'Drugs Death Capital of the UK'. Soubriquets that have consistently defined the town of Brighton – now the City of Brighton and Hove – since Regency days, and with some accuracy.

Two women, separately murdered and stuffed into railway trunks; three members of the same family bludgeoned to death by a fourth; a Chief Constable struck down in his own office with a fire poker and a Prime Minister and her entire cabinet narrowly escaping assassination. All of this happened in and around Brighton.

And as you stroll jauntily down Queens Road from the railway station to the seaside, don't fantasize about building sandcastles on the beach; there is no sand, just the stones that Mods and Rockers hurled at each other during their pitched battles of the 1960s and again in the 1980s. Rising above you to the east is the hilltop racecourse, with its picturesque downland and coastal views; this was where the Razor Gangs prowled in the 1930s, keen to give a 'Glasgow grin' – the scar from a slash from ear to mouth which looks like a joyless smile – to anyone who crossed them.

Aside from these historical horrors, dreadful things still happen in Brighton today. On the surface it is one of the most stunningly beautiful cities in the UK, pulsing with individuality, host to a wide and diverse creative population, a long-favoured home to many great writers, artists and actors, including the late Sir Laurence Olivier, a thriving conference centre enjoyed by both the Conservative and Labour parties, with two renowned universities, one-off shops and a vast array of innovative restaurants and unique hotels. Yet it has always had a contrasting menacing side.

Brighton's dark underbelly has been its defining feature since it was first 'colonized' as a party town in the 1700s by the Prince Regent, who would become King George IV. Following the royal lead, posh toffs from London took to descending on the town for dirty weekends. In the mid-nineteenth century, the new railway line from the capital opened the place to the lower classes, among them, it seems, every enterprising villain who saw opportunity in its riches.

It's a place where for a few pounds ex-employees have snatched their former bosses off the street and beat them half to death, where bodies can be spirited away, chopped up and left as carrion, where you can be gunned down for just trying to sell a van. And, when the local outlaws aren't killing each other, they are robbing the elderly and confused or selling brick dust with a pinch of heroin to make a fast buck from desperate addicts. The grubbiness, the seediness and the violence are so powerfully drawn upon by Graham Greene as the backdrop for the wonderfully dark and evil *Brighton Rock*, the very novel that inspired internationally-acclaimed bestselling author Peter James to become a writer. And he had no further to look than Brighton, his home town, as the perfect setting for the Roy Grace novels.

How do I know all this? I was its police chief for four rollercoaster years. And I had policed its streets for nearly thirty. I loved it. I'm the only person in over a quarter of a century to have served in Brighton at every rank from Police Constable (PC) to Chief Superintendent; I saw it from every angle.

There was never a plan B for me. My mum, I think, quietly worried about my single-minded ambition to become a cop. She always supported me every step of the way, but was anxious of what my reaction would be if I failed. That would never happen.

If Sussex Police hadn't accepted me that snowy February morning in 1983 – the day the arrest of one of our nation's worst ever serial killers, Dennis Nilsen, was headline news – I would have hounded the other forty-two UK forces until one swore me in as a constable. Those constabularies were saved! I joined my home force a month later at the youngest possible age, just eighteen and a half, and weighing a mere 9st 10lbs.

Policing was in my blood. I idolized my Uncle Gordon, a life-long Brighton traffic officer, and my beloved father, John, who ran the Brighton and Hove volunteer Special Constabulary. I grew up wanting to be them. Gordon got to rush around with blue lights blazing and sirens wailing, yet still found time to drop off at our house for coffee and to let me sit longingly in his police car. Dad went to the football for free. His passion for public service, together with so much else about him, made him my lifelong inspiration. It was being a copper or nothing as far as I was concerned.

As my mum never fails to remind me, my first emergency call-out was to escort a family of ducks across a major highway in Bognor Regis. However, I didn't meet many people as inno-cent as those adorable creatures in the ensuing days and weeks of my fledgling career. My love for the job was instant. I was made for it, despite my boyish appearance drawing regular taunts of, 'Does your mum know you're out?' I rapidly hardened into an officer with a reputation as a voracious thief taker, and with it I developed the gift of the gab. I've heard it said many times, and it is without doubt true, that a police officer's best weapon is their mouth, whether negotiating with an armed villain, talking down a would-be suicide from a cliff top, or trying to placate an angry mob.

I was gutted when, after two years' service, I was posted to Gatwick Airport. While always crammed with passengers, the airport had little crime. To alleviate the boredom I joined the firearms team and later a plain-clothes squad. The enforced inactivity did mean, however, that I found Julie, who would become my wife, the love of my life and best friend.

I initially spotted her in her chic British Caledonian uniform checking in holidaymakers to far-flung destinations. It was her sassy smile and sparkling blue eyes that first drew my attention. Plucking up the courage to speak to her, all macho with gun on belt, I was hooked by her confident and playful manner. Nothing I could say drew a serious answer; everything was a joke. Here was a girl who loved life. The fact that she mistook me for another officer when she agreed to my first request for a date still comes up in conversation when I run out of more pithy put-downs.

However, it was after Gatwick, in 1989, that I landed the posting I felt born to. Brighton. I couldn't believe that they paid me to work there. Whether it was at the sharp end of the job, policing its then rough housing estates where returning after ten minutes to your patrol car you might find all four of its wheels stolen, or a year later starting my detective career in the city's Criminal Investigation Department (CID), I felt I had died and gone to heaven.

The thrills, however, were equally matched by fear and frustration.

As a young Detective Constable (DC) I had become exasperated arresting a gay couple for the umpteenth time for a series of horrendous attacks on each other. Their drunken rows would culminate in one or the other furiously stabbing his partner or making a similarly vicious and concerted bid to kill. Once, one crashed a marble chopping board on the other's head, breaking both skull and stoneware. Knowing the lack of protection the police or courts provided for domestic violence victims, particularly gay men at that time, I took the law into my own hands when I heard that our efforts to keep the attacker remanded in custody had been scuppered by the defence solicitor finding a bail hostel, assuring its manager that the crime was just a lovers' tiff.

When Judge Gower discovered I had phoned the hostel and told them the full violent nature of the charges, prompting them to withdraw their offer, he was incandescent with rage. His Honour spelt out all sorts of career- and liberty-threatening consequences to me but he had no option than to leave the would-be murderer in jail. Privately I am sure he was grateful to me, although he never said so.

Brighton was a place that shocked, shamed and enchanted me every day: racing around its streets on 'blues and twos' from pub fight to robbery; dodging bricks and roof tiles thrown by unknown foes while leaping from the police car on the city's run-down estates; or praying that back-up would get to me before the approaching knifeman carried out his threat. It was all in a day's work.

My despair when another thoroughly decent son or daughter, brother or sister, husband or wife had been slain by some drunken, jealous or greedy scumbag was always overtaken by a single-minded obsession to go after the bad guys and see them locked up for as long as the courts dared.

It was much later in my career that I met the novelist Peter James. His Roy Grace books had already topped the bestseller lists world-wide, not least because of the precision with which he describes Brighton and Hove and its policing. As the city's Superintendent, and later its Divisional Commander, I was delighted with the accurate picture Peter painted of the challenges we faced. Together with the Chief Constable, I ensured that we gave him access to every research opportunity we could, while knowing of course that some operations were just too secret to share.

I have had a lifelong ambition to write, but running the UK's second-busiest police station kind of got in the way. Peter and I had often discussed his interest in writing a non-fiction book about policing his home area of Brighton and Sussex. Me hanging up my handcuffs gave us the chance we needed. This book would be an opportunity to chronicle the events that had the most impact on me during my service – the exciting, the intriguing and the distressing. It would set out the inner conflicts of being an operational and high-ranking police officer in a crazy city, as well as drawing parallels with Roy Grace's adventures. We felt it would be an absorbing read both for fans of Peter's crime novels as well as all people interested in the inner world of the police.

For my part, to have such a wise, gentle and hugely successful author as Peter James working alongside me on my first, albeit co-written, book is a huge honour. As he coaxed my style from 'we were proceeding in a northerly direction' to something more readable, and restructured the accounts to achieve greater impact, his patience knew no bounds.

We both hope you enjoy the insight this book offers you. It's been a joy to write but has also awoken some sleeping demons in me. It will show you what it feels like to dedicate your life to policing your own community and the pain, the laughs, the anger and pride that come as part of the package.

I'm going to tell you all about it. I'm going to tell you of the horrors that happen to people. I'm going to tell you what it really feels like having to clear up the carnage caused by others. I'm going to tell you how we cope, what happens when we don't and the personal cost we pay.

I'm going to tell you what it's like to police Roy Grace's Brighton.

1: MAN DOWN

One of the fascinations of policing is that you never really know what is around the corner. A much-loved and respected Brighton public order inspector I knew, Andy Parr – now sadly deceased – achieved his fifteen minutes of fame by theorizing that increases in violence were linked to the lunar cycle. Andy, almost single-handedly, led the fight against the drunken mobs who, each weekend, seemed hell-bent on turning the city into a war zone. His research indicated that people became more aggressive and anti-social around the full moon. While not entirely scientific, his theory attracted a good deal of media discussion and hilarity. It was as valid as any other explanation for when and why shit happens.

The gripping climax to *Looking Good Dead* is a prime example of how events can erupt from nowhere. One minute Detective Superintendent (D/Supt) Roy Grace and Detective Sergeant (DS) Norman Potting are methodically studying a list of sulphuric acid suppliers. The next Grace's sidekick, DS Glenn Branson, bursts in with the final piece of the jigsaw and they race off to evil Carl Venner's lair to rescue the imprisoned Bryces.

Crashing into the warehouse, the team are confronted by not only the imminent deaths of hostages Tom and Kellie Bryce, but their own too. The shout of *'Police, drop your gun'* is rudely answered by a muzzle flash and bullets whistling past. Too late to retreat and yell for back-up. Too late for anything but find cover, move forward and save the innocent. Everyone is a target. Rounds ricochet off walls as cement dust showers the cops.

Branson takes a hit but everyone else keeps going, drawing fire and rescuing the two captives from certain death.

That is the reality of the danger that police officers face every day. In my career I've met many thousands of officers and almost all of them, at some point, have been in a situation where their life was on the line.

Sussex isn't awash with guns. The county averages thirteen murders a year. By comparison Dallas, which has a similar population, has around ten times that. That is dwarfed by Los Angeles where, the Chief Medical Examiner told Peter James on a recent visit to the morgue, there are twenty-five gunshot deaths on a quiet weekend.

Although armed crime in Sussex is rare, when it happens it is terrifying. In 1984, as a very young bobby, I had an early taste of that.

Nineteen years old and with only a year's service I was still wide-eyed at the prospect of booking on duty each day. Every time I donned the blue serge uniform, I would be gripped by a rush of anticipation for the thrills or horrors that awaited me.

One Sunday in the March of that year, I'd just started a late shift. For a change I was allowed the privilege of crewing one of the response cars, rather than plodding the empty streets of Bognor Regis, thirty miles west of Brighton. We used to wonder whether Chris de Burgh had Bognor in mind when he wrote his lyrics for 'Fatal Hesitation' about empty cafes, sodden streets and the desolation of a holiday resort in the rain.

My partner for the day, Steve Clarke, had not been on our team much longer than I. Unlike me, however, he was not an eager youngster. He was a squat, gruff, roll-up puffing, thirty-something joker, whose CID career had come to an abrupt end due to his marksmanship with a bread roll at the 1982 Christmas party. The Detective Chief Inspector (DCI) whose eye he blacked with the flying food clearly lost his festive spirit and busted Steve back to uniform in his first act of the new year.

Despite Steve's fall from grace and sometimes brusque manner, he liked me. I think he saw his own early enthusiasm reflected in my exuberance. He took time to teach me the job, warts and all, and I often wonder whether I would have had such an early eagerness to become a detective were it not for Steve.

That dull, dank day he and I settled into the creaking Hillman Avenger ready for an eight-hour shift of who knows what. I fired up the ageing analogue radio as Steve coaxed the car into life. Immediately we heard the call that we all dread and will never forget.

'Whisky two zero two, ten twenty. Officer shot, offenders made off.' Ten twenty was the code given for a police emergency: one of our own was being attacked. It always triggered a reflex reaction among all cops to drop everything and dash to wherever help was needed.

I instantly recognized the voice. PC Bob Elliott was a dishevelled, battle-worn thief taker; a real old-fashioned bobby who was at home on the streets. Some coppers attract trouble. If it's going to happen, it's going to happen to them, and they have a name – '*shit magnets*'. Bob was, by any measure, king of the shit magnet hill. He'd already won two Queen's Commendations for Brave Conduct. Police officers take the view that there is a thin line between courage and stupidity. Bob was never stupid and he was braver than most. He used to get mercilessly ribbed for the trouble he attracted but this time we knew it was different. This was really scary.

'Bloody hell, Graham, did Bob say what I think he said?' snapped Steve.

'Yes but I didn't catch a location.'

'Right. Let's go!' He flipped the blue lights and two tones on and crunched the gears into action.

I hung on for dear life as we two-wheeled out of the police station back yard. With no location yet revealed, I wasn't sure where we were heading but guessed that Steve's experience told him to just get on the road. My senses battled with the sound of the roaring engine, the smell of burning tyres and the ordeal of being tossed around in the car. I felt as Grace must do when Branson clicks into his red mist driving skills.

Over the radio came a clamour of units offering help, trying to make sense of what craziness had erupted on this sleepy Sunday afternoon.

Bob and his partner Tim Phillips were on an anti-crime initiative which meant they had free rein to patrol hotspots in and around the resort of Bognor, its neighbour Littlehampton and the majestic inland cathedral and castle town of Arundel.

The details emerging suggested that Bob and Tim had stopped a car on the main Brighton to Portsmouth trunk road, the A27, just as it swept into the shadow of Arundel Castle. Something about the two occupants studiously ignoring the marked police car as they drove past, together with them looking just a bit out of place in the Peugeot 604 they were driving, sparked a hunch that all was not right.

Initially the two occupants, both Londoners, had dutifully stood at the roadside while they tried to bluff their way past the officers. However, they had not reckoned on being caught by two of the most intuitive cops in Sussex.

These two took nothing at face value and when the story the men put up of just going for a Sunday drive didn't ring true, Bob and Tim got suspicious and announced their intention to search them and the car. In a flash the mood changed and the men bolted back towards the Peugeot in a desperate attempt to flee.

Bob grabbed one and a furious struggle followed, the two men grappling on the verge with speeding cars whistling past inches away. As Tim leapt for the other, his man suddenly pulled a handgun and aimed it at the startled officer. Both officers desperately lunged towards him, reaching him just in time to divert his aim. A deafening explosion made time stand still. A fiery pain tore through Tim. Then all four men, fighting furiously, fell into a drainage ditch. A passer-by leapt from his car and dashed to the aid of the officers. Thinking only about his safety, they ordered him away fearing he would be shot too. Then Bob was pistol-whipped across the face with the Luger handgun and was stunned by the heavy blow. This gave the assailants the time to break free. They dashed to their car and screeched off.

In horror, Tim looked at the serious gun shot wound to his groin.

I was shell-shocked. The police is a big family and, even though I did not really know Tim at that time, I felt for him like a brother. It was the first and only time in my career that I was on duty when an officer was shot. That shock never left me.

It was only surpassed fifteen years later when I came on duty, again on a Sunday, to find that twenty-six-year-old traffic PC Jeff Tooley had been callously mown down, dragged along the road and killed while trying to stop a white Renault van for speeding. To this day, a memorial stands where Jeff fell, close to Shoreham Harbour. His killer, John Heaton, has long since finished his seven-year sentence. Jeff's family are still serving theirs.

A colleague down and gunmen on the loose, this was big. Very big. A frantic search of the area followed.

Almost straightaway another call came over the airwaves. The fugitives had dumped their Peugeot near Arundel's Catholic cathedral, forced the occupants of a silver/grey Ford Sierra out at gunpoint and sped off in that car.

My instinct would have been to rush directly to the scene but Steve's, honed by years of experience, was that we would be needed elsewhere. He knew a ring of steel was being set up and we would be part of it. Had we all acted like bees to a honey pot, the attackers would have had their pick of exit routes.

'We just have to do as we are told now, Graham,' coached Steve. 'We'll sit up somewhere between Bognor and Arundel until we are sent where we are needed.'

A strange silence descended, no chatter from the radio, nothing to distract us from our anxious thoughts. Even Steve's usual outrageously sarcastic quips had gone. Scouring the road for any sign of the gunmen, we were focused on nothing but what had happened and what we could do about it. We had to find them before they did something even worse. Desperation grew.

Then, about forty-five minutes later, an eerie radio message broke the silence.

'Whisky three zero three, I think we are behind the gunmen's car now. Can you confirm the registration number we are looking for? We can see two males inside. We are on the A29 outside Arundel.'

'Bloody hell, they haven't got far. Less than ten miles. They must be either lost or desperate not to break out too soon,' remarked Steve.

'Shall we head up that way?' I suggested.

'We are no use here now. We'll drift north towards them but let's allow the radio controllers to do their job and tell us exactly where they want us.'

'KB to Whisky three zero three, do not, repeat do not, approach. Keep the vehicle in sight only. Back-up is on its way,' ordered the gruff controller.

Silence.

'KB to Whisky three zero three, I repeat back-up is on its way, keep your distance. Do you receive, Whisky three zero three?'

Silence.

Suddenly the airwaves exploded with desperate offers from other car crews to rush to assist Whisky three zero three.

'This is Ops 1. All units except Whisky three zero three, radio silence immediately. Whisky three zero three, come in … Whisky three zero three, come in,' urged the control room inspector.

More dreadful silence.

'Any unit in the vicinity of Whisky three zero three's last location, come in.'

Again a cacophony of desperate offers to help.

We edged towards the location, hoping that our stealth would allow us to glimpse the wanted men. We were determined to catch them but more so to find Whisky three zero three and the comrades I'd never met. The silence was terrifying. There was nothing. No update, no response to calls. My blood ran cold. It slowly dawned on me that the crew had been kidnapped. Perhaps executed.

Our focus had shifted from concern about Tim to what was happening now. Tim would be treated; he was safe. Now we had two other cops to worry about. This is part of the police way. Emotion and worry are pushed aside when there is a more pressing hazard. Time was against us if we were going to find the crew of Whisky three zero three alive.

Soon reports were coming in from members of the public at a roadside garage on the A29 of two men jumping from a Sierra into a police car and then speeding off. The few witnesses had their wits about them and realized that something was badly wrong with what they had seen. Other officers rushed to the scene and quickly saw the abandoned stolen Sierra with terrified people around it. The silence from Whisky three zero three could only mean that the crew of that car had indeed been kidnapped and were now in mortal danger.

'All units stand by for a description of Whisky three zero three,' came the command through the radio set. We knew it was a marked police car but there were now dozens of those in the area. We needed to be told who was friend and who was foe.

'All units, Whisky three zero three is a marked Sussex Police Vauxhall Cavalier, registration A280 DNJ. Its crew are PC Liam Codling and PC Robin Rager from Petworth. Any sightings report in as urgent but do not, repeat do not, approach.'

The names meant nothing to me but the model of car was good news. The force had only just started to change its fleet from Avengers to Cavaliers and the registration number indicated that it was one of the newer models. At least we could eliminate on sight the aged rust buckets the rest of us were in that day.

Most of the force seemed to have flooded the area and we were all allocated places to search and places to wait. This was before any of the technology that we now take for granted. We were in open country but, in those days, had none of the benefits of helicopters, mobile phones, Automatic Number Plate Recognition (ANPR) or even secure radios. Then, we only had our eyes and ears. At one point my Uncle Gordon drove up in his traffic car to where we were parked. As one of the force's finest advanced drivers I should have realized that he would be drafted in from his usual Brighton patch. Just a quick hello and check on each other's welfare was all we had time for. The task in hand was far too pressing for any more pleasantries.

I tried not to think the unthinkable but as the day dragged on I started to fear the worst. Steve knew Liam and Robin well and was getting more and more anxious. Roles were reversed as I, 'the boy', spent the next six hours trying to reassure him and keep us both focused on the search.

Finally, as dusk drew in, the hopeless radio silence was broken.

'Whisky three zero three to KB, do you receive?'

'Isn't that them?' shrieked Steve.

'It's their call sign. Listen!'

'Whisky three zero three. We are safe and unharmed. We've been released, stand by for details of the targets.'

With a breathtaking composure they announced to the waiting force that they had been taken to a large secluded house where they, and its residents, were held at gunpoint.

They continued, 'The offenders have made off with four hostages in a red Talbot Sunbeam saloon car. There are two adult hostages, male and female, and two children. One of the adults is driving and one is in the front passenger seat. The gunman is in the back seat of the car between the two young children. The other offender is secreted in the boot of the car. All caution must be exercised. The man in the back seat is armed. Repeat, the man in the back seat is still armed.'

Just when we thought this couldn't get any worse we were faced with armed men, mobile, with civilian hostages – including children. However, at least we had a starting point and a swift relocation of officers followed.

Soon, a sharp-eyed police motorcyclist spotted the vehicle. His urgent call drew dozens of police cars to him and a desperate chase through rural Sussex followed. No way were these men escaping.

As we listened to the hurried, brusque radio messages from those units with speed or firepower that were being rushed forward, a very familiar voice stood out. The distinctive Derbyshire brogue could be only one person.

We recently had a cohort of police cadets posted to Bognor Police Station. Jim Sharpe was one of them. He was on my team and became a lifelong friend.

Jim was a scraggy seventeen-year-old who needed a fair degree of help to make his uniform fit for public eyes and often had to be coached not to speak to our old-school ex-paratrooper sergeant 'Chas' MacInnes as if he were some long-lost drinking partner. Jim was a work in progress. That said, he learned quickly and was great fun to be around.

During this period he was on his traffic attachment. That day he was being driven by one of Traffic's most able and experienced officers, PC 'Micky' Finn, in the unmarked car whose call sign was Tango one seven one. As he was in a plain car, the commanders seemed eager to move Micky up close to the target.

They didn't seem to know that, rather than it containing two highly trained advanced drivers, one of its crew was barely out of school. Even the excitable updates did not provide the clue.

The convoy was heading west towards Emsworth Bridge on the border of Sussex and Hampshire. Trying to keep up with the commentary and updates became impossible when Hampshire units started to butt in. As we were about to enter their jurisdiction, they would have a say how this chase would continue.

When we arrived at the bridge, I saw the whole carriageway saturated in orange and white light shimmering with strobing blue beacons. It had the appearance of a movie set. I could just make out in centre stage a small red saloon, alien amid the surrounding fleet of high-performance squad cars. A ring of black-clad officers had their rifles trained on the rundown Sunbeam. Even as a rookie I knew the stand-off was on a knife edge. Any decision to force an ending would depend entirely on the safety of the hostages.

The Ops 1 Inspector ordered everyone just to keep watch and no unarmed units were to move closer to the car. The silence across the airwaves was deafening, contrasting sharply to the clamour that had been the soundtrack to the chase just moments ago.

In frustration the inspector demanded, 'Any unit close to the target vehicle able to provide an update?'

Silence.

'Any unit?' repeated Ops 1.

To my horror, his imploring was answered by that unmistakable Buxton accent.

'Tango one seven one. Well. There's lots of men with lots of guns. I'm only a cadet and I don't know what else to say.'

Unbeknown to most of us, and certainly to Jim and Micky (who'd made the mistake of leaving the cadet alone in the car for that moment), the Chief Constable was at Petworth Police Station listening to the manhunt unfold.

'Who is that on the radio?' he demanded to know.

Feet shuffled and throats were cleared as a local inspector standing at the Chief's side divulged, 'Er, that is, er, that's. Well, that's Cadet Sharpe, sir.'

'Cadet? Did you say cadet?' bellowed the boss. 'What the bloody hell is a cadet doing in the car directly behind two men who clearly want to kill police officers?'

Nothing could be done now but some serious explaining would be required when all this was over.

The order came that only armed units and traffic cars would be allowed to enter Hampshire if the target moved off. Suddenly there was a roar of engines as the Sunbeam darted forward and accelerated away. Jim was rudely ejected from Tango one seven one as four heavily armed officers from the Special Operations Group launched themselves inside a split second before Micky joined the pursuing pack.

We waited for about five minutes before we were all instructed to head back to base. We had done our bit. We now had to leave it in the hands of our neighbours and the specialists lucky enough to be allowed to continue.

The last thing I remember as we turned to make our way back to Bognor was seeing a disgruntled Cadet Jim Sharpe shuffling up to departing police cars trying to hitch a lift back.

We learned that on the bridge, while a brave Hampshire officer, PC George Summers, had tried to negotiate with the gunmen one of them twice threatened to shoot a hostage and George himself. In the interests of safety, they had to be allowed through the road block. As the pursuit continued they ended up on the main A3 road where they tried to hijack a lorry. As they did so, one of the kidnappers held a hostage as a human shield. Miraculously, PC Summers was able to fire off one shot, hitting the gunman in the arm. This gave time for the men to be rushed, cuffed and arrested.

Intelligence suggested they may have been en route to

confront a local drug dealer – a plan that Tim and Bob seemed to have thwarted. The gunmen, Robert Dew and Rudolf Cooke, received eighteen- and ten-year prison sentences and thankfully Tim was able to return to work and managed two promotions before his retirement. Bob, Tim and George Summers were awarded Queen's Gallantry Medals.

While these events are thankfully rare and Brighton is neither Dallas nor LA, it has had its fair share of shootings and grudge killings over the years.

In 1976, my uncle Gordon was the first officer at the scene of a shooting in the car park of Grace and Branson's favourite pub, the Black Lion, on the outskirts of Brighton. Barbara Gaul, the socialite and fourth wife of millionaire property developer John, had been gunned down in cold blood while she was visiting her three-year-old daughter. Gordon had been unarmed and, completely against the safety and forensic conventions of today, had been sent from the scene to the address of a potential suspect. It was almost universally believed that John Gaul was behind the killing. Even some of those who were convicted, as well as Barbara in her dying words, pointed the finger at him.

Another apparent crime of passion involved twenty-four-year-old jailbird Mark Ryder who, in 1993, stalked the sprawling streets of Whitehawk hunting Stuart McCue.

Whitehawk is Brighton's other large council estate. Sitting in the shadow of the hilltop race course, its transition from being the traditional home of the city's roughest and most violent criminals, as so accurately described in *Dead Man's Footsteps*, to a cohesive proud community was complete by the early 1990s. Ryder eventually found McCue outside the Valley Social Club, a community centre crucial to the regeneration of this once run-down area of east Brighton.

Ryder was on the run at the time, having escaped two years earlier during a boat trip organized by Lewes Prison. He had a history of this; he had previously escaped from a Young Offenders Institute in Kent.

While both Ryder and McCue were in prison, they had fallen out over a girl they shared a love interest in, Emma Devoy. Mark was scared of Stuart and therefore spent much of his time in hiding in New Milton, Hampshire. He would only venture into Brighton armed.

That Saturday afternoon, he and two 'minders' cruised the city's streets. Despite claiming to be frightened of him, it was obvious that Ryder was on the lookout for McCue. Spotting him among a crowd outside the club he calmly stepped from the car and blasted him four times with a sawn-off shotgun. As McCue tried to crawl away Ryder fired his final shot. All this in full view of his victim's new partner, his young nephew and nieces and several other shocked bystanders.

Ryder leapt back into the car and, at terrifying speed, wheel-spun off the estate, followed soon by a fleet of police cars. He drove recklessly into the city centre, racing the wrong way round a major one-way system close to the Royal Pavilion and eventually crashing through a car park barrier just as crowds of shoppers were heading back to their vehicles. He and his minders abandoned the car in the multistorey and managed to evade the search that followed.

As a DC by now awaiting promotion, I was called to help in the hunt. One of my tasks was to interview the girl at the centre of it all.

Emma came from a lovely family and was a delightful young lady herself. She was clearly torn between the two rogues and had dearly loved them both at different times. Over a twelve-hour period we had to coax all the painful background from her. It was a long, hard slog and we had to tread carefully. I really felt for her; her twenty-five pages of statement showed that none of this was her fault, only that she had been caught in the middle. We treated her well, shopping for her so that she could have a change of clothes, letting her freshen up and giving her something decent to eat.

Painstaking investigations eventually located Ryder and his cronies. Mark himself was caught days later, holed up in a squat in London. He was tried, convicted and sentenced to life imprisonment. Twelve years later, he won further national infamy by escaping from prison for the third time in his delinquent career, eventually being caught in Malaga, Spain.

Each of these incidents serves as a reminder that with an unarmed police force, it is the courageous thin blue line who risk happening upon tooled-up villains willing to kill in the name of freedom or revenge.

2: A VERY BROKEN HOME

There is never a good time to get murdered. Most people would rather avoid it altogether. But if you were going to be bludgeoned to death you probably would not want it to happen when the police were wrestling with transition and turmoil.

Times were changing. In 1985, when I was posted to Gatwick, science and technology were only just creeping into policing.

For those of us of a certain age the mid-1980s seem like only yesterday. It is worth remembering that much of what Roy Grace's detectives now take for granted, such as DNA testing, had hardly been thought of then.

How would DS Annalise Vineer, Grace's crime analyst, cope with no internet and computers that were just word processors? What could DS Norman Potting do with next to no CCTV, no mobile phone data and no ANPR system to plot villains' movements across the country? How about Glenn Branson not being able to readily access information from the Passport Agency, Department of Work and Pensions or hospitals?

Until the early 1980s most murders were the work of local villains and rarely part of a pattern that crossed county boundaries; people were less mobile in those days. The slaying of thirteen women and the attempted murder of a further seven in northern England, which led to the 1981 conviction of the Yorkshire Ripper, Peter Sutcliffe, was a gruesome exception to that rule. The fact that the investigating police forces operated their own paper-based systems resulted in Sutcliffe being interviewed nine times before being unmasked as the killer. It took this to persuade the police, subsequently, that they had to get their act together and fast.

Detective Inspector (DI) George Smith was a high flyer, the Grace of his time. Quiet, intelligent and ruthlessly professional, he was going places. He was also young and athletic, and a regular starter for the Brighton CID football team. As the perfect role model for any young up-and-coming detective, he was the ideal choice as head of CID training. With that came the responsibility for introducing the technological product of the Ripper failings, the Home Office Large Major Enquiry System (HOLMES), to Sussex Police. The vision was that this computer would be welcomed by all Senior Investigating Officers (SIOs) as the silver bullet to aid any murder enquiry. Sadly, some Luddites saw the system as a needless interference with their tried and tested methods. George, however, was the personification of police modernization.

In early 1985, shortly after the IRA bombing of Brighton's Grand Hotel where Margaret Thatcher's Conservative Government were staying, and after his stint in training and introducing HOLMES, George had earned his first operational CID command in my then home town, Shoreham-by-Sea. This small but vibrant annexe of Brighton, just a mile and a half west of the city's boundary, features heavily in Grace's world. For example, the demise of Vic and Ashley after the car chase in *Dead Simple* and the horrific execution of Ewan Preece that gave *Dead Man's Grip* its name took place in Shoreham.

Real drama happens there too. In a typical blurring of fact and fiction, the hallmark of Peter James' novels, the day Grace turned thirty and his wife Sandy disappeared he was investigating the death of a biker in Shoreham Harbour. That was, in reality, sixteen-year-old Hell's Angel Clive 'Ollie' Olive, who in 1973 made the error of sleeping with the girlfriend of a rival gang leader. In brutal revenge, Ollie had a weighted chain wrapped around his ankles, and was dumped, still alive, into the harbour.

His leathers protected his body from the ravenous lobsters, crabs and eels that inhabit the inky, icy depths but they feasted heartily on his exposed head, providing police divers the grisly find of a skull stripped clean some weeks later.

A few months before that murder, George had dealings with Ollie's girlfriend over an unconnected matter. His skilful and sensitive way with people was such that after Ollie's body was discovered, she would speak to no-one but him, even though he was just a young DC.

George was like a dog with two tails when he was given his own CID. As now, in those days the station DI had status. He was in his early thirties, and had risen quicker than most. Even Grace didn't make DI that swiftly.

Mondays are normally a busy day of catch-up for DIs: assessing the events of the weekend, making sense of crime trends, digesting what the informants are saying and setting priorities for the coming week.

As Grace knows, call-outs have a habit of coming at the least convenient time. Monday, 4 February 1985 was such an occasion. Following a frenetic shift, George was at home slapping coats of paint on the dining-room wall. As he was ruminating on the day that was and the week that would be, the telephone shrilled him back to the present.

'Boss, we thought you might like to know we've had a call to the Lighthouse Club at Shoreham Harbour. There's a woman's body. Seems her stepson and his wife have come home and found her there. Looks like a murder.'

'Right, I'm coming in,' announced George, before reeling off his list of instructions and requirements to safeguard the evidence which, experience told him, might unlock whatever mysteries this tragedy held. Awful though this would be, he was not entirely sorry that he had an excuse to leave the painting for another day.

Satisfied that he had set enough activity in train to buy himself a few minutes, he jumped in the shower to scrub off the splatters of emulsion. However, even those moments of steam-induced reflection were denied him when, again, the phone rang. Hopefully the station sergeant did not guess that his new DI was dressed in nothing but a fluffy bath towel when he delivered the grim update.

'Sorry, boss, we've found another body. The lads at the scene are saying it could be a murder/suicide.'

'OK, we'll see when I get there. Thanks for letting me know.'

This changed nothing at that early stage. One body, two bodies, it didn't matter. The key was to lock the scene down. No-one was to enter without a reason and a white over-suit. Everyone had to be logged in and out, all witnesses identified and whisked off to make their statements. The balloon that Grace puts up when he goes to murder scenes may be much larger now but, even back then, it still went up.

George's personal world had now been put on hold for the foreseeable future. He did not have an assistant to cancel everything as Grace does but, like Grace, he would dedicate whatever it took of his life and his energies to get to the bottom of the horror that was just unfolding.

As you drove along the busy Brighton to Worthing coast road, you could have been forgiven for not spotting the squat cream edifice of the now-demolished Lighthouse Club at the mouth of Shoreham Harbour. Adjacent to where I used to go to Sea Scouts, it was nestled between the nineteenth-century limestone Kingston Buci Lighthouse and the warehouse that hosted the twice-weekly Shoreham Car Auctions. In the 1960s it was a sailing club, of which Peter James was a member. He would delight in rigging up the fourteen-foot Scorpion dinghy he kept there, hauling it down to the water's edge and putting to sea for a day cruising along the Sussex coastline.

By 1985 it had become a private drinking club with celebrity members such as the late world motorcycle Grand Prix champion – and local playboy – Barry Sheene. It was also the place to go for many dubious characters who fancied themselves as movers and shakers. When George arrived just after 9 p.m., it became obvious that no moving or shaking would be going on there for quite a while.

As he pulled up, a dour-faced PC sidled over to him, conscious of the prying ears of the neighbours and would-be customers who had started to migrate to where the action was.

'Guv, there's a third body. A child. It's bleeding carnage in there,' he muttered.

This news had by now permeated through the gathered ranks of officers. Their silence, their shocked expressions and their preoccupied stares were evidence that this place had witnessed the most horrific of deaths.

George was a stickler for forensics. Like Aussie DS Fletcher who finds his riverside crime scene trashed in *Dead Man's Footsteps*, George could explode on sight should an errant PC traipse over evidence in his size elevens. Practising what he preached, George wriggled into the 'one size fits no-one' white protective forensic suit carefully selected from the bin bag of similar garments and slipped on matching overshoes. Providing his name and rank to the well-briefed PC guarding the scene, he climbed the steps and gingerly crossed the threshold through the communal door leading to the two self-contained flats above the club.

Had he not been warned, he would have stumbled over her in the pitch black. If he had, she would not have complained. The dead don't protest. Hilda Teed's skull could never have survived the pounding it had suffered. In her dressing gown, she blocked the narrow hallway, lying crumpled in a pool of her own blood and pulverized grey matter.

George had seen all he needed. It was time to step back and get the 'ologists' in. Then, as with Grace's investigations now, the scientists were becoming essential in demystifying murder scenes. Making sense out of chaos was the domain of the egg-heads who spent their lives poring over the broken remains of humanity.

The first of these to arrive was the renowned Home Office pathologist Dr Iain West. A veteran of countless homicides across the UK, Iain was the 'go to' expert for grisly and complex murders. It always seemed to be either Iain or his wife, Dr Vesna Djuruvic – the real life Dr Nadiuska de Sancha, Roy Grace's favourite death-doctor – who was on call.

To fill the time while Iain made his way to the scene, George drove the short distance to the police station where DS Dennis Walker was already taking a statement from Paul Teed, Hilda's twenty-three-year-old stepson. He and his wife Helen had found the bodies, having apparently returned from a trip to Yorkshire.

Paul struck an unremarkable form. Barely 5'8" tall, pasty and not hindered by excess muscle, his quiet, reserved manner meant he would never stand out in a crowd. However, his lack of emotion was puzzling the experienced detective. Helen, who was being interviewed and comforted in another part of the station, was inconsolable.

Police witness interview rooms are soulless places. The poisonous Ashley Harper's first encounter with the police in *Dead Simple* was in such a facility. Described brilliantly as 'small, windowless, painted pea green and reeking of stale cigarette smoke', they can be a wonderful preparation for a lifetime of imprisonment for those whose dark and macabre secrets are yet to be exposed.

George did not have long until he needed to be back at the scene but he had heard members of staff confiding to officers there that a shotgun was kept on the premises. He was keen to hear what Paul had to say about that. He had offered nothing on this so far. Apologizing politely, George joined Dennis in the interview.

'Paul, do you remember a shotgun being in the club?' he asked.

'A shotgun? No, I don't think so. Why?'

'Other people remember seeing one. Don't you?'

'No. I don't think so.'

'Oh, come on, Paul. You lived there yet you seem to be the only person who can't remember it. Now is not the time to hold back.'

'Oh, right, that shotgun. Yes I do, now you mention it.'

Dennis and George gave each other an almost imperceptible knowing look.

'Right, that's better, Paul,' said George. 'Now where is it?'

'I threw it in the sea.'

'You did what?'

'I hate guns so I threw it in the sea a few days ago.'

'Convenient,' muttered Dennis beneath his breath.

'What did your dad say about that?' insisted George.

'He didn't know,' came the reply.

George and Dennis banked that loose end for tying up later.

Arrangements were made for Paul to stay at the police station. Since he had not yet been arrested, they applied gentle persuasion on him to remain. George made his way back to the club.

Back at the scene, observing the forensic protocols, George, Dr West and SOCO (Scenes of Crime Officer) DI Tilt wrapped themselves in their forensic suits and tiptoed inside. Gently stepping over Hilda, Dr West crouched to examine her injuries by flickering torchlight. They all knew what he was about to say, but he had to announce it nonetheless.

'Killed by extensive and repeated blows by a blunt instrument to the head. No chance of survival.' The formal post mortem would come later but in all probability the cause of death would boil down to just that.

They moved on into the flat. Knowing there were at least two more tableaus of horror awaiting them.

George Teed had had a reputation for being larger than life. Now, in death too, he made an impact.

Usually he wore designer suits and gold bling, but that night he was as naked as the day he was born. Lying on his back, he looked as if he had been caught by surprise while leaping out of bed to meet his murderous attacker. Again, a blunt instrument to the head, with which he was struck many times and with great force, was the last thing he would have known. No chance of retaliation; not the slightest sign of a defence wound. The walls, carpets, bedding and furniture looked as if they had been showered by crimson dye. The scene was straight off the set of Hammer Horror.

The worst was saved until last. David Teed was only thirteen. He had been entitled to look forward to a life of hope and achievement. He had harmed no-one. His last memories would have been of running for his life around the flat.

He was still dressed in his pyjamas, and forensics revealed that he'd had no option but to run through his own mother's blood as she lay dead or dying in front of him. Surely knowing that his dad too had been battered to death, he'd made a frantic attempt to wrench open the patio doors to escape. He had pulled at the full-length floral curtains when his own metal American baseball bat was crunched into the back of his skull. He stood no chance. He died where he fell. There were to be no survivors and no witnesses, apart from the family's black Great Dane.

To most people, such carnage would be overwhelming. It would shroud all rational thought. In the staring, startled eyes of the dead you can sometimes see the horror of their last moments, the disbelief that their life was about to be so brutally quashed. You may detect a fearful plea for help. Police officers know dwelling on that is no good whatsoever. You have to put that to one side. The dead deserve your professionalism. They don't need your tears and pity.

There is always some clue, some mistake made by the killer if you know where to look. As Peter James often reflects, the perfect murder is the one that never comes to the attention of the police so with all the others there is always a giveaway, a product of the killer's panic or poor planning. In the same way that Grace looks for that tiny slip-up when analysing the chicken shed torso murder in *Not Dead Yet*, so twenty-seven years earlier George had to find the murderer's Achilles heel by thinking outside the box.

It's often the simple things that get missed. Some people try to be just too clever. There is a reason Grace talks of 'clearing the ground under your feet'. The clues are invariably there. You just have to know how to look for them.

Such as the flashing digits on the radio alarm clock that George had spotted, possibly indicating a break in the power supply. Not unusual in itself but, applying the dogged determination of the inquisitive detective's mind and by layering the little things together, significance starts to shine through. The detectives' code: ABC – *Assume nothing, Believe no-one, Check everything*.

He looked at clues, like that flashing clock and the normally ferocious black dog that witnessed the slaying, from a slightly different angle. They started to take on new meaning. Did the clock indicate that something had happened to cut the power temporarily? Assuming the clock reset itself at 00.00, could it be telling George how long it was since the brutal attacks? Did the fact that the guard dog had seemingly not intervened indicate that he knew the killer?

A story was starting to emerge but it triggered two very different and conflicting hypotheses among the investigators: two versions of events that would create irreparable divisions in the senior team, threaten careers and almost deny justice to the mother, father and son lying broken and butchered in their own home. A struggle between the old and the new. One thought the answer lay in some as yet unknown murky gangland feud and the other within the emerging facts.

The Teeds came from Bradford, West Yorkshire. Paul's parents had separated when he was young and, initially, he and his brother had lived with their mother and stepfather. Paul didn't take to his mother's new husband and they regularly fell out. Unlike his brother, he would not accept the bullying by his stepdad but often that meant fleeing home. He got into trouble from time to time, including a bungled burglary of a butcher's shop where the fact that all but a fraction of their haul was in unusable cheques should have taught him to follow another career. Amazingly he avoided prison for this. Perhaps that gave him a sense of invincibility.

Things weren't much better for him in Shoreham. Despite finding love and marrying his girlfriend Helen, his high hopes for a new life away from his troubled past were soon dashed. His father had reluctantly allowed him to work at the club. He and Helen had moved into the second flat but literally living above the shop he was unable to escape his father and Hilda, and had become fed up with their drinking and arguing. By now, he and Helen had a three-year-old daughter and he knew he had to make his own way in the world – he just didn't need his dad constantly reminding him of that.

George Teed was a big, brash self-made entrepreneur with fingers in more pies than Mr Kipling. He seemed born to run this small exclusive, but seedy, nightspot whose membership defined much of the society scene in Brighton at the time.

Dripping with gold and with pockets full of cash, he embodied the work hard/play hard philosophy of the early eighties, not as brash as Harry Enfield's 'Loadsamoney' but equally flamboyant. Nothing in his life was understated. He was a heavy boozer, as was his wife, and they frequently had violent alcohol-fuelled rows. Such garishness inevitably attracted the attention and envy of rivals, enemies and even the downright greedy. Of course, that was bound to be one line of enquiry. Any SIO would be mad not to look hard at that as a motive. *A* motive, but not *the* motive.

The early evidence was, however, pointing at something much closer to home. The successful Teed's disappointment with Paul was no secret. He was often heard deriding his son as a sponger, and had just given him three weeks' notice to quit the flat, forcing him to put his name down for a council house. 'Stand on your own two feet,' he had repeatedly insisted.

Every family has its problems. There are always skeletons to be found, if you know which cupboards to look in. It does not mean, however, that they all go round killing each other. Indeed, leaping too quickly on family discord has derailed many an investigation. Conversely, many have been scuppered by being too timid to confront domestic strife. It is a stark reality that most people are killed by someone they know. Could this be a case of a son trying to expedite his inheritance while eliminating some major grief from his life?

As a DI, George Smith was not senior enough to run a murder enquiry so was asked to lead the outside enquiry and interview teams. A D/Supt and a DCI were appointed as SIO and deputy.

However, there was real tension. Many highly experienced senior detectives had reservations about HOLMES. They had been used to applying their 'detective's instinct' and gut feeling in murder enquiries. They saw that influence being chipped away with the introduction of computers and incident room staff who, they feared, might undermine their leadership. George, the champion of HOLMES, was acutely aware of this risk and soon realized that his sceptical bosses had set up a second 'incident room' operating in the old way from the DCI's office.

Members of the official murder investigation team spotted Regional Crime Squad officers visiting this second incident room but details of the actions they were undertaking or the intelligence they were supplied with were not shared with the HOLMES team. This was the worst of both worlds; each room in ignorance of what the other was doing.

Foremost in the minds of the 'old school' was the gangland massacre theory. The DCI, with years of experience investigating organized crime, was comfortable dealing with the dark and grubby landscape of vendettas, hit men and dirty money. He was in his element investigating this hypothesis. George and his team on the other hand were making progress elsewhere.

Helen would often stay with friends and relations in Yorkshire, as she had that weekend. She didn't fancy going to the big reunion of Teed's South London friends that the Lighthouse Club was hosting. It wasn't her scene. It was not unusual, following these visits, for Paul to make the 500-mile round trip when she needed collecting. And, so he said, that was exactly what he did in the early hours of that fateful morning. Grateful that his dad had let him drive his brand new distinctive Range Rover, he claimed that about 1 a.m. on the Monday he left George, Hilda and David safely tucked up in bed and drove north.

In his mind he believed he had constructed a perfect alibi. If to the outside world he could put himself 250 miles away when the killing was supposed to have happened, he hoped he would get off scot-free. Luck goes both ways in murder investigations. Both police and assailant rely on it in equal measure.

Almost anyone who has just committed a violent crime will be uptight and jittery. They will inevitably drive differently – too fast, too slow or plain erratically. Any sharp-eyed beat copper spotting this will at least note down the licence number and check it through the Police National Computer in case it is stolen. Just as the PC outside Buckingham Palace did on seeing a Range Rover at four o'clock that morning.

Other, normally insignificant, factors were becoming relevant. The £370 young Teed had in his usually empty pockets (about my monthly take-home pay at the time) was in stark contrast to the paltry 53p his successful father had in his trousers close to where he lay.

It did not seem right either that at the end of his marathon drive Paul would feel the need to take in the washing before he went indoors, leaving Helen to be the first through the communal door. It turned out that he had expected the bodies to be found by the cleaners, hours earlier. The absence of police activity when he pulled in told him that the staff could not have turned up that morning.

He panicked and left the discovery to Helen. He would have known the scream was coming. He knew the House of Horrors he had left as a welcome for her. The bloodbath his darling spouse was about to walk into would be branded on her memory forever. His reaction to her terror however was yet another example of his odd behaviour.

'Paul!' she had hollered. 'Paul, help. Hilda's on the floor. She's covered in blood. Oh God, no. Paul, please come and help,' she implored.

'Oh Christ, phone 999,' was all he replied.

No rushing in to check on his stepmum. No looking for any sign of a break-in. No concern that there might be an intruder still inside. No thought for his dad or brother. Nothing. From what his wife had said, an innocent son would have presumed a nasty fall. An innocent son would have dashed in to help. But that wasn't Paul. He knew what was behind that door. He knew that no amount of CPR could save Hilda. He knew of the massacre he would face should he venture in.

When the first PC had emerged, horrified by the carnage she had stumbled across, Paul hadn't even bothered to ask what had happened to his family and whether his dad and brother were

OK. A person's inactions can be as damning as their actions. Paul was already slowly but surely sealing his fate.

With all of these anomalies, by the early hours of the following morning, George Smith had had enough. He strode back into the interview room where Paul was resting his head on his folded arms.

'Paul Teed, I'm arresting you on suspicion of the murders of George Teed, Hilda Teed and David Teed. You do not have to say anything unless you wish to do so but anything you do say may be used in evidence,' he declared with all the necessary formality such a step warranted.

Stunned, Paul was taken, quietly protesting, into the tiny cell block at Shoreham Police Station, not realizing he had just drawn his last breath as a free man for the next quarter of a century.

Over the next thirty-six hours, Paul faced a series of interrogations designed to scrutinize every detail, every comment, every last piece of evidence to test his truthfulness. None of the modern-day techniques that Grace insists on were available then. No profilers like the fictional Dr Julius Proudfoot, no advanced interviewers, no online volumes of case law to refer to, no tape recorders. The Police and Criminal Evidence Act, which governs how the police interview suspects, had yet to take effect.

This was an intellectual duel, a game of poker with the highest stakes imaginable. Neither could lose. For one it would smack of failure in the eyes of his bosses – it was unthinkable in those days to fail to elicit a confession from such a high-profile suspect. For the other, second prize would lead to a lifetime behind bars.

The questioning covered everything: the timing and exact route of Paul's trip to Bradford, his reaction to Helen finding Hilda, his acrimonious relationship with his dad, even the small amount of cannabis found in his bedroom. Paul remained resolute. Other than the dope, he thought he could explain or deny everything. He believed he had the upper hand. He was convinced he was walking. Then came the killer question:

'Paul, you've been here for two days. We've interviewed you many times. We've listened very carefully to your answers. We have made you go through every detail time and time again. You have continually tried to assure us you had nothing to do with the murders. You've been certain of that, Paul. If that is true why have you, not once, asked us how your dad, stepmum and brother died? Why is that, Paul?' George queried softly.

Silence.

'Paul?'

Silence.

'Paul, why have you never asked?'

'I think I'd like to see a solicitor now, please, Mr Smith,' was all the crestfallen prisoner could mutter.

'I'll see what I can do. Just think about it,' insisted George as he walked the tearful Paul back to the cold, lonely cell.

'Sir, he has asked for a solicitor,' announced George as he entered the makeshift incident room.

'I didn't hear that,' replied the clearly irritated DCI.

'He has asked for a solicitor. He knows his rights. He's got previous convictions and he's in custody for three murders,' said George.

The atmosphere was tense. The seated D/Supt was conspicuously ignoring the argument that was brewing. The stifling silence was eventually broken when the DCI brusquely ordered George, and Dennis Walker who had witnessed the whole confrontation from the open doorway, out of the office.

George was taken aback. He knew he was of a different generation to those above him but surely they could see the risks in such a denial. Assistant Chief Constable (ACC) Alison Vosper treated Grace badly on many occasions, pressurizing him to get results and get them at all costs. The priority would be to make the boss look good, deliberately ignoring that a conviction attained through dubious means is a hollow victory.

With no choice, George obeyed but not before writing every word down in his notebook as a precaution – as Grace did in *You Are Dead* when protecting himself against his nemesis ACC Cassian Pewe. Despite the overwhelming pressure later to remove it from his witness statement, he had a Pontius Pilate moment – 'What I have written, I have written.'

More interviews with Paul followed, including one led by the Detective Superintendent, but they yielded nothing more, just denials and him glossing over inconvenient facts, protesting his innocence.

Faced with no firm admission, no forensics yet – that took weeks in those days – and no eyewitnesses, George had little choice but to bail him from custody. However, Paul went nowhere. Some warrants for non-payment of fines had been discovered in Leeds, and this meant Sussex Police could instantly rearrest him.

Over the previous two days, some of George's team had been in Bradford, ten miles from Leeds, making enquiries. Their brief was to speak to anyone and everyone who knew the Teeds, to get under their skin, find out what Paul had been doing there and leave no stone unturned. Now, George volunteered to drive Teed up north to answer his warrants, which conveniently would give him a chance to see how the Sussex detectives were doing but more importantly would give them five hours in the car together, perhaps giving him the chance to open up. This close contact between investigator and suspect would never be allowed now, but at the time it was not uncommon.

The car journey did give George and the highly respected Dennis Walker an opportunity to get to know their frightened yet stoic suspect better. Paul's tongue loosened but he kept his counsel about any involvement in the bloodbath.

Lady Luck visited again just as George had handed Paul over to the burly Yorkshire custody sergeant.

One of his team slipped him a folded scrap of paper which George hurriedly opened, reading the scribbled note as he strode out of the cell block.

'*Guv, pls phone DC David Gaylor in the Shoreham incident room – URGENT!!*'

Darting into a nearby office, George grabbed a phone and dialled the number he knew by heart. He listened intently and a rare smile broke his usual dour expression. He called his team together in the Bradford CID office to update them on the news.

'Chaps, we have a breakthrough. We know that these killings have aroused the interest of the national press. Well, it seems that has got someone a little scared. One of Paul's friends has become spooked that we may be looking for him.'

'What, have we got the wrong man?' came a voice from the back.

'Let me finish,' George insisted. 'This fellow, Larry [not his real name], says that Paul approached him some weeks ago. They are old friends but he now lives in London. Paul asked him if he would kill his dad for the insurance.'

You could hear a pin drop.

He continued. 'He told him there would be £1,700 in the safe and he would give him another £5,000 when the insurance came through. He even offered Larry a sawn-off shotgun and a map of the flat. When he turned it down he thought that would be the end of the matter. Until he saw the news, that is. He got scared. He's no angel; he has form for armed robbery but, as he said, he's no killer. For the first time in his life, Larry has provided a full witness statement and has handed over Paul's sketched map. Gentlemen, we've got him, well, almost.'

Meanwhile, DC David Gaylor – who later in his career would become the inspiration for Roy Grace himself – DC Chris Cox and the rest of the incident room team back at Shoreham were beavering away, trying to turn suspicion and intelligence into something that might stand up in court.

A careful count back from the time flashing on the alarm clock had led them to the moment that the power had been restored to the flat – 3 a.m. That gave them a possible time of the killings.

Through the Police National Computer, they had discovered the check carried out by the cop on George Teed's poorly driven Range Rover outside Buckingham Palace. Paul's alibi depended on the police believing that he could not have committed the murders as he had been in Bradford. The witnesses there were not providing much help but the timings of those two events showed that he could have wiped out his family and then made the journey north. A case was starting to build.

After a restless night planning his next move, George steeled himself for what he knew would be a landmark interview.

Soon after Paul had arrived in West Yorkshire the police had allowed his uncle, Frank Towel, to visit him. Frank brought with him a friend, John McKenna, who happened to be a solicitor's clerk, as well as a retired police inspector. George met both and was struck by how caring and genuine they were. They were allowed a private visit with Paul at which no police officers were present.

Following that visit, it transpired that something had been said that had troubled John and after much soul-searching he told George that Paul had admitted the murders.

George stepped into the dark, grey, airless interview room at Leeds Police Station. Paul agreed that John could be there, as a friend rather than a solicitor, to support him through what would doubtless be a very difficult few hours. The prisoner sat ashen-faced and trembling on a cold metal chair that, together with the scarred and scorched table, was shackled to the floor by rusty chains.

Taking the only other seat, George built up the tension by

arranging his papers into neat piles. The silence was only broken by the distant slamming of a cell door and the plaintive cry of another inmate demanding a light for his cigarette.

George cleared his throat, then in a quiet, fatherly tone he rearrested Paul, reminded him that he was under caution, then revealed that John had told him of the admission he had made.

Paul became furious, glared at John, turned to George and demanded, 'I don't want him here. Can I see you alone?' Without another word John slipped out leaving just George and the very frightened young man in the room.

'Paul, for the past few days you've been bottling it up, something has got to give. Look at the state you are in. Would you now like to tell me?' said George.

'Mr Smith, I'm frightened,' Paul confided, tears spilling from his bloodshot eyes.

'Shall we discuss what happened?'

Desperately he replied, 'I don't know if I can trust you.'

'Hopefully over the past few days you've got to know me. I've treated you with consideration and compassion. I'm not going to act any differently whatever you decide to tell me,' George reassured him.

'How can you say that, Mr Smith? It was so wicked,' cried Paul.

The cracks were starting to show. Those last four words were the first glimmer of truth. George knew he had to strike now or risk losing his chance forever.

'Paul, why did you do it?'

A wild and uncontrollable wail was all Paul could offer. He wept from his very core. George sat there silently, feeling sorry for the young man. This conflict is quite common in the more humane officers. It is not our place to forgive but equally we are not there to hate or condemn. George could see Paul's conflicting grief and guilt but knew he was seconds away from the elusive confession he needed.

Pulling himself together Paul continued between the tears.

'I'm so frightened, I feel so cold. What's going to happen to me? I'm not mental. I don't want to go to a loony bin. I don't want to be locked away for thirty years. Be honest with me, Mr Smith, what's going to happen to me?'

Sensing that Paul was veering away from the facts and focusing on himself, George steered him back on track.

'Let's sort it out first and we can deal with that matter later. Why did you do it?'

As if it suddenly dawned on him Paul declared, 'I loved them! I loved them both. They both told me to clear out and never come back. Dad was sloshed and he was shouting at me. He said I was lazy and never had been any good. They were both shouting at me and treating me like a child. I couldn't handle it. Then she was dead on the floor, all covered in blood. I was standing there holding the bat. It was horrible.'

Crestfallen he went on to describe how he had snapped under a torrent of abuse and lashed out wildly with his brother's metal baseball bat. The strategy he was using was now becoming clear. He was trying to mitigate the horror by implying impulse and provocation. It's rare that people in such tight corners have the clarity to think these things through though.

Was it really likely that they had such a row at that ungodly hour of the morning? What about the convenient fact that his wife just happened to be away? What about that shotgun? Why was all the money in his pocket and none in his dad's?

It was time for the sixty-four-thousand-dollar question.

'Paul, tell me about Larry. What do you know about him?'

'Who? What's this about?' a startled Paul replied.

'The man you tried to get to kill your dad,' George continued. 'The man who let you down at the last minute. The man you gave your shotgun and this sketch to. Ringing any bells?' he queried, laying a faxed copy of the drawing in front of him.

Paul's world crumbled. The game was up. No more excuses. No more lies.

Piece by piece, Paul tearfully confirmed Larry's account, that it was not an impulse crime but a cruel, cynically planned execution for revenge and a few thousand pounds. Defeated, he wrote a statement. With Paul's permission George invited John back into the room, whereupon the account was read out and endorsed by all.

Years later, Paul was adamant that if his request for legal assistance had been met in Sussex, this could have all been wrapped up very quickly. He had only wanted someone by his side, he claimed. He knew what he had done was evil and unforgiveable but just needed some support.

On his arrival back in Shoreham Police Station the next day, Teed asked to see a vicar. Paul would assert in 2014 that in the course of the killings something deep had happened within. In his words, 'I went through the door of the flat an atheist and came out a believer.' But at the time his ecclesiastical consultation, rather than eliciting a deeper confession of what drove Paul to do what he did, only triggered a further demand for a solicitor and an attempt to retract his admissions.

This time his request for legal advice was granted. In a further confirmatory interview Paul resorted to a cornucopia of lies, denials, half-truths and silence. George wasted no more time; Teed was charged with the three murders just half an hour later.

Cadet Jim Sharpe had now become PC Jim Sharpe and had recently been posted to Shoreham. One of his first tasks was to escort Teed to court for his initial remand hearing. Handcuffed to him on the bench seat of a rickety blue police prison van Jim, in his customary convivial way, struck up a conversation. While his memory of the exact nature of that chat is less clear now, he recalls the empathy he felt. Here were two young men about to start on very different life journeys, one in the police, the other in prison.

Jim met Paul many times over the ensuing months. While in police custody in Shoreham awaiting further hearings, Paul grew to like young Jim. His easy style, not common among police officers those days, together with him allowing Helen to visit, made those court appearances more bearable.

The subsequent trial wrestled with all sorts of issues such as the retracted admissions, the refusal of legal advice initially, and the status of John McKenna. Many trials collapse following a successful assault on police and prosecutor practices. Once George's team had eliminated every possibility other than Paul being the killer, such an attack was the only tactic left if there was to be any hope of the defence winning him his liberty.

George had to front this for Sussex Police. It isn't unusual for a senior officer to be set up to draw the venom of defending counsel. I have done it often, absorbing all the criticism personally, and, in most cases, it protects others.

Pummelled in the witness box, as Grace has been on many occasions, George had to bob and weave. He had to explain and re-explain every decision, every act, hoping that his honest accounts remained consistent in the eyes of the jury. This included the denial of access to the solicitor, which was a particular worry for him.

His meticulously written notebook and seventy-eight-page witness statement certainly helped, as did his conspicuous integrity and obsessive attention to detail. The arguments lasted for hours but George won every point.

His bosses' scrutiny of their young DI's performance during the trial reminded George that the outcome of this contest would determine his future career. Everything was on his shoulders. Resolute yet isolated, George knew who was going to be the fall guy if Teed walked free. Despite his unerring honesty and professionalism George felt angry, lonely and vulnerable. If the old triumphed over the new he, and many like him, would be finished.

Thankfully, despite all the grubby accusations thrown at the police by the defence, the jury saw sense. Three clear cries of 'Guilty!', one for each victim, rang out from the jury foreman across the hushed Lewes Crown Court. Justice delivered for George, Hilda and young David Teed.

A mandatory life term followed but, stunningly, no appeal. No desire to overturn verdict or sentence. Just a solemn acceptance of his fate and twenty-three years to dwell on his evil was how it ended for Paul Teed.

George felt he and his modern tactics had been vindicated. Two years later he worked with the Deputy Chief Constable to take charge of a major review of Sussex CID. Promotion came soon after and he became the first serving UK police officer with 'special dispensation' from the Home Secretary to operate as a full member of the Security Service (MI5). He operated as a member of K2 Branch (Counter-espionage), which also saw him work with MI6 and, in the USA, with the FBI and CIA. On his return he headed Brighton CID then moved on to work in other sensitive areas of policing. He was my boss when I was a DC and I held him in the highest regard. His sense of justice, fairness and respect were a huge influence on me as I matured in service. His bosses went on to embrace the new world, both achieving further promotions.

Paul is now free. I was fascinated by what becomes of a person who has wiped out his family once they have been released, so I tracked him down. Although I doubted that he would agree to meet, incredibly he was very keen to.

Peter James and I have, over the years through our different professions, met many killers, but not mass murderers and certainly not those who have had twenty-three years of incarceration to contemplate their act.

We met Paul in an austere roadside pub half way between

Leeds and York. When we drove up in a black Mercedes it must have looked like we were carrying out a drugs deal. We didn't know what to expect, we didn't even know what Paul would look like now. As a thin, gaunt man in his fifties climbed out of a rackety Ford Fiesta that had lurched into the empty car park, blue smoke spewing from the exhaust, we guessed we hadn't been stood up.

He was much cheerier than I had expected, but Paul's prison pallor bore testament to the way years inside, with the stale air, drug culture and diet of cheap food sap the vitality from every pore.

Over the next three hours he laid bare his life before, during and after the slaying. He knows what he did that night was truly bad. He accepts that he meticulously planned the deaths yet, despite the evidence, maintains that neither his father, Hilda nor David had any idea what had happened to the others, such was their clinical yet brutal execution. He blames his actions on a slow build-up of tension, animosity and jealousy. The seed, he says, was sown months before with every cross word or fallout thereafter fuelling his determination to take their lives.

He is philosophical about his life in prison. He talks about inmates being broken machines and needing their software fixing (as opposed to those in psychiatric hospitals who he says have hardware problems). He is less convinced that jail is effective at the reprogramming prisoners so need.

Nowadays he is forever trapped, defined and scarred by that moment of evil madness. He struggles to find employment; he secured a job once in a garden centre but they got cold feet when they found out he had battered three people to death. He has turned to painting and tries to sell his abstract artwork online.

He has become deeply spiritual; he believes in signs and portents such as black dogs – like his father's Great Dane and one he owned that was crushed by a train in 1984 at the site of the 1989

Purley rail crash – and the number twenty-three, his age at the time of the murders and the time he spent incarcerated.

He is a great believer in destiny but, above all, he is clear that he chose to do what he did; no-one forced him. He accepts that he had no right to do it and insists that he regrets it every day. Only he knows how much.

He wonders what life would be like if he had made different decisions. The true tragedy is however, whatever was going on in his head, he denied the others any choices; he took those for himself with every swing of the bat.

Unlike several killers I've met who are clearly psychopaths and have no conscience, enabling them to live guilt-free with the knowledge of what they have done, Peter and I both got the sense from Paul that he is, deep inside, consumed with remorse. His victims are long dead and buried, and Paul is now at liberty. But I don't see him ever being a free man. He will be chained to his conscience forever.

3: KNOCKERS AND NOBLEMEN

I recall in my childhood my dad insisting, in his usual no-nonsense way, that every Sunday evening we all sat down to watch BBC's *Antiques Roadshow*. In my boyhood naivety I believed that the world of antiques was populated by quaint gentlefolk receiving honest windfalls. The one I later battled with in Brighton was riddled with deceit, extortion and violence.

In the years following the Second World War, rag and bone men, of the kind immortalized in *Steptoe and Son*, were a familiar sight. They would traipse Britain's streets with a horse and cart, yelling 'rag and bone!', inviting people to throw junk such as broken vacuum cleaners out of their houses. But a group of low-lifes in Brighton decided they could enjoy a much more lucrative door-to-door trade by conning unsuspecting people out of their antiques. They became more proactive knocking on front doors, frequently targeting the frail and elderly, offering to buy their antiques and valuables for instant cash.

These 'knocker boys', as they became known, had only a rudimentary knowledge of antiques – enough to spot items of value – but their game was to cheat people. A particularly pernicious trick was to carry a bag of sawdust in their pockets. On entering the house of an elderly person, they would furtively pour the sawdust on the ground beneath the best piece of furniture, then warn the victim they had woodworm, and offer to take it off their hands before it spread to all the other furniture. If an owner refused to sell any high-value items the knocker boy would pass the details to a burglar, who would later steal them and give the knocker boy a cut.

Some of these knocker boys graduated into a life of faux-respectability, setting themselves up as bona fide antiques dealers in well-stocked shops in Brighton's famous Lanes.

In Regency times privileged classes would divide their balmy days between their modesty-saving bathing machines on the beaches and strutting around The Lanes. This compact network of fisherman's cottages would evolve into a market place crammed with a delightfully eclectic mix of art dealers, furniture shops and bric-a-brac stalls. As time passed and Brighton grew, The Lanes gained the reputation as the go-to place for classic collectables – and so it remained until recent years, when most dealers turned from the failing antiques market to the more profitable second-hand jewellery trade.

However, this warren of Aladdin's caves had a dark side, and it soon became the go-to place to fence stolen property. I was struck by the insightful 1996 *Independent* newspaper headline that proclaimed:

> **If your antiques have been stolen, head for Brighton**
> **– the Sussex resort is now a thieves' kitchen for heirlooms.**

It was fair advice.

While enjoying the latest gripping crime novel it is sometimes tempting to write off some authors' extremes as poetic licence, the writer getting carried away with the story and leaving reality at the door. However, Peter James throughout the Grace series shows flawless authenticity in his depiction of the evil that some are capable of in the pursuit of wealth.

From my days as a DC with Brighton CID, amid catching rapists, robbers and burglars I became very familiar with the vermin who preyed on the lonely and the vulnerable.

The image of Ricky Moore, the slimy antiques dealer in *Dead Man's Time*, is one I recognized immediately: 'Fifty-three, balding, long, lank grey hair, shiny white open-neck shirt undone to show his medallion, cheap beige jacket, fingers adorned with chunky rings, booze-veined face and sallow complexion *but* he knew how to charm his way into any old lady's house no matter how canny she was!'

From eyeballing them across an interview room table in the dank grey Brighton Police Station cell block, I could conjure up many a real villain matching this description.

There may well be antiques dealers who are loveable rogues. You have to laugh at some of their nicknames, 'Two-fingered Wadey', 'Banjo Banham', and 'The Dude' for example. Some will be straight, with a genuine passion for making profits for themselves and their grateful vendors. But many are just crooks, plain and simple.

I hate to think how many trusting and gullible grandmothers and war heroes I met whom these chancers had fleeced. Far too late, they realized they had been duped and I found it heartbreaking when spelling out that the odds of recovering their treasures were hovering just above zero.

The ruse relied on careful target selection, the ability to pass themselves off as experts, and of course plenty of charisma. However repugnant the inner person may be, like Ricky Moore, the knocker boy must come across to his target as a favourite son.

Many were able to pull this off, but several simply skipped the charm and relied on unadulterated violence and intimidation.

Terry Biglow is described in *Not Dead Yet* as being from one of the biggest crime families in the city, whose activities included protection rackets, drug dealing and of course the illicit antique trade – not a person to be messed with. No surprise that the Biglows and the repulsive Smallbone family (of which the hateful Amis is portrayed as particularly contemptible by James), had Brighton crime sewn up.

There were at least four similar families in my time in Brighton CID. Their tentacles spread into almost any scam you could mention and their reputation for extortion was notorious among would-be challengers. The slam of the cell door on these heartless villains was such a sweet sound.

All through my early career as a detective at Brighton there was a small but highly functioning specialist team who had these criminals firmly in their sights.

The Antiques Squad was housed in a sweltering broom cupboard on the first floor of the imposing Brighton Police Station overlooking the palatial and airy American Express building. Its DS and four DCs held the most complete and sophisticated intelligence of every known criminally active antiques dealer and knocker boy in the UK.

They reflected the more positive traits of Peter James' DS Norman Potting and I looked up to these old-school detectives. Most of the time they kept themselves to themselves but their knowledge, expertise and intuition were awe-inspiring and I wondered if I would ever have it in me to graduate to their level.

One of the stars was DC Nigel Kelly. He was like a terrier. He would overwhelm his adversaries with a racing intellect and his awesome grasp and recall of every tiny detail. Even the wiliest crooks would need to have their wits about them if they wanted to pull the wool over Nigel's eyes. I took over an investigation from him once and I will never forget the exasperated look in his eyes as he briefed me when I failed to follow each intricate twist and turn as it was fired at me like a Gatling gun.

As well as being looked up to by rookies such as me, the Antiques Squad was the peril of many a villain. So feared were they that many ne'er do wells would sell their own grandmothers, in an effort to divert the squad's attention to someone else.

However, in the early nineties their very existence was in jeopardy. They knew only too well that Brighton's knocker boys were venturing further afield. Pressure was coming down from the big UK cities for the squad to get a grip on its bad boys, who were causing havoc far and wide. Officers up and down the country started to target cars with Brighton registration plates and, if they suspected a link to the antique trade, would order the occupants out of town. Questions were being asked. The squad needed a big result and fast. They had to prove their worth to those who were eyeing them up for the next efficiency saving.

With the eyes of their bosses, as well as those from other forces, on them, the Squad seemed to have hit the jackpot out of the blue. Through their tried and tested technique of striking their prey at their lowest point, they found themselves to be on the verge of a coup that would turn them from zeroes to heroes in a matter of days.

The Squad's network of informants gave them access to around thirty 'grasses' and the team could rely on daily contacts from their snitches. Two in particular were so productive, so reliable that they were afforded 'agent' status – effectively on a retainer to gather and pass on information about Brighton's bad and bold.

As part of an attempt to shift attention to bigger fish, a snivelling thief had blabbed to Nigel Kelly about a huge theft at a stately home in the north of England, which had netted a legendary sapphire stone nicknamed 'the Plum'. He bragged that this gem, set in a beautiful necklace, was a whopping fifty-nine carats, worth over a million pounds in today's money, and truly unique. This might have seemed like a desperate boast from a man in a corner but when he described the magnificent house, his tale became more plausible.

To put the size of this stone into perspective, Julie and I considered we had pushed the boat out when we bought what I thought was a massive sapphire set in her engagement ring that had cost £450. I say *we* bought it as the day we actually decided to take the plunge and select the symbol of our love and commitment to each other, I forgot my credit card. So, in the spirit of sharing, she paid for it. I knew I would never be allowed to forget that so, as soon as I had amassed enough overtime in my new job on CID, I promptly paid her back. I still haven't been allowed to forget it.

The informant had certainly whetted the Squad's appetite but they were too long in the tooth not to test these extraordinary claims. These were the days that dear old Norman Potting and our hero Roy Grace were brought up in; detectives were expected to be able to reach out to the underworld to pick up the whispers of who was up to what and when and where. Some had the Midas touch and found that crooks just couldn't help spilling their guts to them. Others, like me, struggled somewhat but our talents lay elsewhere.

It soon became plain that the underworld chatter was indeed rich with stories of 'the Plum', as well as others of manor houses and safety deposit boxes crammed with stolen gems. Electrified by this, Nigel rushed to obtain a warrant to search a Brighton bank's vault.

The chosen magistrate, who was used to authorizing the searches of homes, offices and warehouses, was stumped as to whether he had the authority to grant search powers in such a secluded hideout. Luckily, a check of the law confirmed he could, and he readily signed the warrant. So, armed with this, and filled with almost childlike excitement, Nigel and his colleague, the burly DC Alan Reed, dashed to the bank whose cellars were unwittingly concealing their prize.

These places, like Southern Deposit Security, the intended venue for Abby's stash of stamps in *Dead Man's Footsteps*, consist of discreet and secretive strongrooms and owe their very being to the anonymity they provide. Uncovering a stash of ill-gotten gems in one of these places would not be straightforward but the Squad knew that justice and their very existence depended on it.

Those entrusted with safeguarding such places are not keen on flinging the door open to any passing detectives to allow them free access to their depositor's property. Call it protocol, call it polite obstruction, they will do what they can to put barriers in the way rather than be seen to be too accommodating to Plod.

Eventually, the posturing out of the way, entry was reluctantly granted and the search could start. This wasn't a door-busting raid as in the hunt for Ewan Preece in *Dead Man's Grip*. This was a search of one box in one vault where access to the necessary key was, while not easy, at least possible.

Nigel's heart raced in anticipation as the tumbler bolts fell. The nervous tension was almost unbearable as the tiny safe door gave way, surrendering its secrets.

The contents glittered like an over-lit Christmas tree.

The box was rammed with a stunning array of rubies, diamonds, emeralds and a plethora of equally exquisite jewels that glistened in the half-light – a breathtaking haul of ill-gotten gains, each item representing a victim's loss and anguish.

But among it all was the prize they were seeking. Proudly dwarfing the array of precious stones, nestled amongst them, sat a bright blue beacon that needed no introduction. The Plum.

Salvation was theirs. Surely now justice would be served and the Squad would regain their reputation as premier league crime fighters.

All the gems were carefully photographed, catalogued and seized, much to the chagrin of their powerless protectors.

Painstaking efforts were made to identify each and every item in the hope that they would reveal further victims whose heartache the jewels' return might go some way to salve. Sadly, the vast majority of stolen property is not identifiable, either due to it not being distinctive or the owners never having thought it necessary to record the details of its existence.

Thieves rely on this. And there was no greater thief than the lessee of the box. He was a big name, a top-level target. His scalp would prove to the world that the Squad had lost none of its edge.

True to form, though, once arrested his interview strategy was simple; say nothing and let the cops prove it. If guilty, only fools protest their innocence and try to explain. Top villains sit back, listen and keep it zipped.

Our misnomer of a criminal justice system encourages this, with it being incumbent on the prosecution to prove beyond reasonable doubt any case they bring, while the defence merely have to introduce a grain of uncertainty from any quarter. This creates a courtroom combat rather than a search for the truth. In the troublesome trial of Suresh Hussain in *Dead Simple*, Grace is on the wrong end of the same kind of joust that I became very familiar with, where all sorts of allegations are thrown in the hope that they damage a perfectly just case.

It is important for charges to be properly proved within the rules. But when ethically brought prosecutions fail because a witness has a dodgy past, stolen property remains unidentified or suspects refuse to account for their actions, this cannot be defined as justice being done, especially for victims. They too often become forgotten bit players in the duels between the bewigged combatants. As the twentieth-century poet Robert Frost noted, 'A jury consists of twelve persons chosen to decide who has the better lawyer.'

I have, on many occasions, had to sit down with people who have lost their life savings, their privacy and sometimes their innocence and gently explain to them that a not-guilty verdict is not the same as them being disbelieved. To these tearful, dismayed victims it is little comfort that the justice they sought has been denied purely because one barrister argued his or her case better than the other. It's a tough message to give and one that I could never deliver with any conviction that the system was fair.

Devastated at being unable to locate anyone with a claim to the other gems, Nigel and Alan's last remaining hope was pinned on the Plum. Surely their just rewards were now a mere short flight away.

Years of their man having slipped through the net, of victims being robbed of their treasures by his arrogance and his apparent immunity from prosecution were about to come to an end. They could almost taste sweet justice as they stepped off the commuter aircraft, the Plum securely but anonymously nestled in the carry-on bag that never left their sight.

If only they had known how misplaced their optimism was. This should have been straightforward yet no-one could have anticipated the massive shock that awaited them.

After the customary hospitality from their locally based colleagues, Nigel and Alan swiftly made the short journey to the wonderful mansion. Having finally reached the top of the ludicrously long drive, they rapped on the huge door.

Knowing they had to go through the formality of introducing themselves to the butler did not make the wait any easier. They were desperate to secure that final confirmation which would turn the jailer's key once and for all on their nemesis.

As they were ushered into the cavernous hallway they could not believe their eyes. They nudged each other, barely able to contain their delight.

This was surely a gift from God.

In pride of place beside the sweeping staircase was a huge portrait, probably from the nineteenth century, depicting an alluring young woman dressed in the finery of the day, adorned by the most magnificent necklace, the centrepiece of which was the Plum sapphire. Its distinctive size, colour and cut had been beautifully reproduced by the artist. Surely, Nigel and Alan couldn't be this lucky. But there it was, if ever they needed it, proof that they had won the lottery. The Plum was clearly one of a kind and its owner would very shortly be moved to tears upon its return.

The strangely edgy and uncomfortable aristocratic owner emerged into the hall from one of the many doorways, unnerving them.

'Good day, gentlemen. I trust you have had a pleasant journey. I do hope you haven't had a wasted trip.'

This seemed an odd greeting, but sometimes people behave oddly in front of detectives.

Perhaps he had not been told the wonderful reason for their mission. They soldiered on and proudly explained the whole story. The intelligence, the hours of investigations, the recovery of the Plum, the arrest of the suspect, and now – building to the climax – the spectacular sapphire reunited with its rightful owner. Victory was theirs.

'That's not mine,' said the gentleman. 'That hasn't come from here.'

Stunned, Nigel and Alan could not believe their ears. Surely they had misheard, somehow misunderstood.

'But it must be yours. All our enquiries show it is, we even had a detailed description of the inside of this wonderful house. It is definitely yours!' Nigel pleaded.

'I'm very sorry, gentlemen, you have been misled. It's not mine.'

'But how can that be? This sapphire is the one shown in the Victorian painting by the staircase. That lady is wearing this stone. Please look again. We know it's yours,' Alan begged.

'All I can say is it's not mine. I can say no more. I am sorry you have come all this way.'

'You must think again. I couldn't begin to explain how much misery the person behind this theft has caused. You could end all that, for Christ's sake. What's more, this beautiful stone, which that picture tells me is a family heirloom, will go straight back to him. You cannot want that to happen, surely?' implored Nigel.

'I'm sorry, gentlemen, I can't help you any further,' was the terse reply as they were shown the door, the wind off the hills now more chilling than it had been a few minutes earlier. Hundreds of hours of work, dozens of enquiries and a six-hundred-mile round trip, together with a cast-iron belief that they would get their man, all wiped out in an instant.

Their world had come crashing down. Just as the net was about to close on the big fish they thought they had landed, he slipped away once more. Crestfallen and confused, Nigel and Alan's journey back south was silent, with each lost in his own thoughts. They knew, for certain, that they had spoken to the owner of the Plum. But if he would not identify the gem, they could not prove that any theft had taken place; suspicion – even 100 per cent certainty – was not enough in the eyes of the law. The absence of a statement confirming ownership meant the Plum had to be returned to the person in whose deposit box it was found. It made them sick that one of their most prolific criminals was going to get a massive payday he was simply not entitled to.

Try as they might, they never did get to the bottom of why their victory was so cruelly snatched from them. The detectives were puzzled by the householder's flat denial that the gem belonged to him. Was *his* ownership of it dubious? Did it hold some age-old family secret that would be best kept buried?

Could the acceptance of his ownership of the Plum and its theft *really* be that devastating? Did he actually give a moment's thought to the ordinary people who would go on to be further victims? It was anyone's guess.

The anger and despondency felt by Alan and Nigel was only matched by the sickeningly smug glee shown by their Mr Big as he flourished his signature on the paperwork that would return the Plum to him.

You can rarely predict the reception you get from the public. Experience taught me that not every victim regards the police as knights in shining armour. A thorough investigation, for example, can scupper a nicely inflated insurance claim. Some people are just too wealthy to bother worrying about their missing valuables and all the inconvenience police intrusion brings. Some just hate us and won't give us house room, whatever the consequences or losses that entails.

It's bad enough to be thwarted by smart lawyers or a sceptical jury, but it is most galling of all when the victim or a potential prosecution witness clams up. It happens time and again, often for no understandable reason – it could be threats made, fear or embarrassment or some other well-concealed reason. People are fickle and there is never enough time to fully understand the motivations of everyone we come across. Sometimes you just have to accept that it takes all sorts and move on. Policing Brighton is much too frantic to allow much time to do otherwise.

4: LAUGHING POLICEMEN

It's not all death and misery. Sometimes policing can be fun. As a species, emergency service workers find their light relief in the most bizarre places.

Special (or volunteer) police officers were not always as respected as they should have been. I found this frankly insulting as they put themselves on the line as much as we who were paid did.

I had a very personal reason to admire them. My father, John, always wanted to be a police officer but back in the 1960s the pay was poor and he wanted a family so he let his head rule his heart and instead qualified as a chartered surveyor. However, he and my mum Hilary instilled in me, and my older siblings Martin and Carol, a deep respect for the law and policing. This sparked a single-minded desire to tread the path that he was denied. My parents could not have been more proud of the choice I made, nor I of them.

My Dad decided, later in life, that he could live out his dream by joining the Hove Special Constabulary. Unpaid, the job mostly entailed attending fetes and public events. However, never one to miss an opportunity, Dad volunteered for fortnightly football duty at Brighton and Hove Albion home games. He loved football and loved policing; who needs paying if you can combine your two big passions? When my Uncle Gordon, Dad's brother, took me to the games Dad was working at, I would stand on the terraces on a crate to give me extra height, and enviously watch him as he patrolled the perimeter of the pitch. I so wanted to be him.

As a natural leader (he became a Director of Brighton Borough Council) he never accepted the status quo. His insistence that 'Specials' could do more than just be rolled out for the soft events, such as being a token police presence at church fairs, provided him with the profile of a modernizer and he soon won promotion to head up Brighton's Special Constabulary.

He could be quite ruthless, never suffering fools gladly, but he was fair. He saw that a number of colleagues were interested only in the status of being a Special, not actually the reality of doing the job. They did not last long but those who genuinely wanted to be part of the wider policing of the city were nurtured and encouraged. Dad would vehemently negotiate their rights and promote the profile of Specials. Many of my Divisional Commander predecessors still speak highly of him for this. He brought the Specials out of the dark ages and set them on the path to what they are today.

One Saturday afternoon, my partner, DC Dave Swainston, and I were in the Brighton CID office reading through witness statements regarding a prisoner we were about to interview for robbery. Suddenly the tannoy crackled into life: 'All units, ten twenty Queens Park Road. Traffic warden being attacked. All free units to attend.'

And that is exactly what Dave and I did. Grabbing a set of car keys we joined the mass exodus all heading for the car park to race the short distance up the hill to assist the warden. Despite Dave being a former traffic officer, it was I who had the keys and therefore I who took the wheel of the CID car.

As I revved the protesting 1100cc engine, I gave way to the better-equipped and more powerful marked response cars then fell in behind them, using their wake of sirens and blue lights to force my way out on to the roadway.

As I raced up towards Queens Park Road, I noticed a very

familiar uniformed figure running in the same direction. Dad was never an athlete but neither was he unfit. However, he was thirty-two years older than me so would have been knocking on the door of sixty at this time.

A wave of protectiveness engulfed me and temporarily I forgot about the poor traffic warden. My dad, fully kitted up with radio, truncheon and chunky jacket, would be thankful for the respite I could provide.

I ground the car to a halt next to him, noticing him sweating and panting like a bloodhound.

'Dad, Dad,' I shouted, 'get in, we'll take you up there,' expecting him to fling open the back door and gratefully throw himself across the bench seat.

However he broke stride momentarily, took one look and bellowed, 'You can fuck off, son. I've seen your driving. I'm safer risking a heart attack!' His pace seemed to quicken as if to put as much distance between him and me as possible.

'That's bloody charming,' I remarked to Dave as I accelerated the car away. 'That's the last time I offer to help the old timer!'

As I glanced towards him I saw Dave was in no state to reply. He was creased up, convulsing with hysterical laughter, eyes streaming and fighting for breath.

I drove on, silently rueing the lack of respect the older generation was showing me. Even the traffic warden didn't prostrate himself at my feet with gratitude. His assailant had already been handcuffed and was being squeezed into one of the other police cars.

I got back into the car and sloped down the hill to the police station, feeling distinctly unloved and unneeded. The homecoming warmth that Grace and Branson feel every time they arrive at this strangely welcoming concrete carbuncle escaped me that day.

One of the most common saviours of our sanity is gallows humour, or the hilarity found in the macabre. We hear in the

Grace novels dozens of instances of this and all evoke in me memories of how it helped us cope, free from today's political correctness Gestapo bearing down.

Some of the acronyms that describe the various states or liabilities of those involved in road crashes may seem insensitive. FUBAR BUNDY – *Fucked Up Beyond All Recovery But Unfortunately Not Dead Yet* and DODI – *Dead One Did It* are both examples of the dark wit of all emergency service workers, but they serve a purpose in keeping us sane amid the horrors we face.

Like so many of my colleagues, several of the characters in the Roy Grace series would be either the instigator or the target of merciless banter.

DS Norman Potting, with his old-school roots and his crass political incorrectness, shows his colours throughout with his injudicious comments in briefings, some of which are shocking, but many display the hilarity required to survive consecutive murder enquiries.

DI Glenn Branson, with his sharp dress sense, encyclopaedic knowledge of the movies and his background as a club bouncer, receives as much teasing for this as he doles out to his friend and boss, Roy Grace, over his age and musical tastes.

I hate to think what revolting substitutes would have been placed in DS Bella Moy's ever-present Malteser box, just waiting for her hand to spontaneously grab while beavering away in the incident room.

When I was a patrol officer most police stations had social clubs. Those who never had to face the misery and violence that frontline policing dishes up in spades saw these bars as a luxury.

However, after a frenetic late shift I, and many like me, found them a welcome sanctuary where our unofficial debriefs could be held in relative privacy. We had to unwind and the stuff we needed to talk about was not fit for public ears.

The healing properties of a couple of pints of warm flat beer, supped in the austere surroundings of the fourth-floor Brighton Police Station bar, spiced with an hour of merciless mickey-taking, worked wonders in normalizing the mind after eight hours immersed in human misery.

There was no seniority or pecking order; no-one was immune. I was as guilty as the next person of homing in on those who'd had an unfortunate shift. You were an obvious target if you had been assaulted, crashed a car or let a prisoner escape – all thankfully rare, hence all the more ripe for a torrent of relentless ribbing.

None of this was serious. We all knew that 'there but for the grace of God go I' but as it was not us on those particular days, why not give the luckless ones a hard time and everyone else a good laugh?

However, this could occasionally become abhorrent. Some would ridicule their colleagues or members of the public for just being different. Women, gay people or those with a different colour skin had a torrid time at the hands of the ignorant. This wasn't banter, it was bullying plain and simple. My experience now is that this bigotry is stamped on the second it surfaces. Others may disagree.

It's a shame, however, that the positive camaraderie that team bonding brings is waning. Some officers feel shy laughing off the trials they have faced in case some clinically minded, desk-bound manager takes offence.

Often, it's the members of the public we deal with who provide the richest material for laughs. The lighter moments can spark from a particularly dumb villain, a helpless inebriate as well as from the idiocy of a colleague.

Show me a cop who doesn't relish the sights and sounds of Brighton's notorious West Street late on a Saturday night when the drunks start to spill out from the countless clubs, and I will show you a misery-guts.

A few punters want to fight but most, in their own woozy way, just 'wanna be your mate'. Scantily clad women, and men, insist on being photographed with 'the best bobby in Brighton'. Some confuse the rooftop 'Police' sign with one signifying a taxi and demand to be driven 'Home, James' while others insist you have 'a bite of my kebab, mate, 'cos you must be bloody starving and I bloody love the Old Bill, I do!' The banter is just fabulous and I always imagine their reaction the next morning when reminded of this by friends who would no doubt add, 'I can't believe you said/did that to that copper. You were lucky not to get nicked.' Never a chance of that from me. These people made my evening.

It was rare to see the blueprint for Roy Grace, David Gaylor, lose his sense of humour. He was normally at the centre of most of the pranks but on one occasion, while the rest of us were revelling in a colleague's misfortune, his was the only stern face.

I was a DS and David was the DCI at Hove CID. I'd known David since we both served in Bognor together, him on CID and me as a wet-behind-the-ears probationary constable. He has always been a very self-assured and superbly gifted detective. His reputation for getting things done earned him many promotions. He would always find a way to reach an objective and that, in the policing culture, is a highly prized gift. He ran a very tight ship and we all knew where we stood. That said he was great to be around, always quick with a joke, and could not resist a wind-up when the opportunity arose.

My very good friend and constant colleague DS Bill Warner was normally very close to David. For years David allowed the office to believe that when he went on holiday, as well as Bill ferrying him to and from the airport, he would task him with various chores at his home such as cutting the grass and keeping the house ship-shape for his return. He would even send him a postcard reminding him. Many thought that this was what actually happened and counselled Bill to stand up to these over-bearing and outrageous expectations. It was only when someone threatened to blow the whistle that they both revealed it was all a jape and, as one, everyone had fallen for it.

Bill was a late entrant to the police. His previous careers running his own contract cleaning business, as a Brighton taxi driver and professional boxer gave him a street credibility that was rare among most of us. He was in his late forties when he became a DS but, as he once represented Great Britain at water polo, he was fitter than most of us.

Always immaculately turned out, he struck a fearsome form. His broad frame, flattened nose, pencil moustache and tight buzz haircut gave him the look of a high-class bouncer.

His quick and acidic wit spared no-one. From the Chief Constable to the cleaner, we all had to be on our guard when Bill was around. In my later years I found I was safe from his sharp-witted retorts only when in the relative, yet temporary, protective formality of official meetings. If I managed a swift put-down towards him he would march into my office after-wards and remind me that 'you are only the Chief Superintendent because I told the Chief Constable to make that so. You know I run this force and you are all subject to my will and I can with-draw rank as quickly as I bestow it!'

That was his fantasy world. In reality he was a hard task-master and he ensured that people knew that his respect had to be earned; rank alone did not guarantee it.

We were suffering a spate of frauds at banks along the main drag running from Brighton to Hove. These would, invariably, be just as the bank was closing. It was becoming a real problem and the pressure to catch the offender was growing. David Gaylor made it our key priority to apprehend whoever was responsible and see him locked up for many years.

Intelligence seemed to suggest that the bank on Holland

Road, just down from the police station, was going to be targeted late one Friday afternoon. David was beyond excitement. Not only was this his chance to arrest a very prolific villain, but also an opportunity to get one over on his smug counterparts over the border in Brighton.

Two of the most vigilant detectives, Simon Steele and Rachel Terry, were chosen to sit in the bank and wait for the inevitable; the trap was set.

Now Bill appeared to have no life outside the police. Despite being officially off duty, he would often pitch up at the police station and assist, or rather interfere, with whatever was going on. Such was the case on this day.

His presence was not something you could ignore. He was loud, gregarious, nosy, uber-confident and very, very funny. I loved the big old bear!

While holed up in the bank, Simon and Rachel were getting concerned that they both had prisoners coming back on bail later that day and needed to be ready for them. So, just after 3 p.m. they phoned the DS's office. It was no surprise to them that the off-duty Bill answered the phone.

'Hi, Bill,' said Simon. 'Any chance Rachel and I could come back to the nick? It seems all quiet here and we both need to get some stuff together for later.'

I had stepped out for a while so, not bothering to check with someone who actually knew what was going on, Bill glanced at his watch and gave them the OK. Not ten minutes later they strolled back into the office and quietly settled down to their more pressing commitments.

On the stroke of 3.25, the tannoy broke the silence throughout the police station.

'All units make for Holland Road, fraud in progress.'

'Yes,' shouted David, punching the air, as he dashed from his office to the open-plan DCs' room, knowing that his hunch had paid off. We had him. Simon and Rachel would be bursting from their cover ready to slap the handcuffs on the offender once and for all. I followed him, sharing his exuberance and delight.

It took David a second to register what he was seeing. Who were those doppelgangers sitting at Simon and Rachel's desks?

'What the hell are you doing here? Why aren't you at the bank?' he yelled.

Seeing their boss's rage rise, they knew it was time to deflect his wrath.

'We phoned Bill and he said we could stand down,' Rachel wisely explained.

'Bill's not even here, he's off today,' retorted the incandescent David just as the workaholic DS sauntered into the office.

'Control must have got it wrong. The banks shut half an hour ago,' he pronounced.

'Bill, what are you doing here?' demanded David.

'You know me, always here to help,' quipped Bill.

'Not this bloody time you haven't. Did you let Simon and Rachel come back?'

'Yes. No sense in them sitting there in a closed bank,' he scoffed.

'Bill, in your world what time do banks close?' asked David, smelling blood.

'David, all banks close at three. I know you probably have people to do your banking for you, but us mortals need to know these things!' joked Bill, now playing to his audience.

'Bill, I'm not in the mood for your piss-taking. This bank, as well as every other one I know, shuts at 3.30. That is why *I* authorized an operation to run to 3.30 as that is the time our target has been striking,' replied a stony-faced David.

By now we could all sense that the viper was about to strike and Bill's ignorance and self-assured assertions were bringing that moment closer and closer. We were spellbound. I was loving it – it wasn't often Bill was in the spotlight like this.

Quietly, the northern drawl of DC Mick Burkinshaw, a rugby-playing, hard-working, brash Yorkshireman, could be heard. 'Cut your losses, Bill. It's 3.30. Face it, you're in the shit.'

'Are you sure?' demanded Bill.

'Sure as eggs,' came the reply, this time from Irishman DC Dave Corcoran.

'Shit. I don't normally do this but is it too late for an apology, David?' asked Bill, clinging onto the last vestiges of his dignity.

'It's not David, it's *sir* to you,' bellowed David. 'Get out of this police station now. Get out of my sight and don't come back until 8 a.m. on Monday when I want you in my office. If you stay a second longer I will say or do something we will both regret.'

Bill shuffled out of the door and sloped off down the back stairs to his car and away in search of sanctuary. David left the office and the DCs roared with laughter at the slaying they had just witnessed.

Unable to stand a weekend of angst, contrary to his orders and knowing David was working, Bill braved a visit at 9 a.m. the following morning.

He gently tapped on the DCI's door.

'You're late, Bill,' mumbled David without looking up.

'But you told me to be here at eight on Monday, I thought I was two days early.'

'I expected you here apologizing an hour ago. There is no redemption for what you did. I will never let you forget it. I will be angry with you forever more, while all of your colleagues will, in time-honoured fashion, rip the piss out of you at every opportunity especially when you next dare to become the big "I Am" in their presence. Now, this time I mean it – get out and don't you dare come back until Monday.'

Happy to have survived with his most delicate parts intact, Bill slid out of the nick and did something he had never done before or since – he took the weekend off.

Of course, good as it is to laugh at each other, it's even

sweeter to revel in the crass stupidity of villains. We often rely on a degree of foolishness to assist us in solving certain crimes but some take that to extraordinarily helpful extremes.

It was a cold, windy winter night in Brighton, the glare of the street lamps creating a glow on the damp pavements of the Kemp Town area as it rose from the seafront to the sprawling Whitehawk council estate. PC Rain, as cloudbursts are often called given their effectiveness in keeping drunks off the street, had done his job.

Dave Cooper, a tough and canny probationer who had recently joined Sussex Police from the French Foreign Legion, was in a panda car with his tutor. This duo were not your ordinary pair of cops, they shared a number of things, a quick wit, deep inquisitiveness and the same surname. Dave's tutor was a Cooper too, Geoff Cooper.

In those wretched early hours where everything is either kicking off or dead as a dodo, the Coopers were trying to make their own luck. Drunk drivers were always fairly easy pickings on cold Monday night shifts. For some reason irresponsible motorists feel less vulnerable when the streets are deserted, unaware they stand out like sore thumbs.

Suddenly as the Coopers inched eastwards along Eastern Road towards the Royal Sussex County Hospital, a car behind them flashed its headlights. Geoff pulled over and the other car followed suit.

Both cops stepped out of the patrol car and strolled to the vehicle behind, a Ford Escort. Geoff approached the driver and, true to his training, Dave engaged the passenger in conversation. Immediately both officers realized from their chirpy accents they were dealing with two Scousers – Liverpudlians.

'All right, mate, where's Newhaven?' asked the driver, clearly lost.

As Geoff chatted to the driver Dave succumbed to his natural distrust of just about everyone. Firstly, he decided to carry out a Police National Computer check to find out who owned the vehicle. He edged out of earshot and radioed the control room, giving the registration that started with an E.

In no time the radio crackled back. Not good news. There was no record of the number Dave had read out. With his military training he doubted he had got it wrong so he took a closer look at the registration plate.

Despite the pervading darkness, broken only by the glow of sodium from the street lights, Dave spotted something odd on the plate. He rubbed his fingers over the E and, rather than the smooth surface he expected, the bottom bar was raised. He picked at the imperfection and soon found that black masking tape had been stuck across the letter. Peeling it away he saw that the real registration started with the letter F, the tape creating the illusion of an E.

He re-ran the check and was delighted when the call came back; the vehicle had been reported stolen. Dave was elated, but needed to hide his glee for just a moment longer.

He stepped over to Geoff who was by now boring the two Scousers describing the large collection of cars he had restored. They looked relieved that Dave was about to interrupt his colleague's monotony until he proudly announced, 'Right, you two, you're nicked!'

As the cuffs were slapped on, Dave could not help but mercilessly rib the two hapless thieves. Exactly how stupid do you have to be, when driving a stolen vehicle, to stop a marked police car to ask for directions?

Back at the police station, Dave and Geoff summed it up when recounting the story for the umpteenth time – Papa Oscar Charlie; meaning (and I have provided the cleaner version) Pair of Clowns.

*

Christmas is a time for families, a season of goodwill to all men. It's also a great time to catch elusive fugitives as, like homing pigeons, they can't help but migrate back to their kith and kin.

One December DS Julian Deans was becoming exasperated hunting down a particularly slippery suspect.

Deansy, as he is affectionately called, is one of the drugs investigators in the city. He is a man's man. His passion for golf and football slightly exceeds his ability but, nonetheless, he has a competitive spirit that permeates every fibre of his being. His tendency to say what others only think is not always popular with his bosses, but I found his frankness and his disdain for bullshit refreshing and sobering in equal measures. He has an intense sense of right and wrong and always takes the battle to the villains.

Yet again, he wearily rapped on the door of the flat where he knew his prey lived.

'Fuck off. He's not here,' yelled the delightful wife, in tones reminiscent of Evie Preece when she was raided by police in *Dead Man's Grip*. 'You're wasting your fucking time!'

'Well you won't mind me coming in to have a look then, will you?' implored Deansy, sensing as he gently wormed his way in that this was going the same way as every other visit he had made.

'Help your fucking self.'

As he walked into the hall, Deansy was met by a five-year-old girl, dressed in all her festive finery and looking like a little angel. Her sweetness and innocence seemed to be in spite of, rather than a consequence of, her upbringing. She stared up at him with her bright blue eyes, smiled and gently asked, 'Are you looking for my daddy?'

'Yes, I am, sweetheart,' replied Deansy, feeling faintly optimistic.

As if giving away a game of hide and seek, she pointed and

her voice dropped as she giggled, 'Oh, he told me not to tell you but he's hiding in that cupboard.'

The look of fatherly love was distinctly absent as the runaway was dragged unceremoniously from the under-stairs closet and off to the cells.

Gus Chiggers was a careful chap. He knew that crime was everywhere and opportunist thieves were not terribly choosy who they targeted. He also knew, despite being from South London, that Brighton had a certain reputation. If you didn't want to become a victim there, you really couldn't be too cautious.

One Monday lunchtime in late July 1990, PC Paul Norlund was enjoying a reasonably peaceful shift, riding shotgun in the city centre response car. The usual band of shoplifters, nuisance beggars and domestics had been dealt with and dispatched with relative ease. He and his colleague Sam, a gentle fellow whose quiet manner thugs often misread to their cost, were parked in a police bay close to the main shopping mall, Churchill Square. Both had the end of the shift in their sights and were hoping to catch some rare summer sunshine in just over an hour's time.

Paul was one of those sickening people: tall, athletic, an all-round accomplished sportsman and far too handsome for his own good. Add to that his natural skill at picking out wrong'uns in a crowd, his innate easy style with all manner of people and the fact he was great company, humbled us lesser mortals.

'Any unit for an armed robbery Lloyds Bank North Street?' crackled the urgent call over the radio.

'Bloody hell. I suppose that will be us then,' he remarked to Sam. 'Yep, Charlie one zero one, we are just by the Clock Tower now. ETA about a minute. Have you got any more details?'

'Not much but it seems that the offender has been detained by staff,' came the controller's reply.

Sam put his foot to the floor and they raced towards the

iconic Victorian memorial that marks one of the busiest road junction in Brighton. As they crossed it, lights flashing and sirens wailing, the more astute pedestrians and motorists cleared a path for them. All except a startled French student, equipped with language school rucksack, frozen astride her pushbike in their path. As Sam swerved to her left, saving her from certain death, Paul bellowed something less polite than 'Please give way to emergency vehicles with their sirens on.'

They hardly got out of second gear as they raced the short distance down the hill to the bank in question.

Partly frustrated that their afternoon plans had been scuppered they were nevertheless fired up with the adrenaline now surging through them in expectation of the drama that lay ahead. Leaping out of the car milliseconds after it came to a halt, they sprinted for the half a dozen steps that led to the banking hall.

As they did so Paul privately cursed the selfish cyclist whose bike was locked to the lamppost as he clipped his leg on its back wheel on his way past.

Bursting into the public area, the scene that greeted them was surreal. It was packed, not wholly surprising given it was a summer lunchtime, but business seemed to be carrying on as normal. Was this a hoax call? They had said *Lloyds* Bank, hadn't they? Their finely tuned ears had never before misheard a location, even in the heat of the moment.

Having quickly closed the bank's doors to prevent any witnesses or suspects slipping away, Paul became aware of a bundle of bodies on the floor close to the quick tills – the unscreened counters where people could make transactions up to £200.

As he made his way over, he heard a plaintive cry of 'Help' coming from somewhere near the bottom of the pile. 'Help me. Get them off.'

'Let me through,' Paul ordered in his lilting Geordie tone.

As the heap of people started to untangle, he realized that at the bottom was a very frightened-looking young man.

'OK, what's going on?' Paul enquired as Sam, guarding the doors, watched on.

'This bloke just tried to rob us,' a suited gentleman wearing a Lloyds Bank name badge replied.

'What, him?' Paul queried incredulously.

'Yes, he tried to rob one of the quick tills. We jumped on him as he walked away. He had this.' The gentleman suddenly brandished what was clearly a toy gun, the red stopper in the muzzle giving it away. Paul grabbed it.

'Bloody hell,' Paul muttered as he pulled the crushed robber to his feet.

'What's your name?' he asked, sensing he was not dealing with a top-level gangster.

'Gus Chiggers,' came the frightened reply.

'Well, Gus Chiggers, I'm arresting you on suspicion of armed robbery.' Following the caution, the hapless gunman was hand-cuffed.

By now back-up had arrived and Paul's colleagues had started to identify witnesses, close off the till area and secure CCTV. Paul took the opportunity to search Gus and the holdall lying at his feet.

The bag was heavy and from the feel of it contained an object that seemed to have a long barrel-like structure.

Cautiously, Paul unclipped the flap and peered in. Firstly he saw a Tesco carrier bag that seemed to contain a few handfuls of 1p and 2p pieces.

'Whose is this?' asked Paul.

'It's what they gave me,' said Gus.

'Who?'

'The bank.'

'Is that it?' queried Paul.

'Yes, they said they didn't have any more money as they had a rush on.'

Paul held Gus's gaze in disbelief then gently removed the structure he had felt from the outside, still not guessing its identity.

'That's my bike seat,' volunteered Gus just as Paul was inspecting it.

'Your bike seat?' asked Paul, now aware that he could be the target of an elaborate *Candid Camera* stunt. 'Why is your bike seat in your bag?' he continued, fearing a bizarre answer.

'It's off my getaway bike,' Gus explained.

'Your getaway bike? You've got a getaway bike? Why isn't the saddle on this getaway bike, then?'

'It might get stolen.'

'What, the saddle?'

'No, the bike. There's a lot of crime in Brighton and it's a nice bike. I've padlocked it outside and taken the saddle off so no-one nicks it.'

'Won't that slow your getaway down?' Paul could hardly believe he was having this conversation.

'Not as much as if it was nicked,' came the obvious response.

'Right, out to the car, you,' demanded Paul, tightening his grip on Gus's arm.

As they emerged into the blinding sunlight, watched by dozens of onlookers, Gus pulled back slightly.

'What are you doing?' asked Paul, fearing an escape.

'That's my bike,' announced Gus proudly, indicating the very machine that Paul had nearly tumbled over on his way into the bank. 'Can you look after it? I don't want it stolen.'

'For God's sake. Yes, yes, get in the car,' muttered Paul, realizing how bad he must have been in a previous life to deserve this.

Back at the police station, DC Peter Smith and I were the only detectives available as there had been a major incident in

East Sussex and everyone else had been seconded over there just hours before. We were gutted that we had been told to stay back and hold the fort.

Word had reached us about an armed robbery at a major bank in the city centre. We were salivating with excitement, hoping this would help us get over our disappointment at being left behind. With an arrest already made, this was not only looking interesting but also, with luck, a nice little overtime earner.

Paul, who would later become a fine detective in his own right, was usually able to talk up any job to get the CID to take it over but, for once, the look on his face took the wind out of our sails.

The fact he was starting with an apology didn't bode well and as he recounted the whole story a feeling of 'why us' engulfed me. I was still in my first year in CID but even I knew this was never going to be an investigation to tell my grandchildren about.

Reluctantly Smith and I took the job on and sloped off to the bank to take some statements and seize what evidence there was.

Despite the seriousness of the offence, Gus's modus oper- andi just got more comical the more people we spoke to.

Gus had entered the bank about ten minutes before he struck. It was, as we had already established, incredibly busy. The queue for the quick tills was almost out of the door. Not wishing to upset anyone, Gus did the British thing – he stood at the back of the queue and patiently waited his turn.

As he shuffled his way towards the counters he drew no- one's attention. After all, he was behaving like everyone else, quietly queuing in line.

As he reached the front the tannoy announced that cashier number five was now free. So, with his hand in his bag he stepped up to the counter. With no hint of drama, he slipped his red-stoppered pistol from the satchel and pointed it at the young man waiting to serve him.

Terrified, wondering what was going to happen next, the cashier discreetly pressed his alarm button under the desk and waited for the demand to be bellowed at him.

Silence. Gus just stood there.

The young man sensed this was not the normal type of stick-up he had been trained for.

'Are you robbing me? Would you like some money?'

Gus nodded.

Recognizing the dissipating threat, the cashier took a chance. 'I haven't got very much left. I'll give you what little I have. Have you got anything to put it in?' he asked, spotting some senior colleagues closing in. A scrunched-up Tesco bag was placed on the counter into which he put some small change. Gus stepped away, still not having said a word, whereupon he was pounced on by the waiting crowd.

Back at the nick, we were so looking forward to the interview. Surely Gus had a reason for being such a cautious, considerate, polite robber. Perhaps this was some kind of social experiment, albeit one which would certainly see him jailed.

Peter, being the more senior detective, took the lead. With a wicked personality, he was a vivacious joker. Having a sense of humour drier than the Gobi Desert and being infinitely better than me at keeping a straight face were two other reasons why he was best placed to ask the big questions.

We implored Gus to get a solicitor but he thought we were a nice couple of blokes and would help him if he got stuck – we were and we would, of course.

Any chance he had of finding a psychiatric excuse for his peculiar behaviour was dashed by his incredibly lucid, detailed and consistent explanation. He said he needed some money, treasured his bike, didn't want to upset anyone in his native London so came here and then wanted to make as little fuss as possible. On hearing this, despite his eccentricity, no doctor would have certified him as mentally ill.

We had no choice but to charge him with robbery and a number of other linked offences and let him take his chances in court.

True to form, in front of His Honour Judge John Gower, a fearsome but fair man I had crossed previously, Gus pleaded guilty at the first opportunity. Peter and I did not feel the need to attend court as there seemed nothing contentious about the case, but word soon reached us that our presence would be required at the sentencing hearing a few weeks later.

'I want the officers to bring the gun along so I can determine a proportionate sentence,' the judge commanded.

Well, this should go in Gus's favour, I thought as I entered Lewes Crown Court on the day the prisoner would learn his fate. He was a poor excuse for a robber, he had admitted the offence at the very first opportunity, he had stolen just pennies and no-one really believed he would harm them. Although armed robbery was very serious and attracted long prison sentences, Gus must pose a comparatively low risk.

As the judge entered, I duly handed the toy gun up to His Honour. He examined it carefully from all angles, paying particular attention to the red stopper. I wished the ground would eat me up. Surely I was in for another roasting, this time for bringing charges against this inept villain.

'Stand up, Mr Chiggers,' ordered the judge.

Gus stood.

The judge then went through the horrors that befall people faced with armed gunmen and how some never recover. He took into account the early guilty plea, the crackpot getaway strategy, the paltry amount gained and the robber's demeanour throughout. He then turned to the gun.

'I can clearly see that, by this red stopper, this gun is nothing but a toy; incapable of harming anyone.'

Here it comes, I thought. I put on my best sheepish look.

'However neither I nor you know how other people would react when such a weapon is pointed at them. You are lucky that the person you chose to rob did not fall for it. Others might have. Therefore I judge this to be a most serious offence carried out in a crowded place in the middle of the day. Despite all the mitigation, I have no option but to sentence you to four years' imprisonment. Jailer, take him down.'

I saw the confused look in Gus's eyes and the whispered apology as he went down the steps. I spared him some sympathy, conscious that only then had he grasped the stupidity of his actions.

Farcical as Chiggers' escapade was, Judge Gower was right of course. Not even a highly trained firearms officer will claim to be able to determine a fake gun from a real one at a glance. Sometimes they have to make a split-second decision whether or not to shoot someone brandishing a weapon.

At the New Scotland Yard Crime Museum, the curator, an ex-detective himself, put Peter James through a test. Standing just ten feet away he pulled a gun from inside a box on Peter, calling 'Real or fake?' There was a one-second pause. 'You're dead.' No time to decide. No way of telling. That was play-acting, but cops have to decide in real life. And they take no chances.

5: BAD BUSINESS

Never underestimate the power of the criminal mind.

Crime can realize profits that would shame many FTSE 100 companies. With the international drugs market worth an estimated £320 billion per year, it's no surprise that disrupting and dismantling organized crime has been one of the most enduring challenges and priorities for governments across the world in recent times.

Major league criminals operate on a truly global scale. Grace finds himself reflecting, while waiting for Amis Smallbone to emerge from a pub full of old-world villains in *Not Dead Yet*, on how local criminal rivalries in Brighton had been surpassed by the pressure brought by faceless yet ruthless overseas mobsters.

A huge number of people amass fortunes through top-level crime. It would be foolish, however, to assume that comes from next to no effort. Far from it. Only the strong survive. Weak, lazy criminals wither into oblivion, jail or an early grave thanks to turf wars and smarter opposition.

To be a successful criminal requires acute business acumen worthy of any multinational conglomerate's boardroom. A forensic understanding of profit margins, risks, opportunities, markets and one's competitors is the lifeblood of all successful entrepreneurs, on whichever side of the law they operate.

Business guru Alan Deutschman coined the oft-repeated catchphrase 'Change or Die'. Indeed, in 2007 he published a book on this philosophy. Never has this been taken quite so literally as in the criminal world. Villains who fail to adapt to keep one step ahead of the law, to have the edge over their rivals or to capitalize on new opportunities are never far from a cell door or an early grave.

Brighton and Hove has always been a nest of enterprising speculators. The vibrancy of the place, coupled with a ubiquitous can-do attitude, means that if you can't make it here, you can't make it anywhere. There is a reason why it features in the www.startups.co.uk list of the 'top twenty places in the country to start a business'.

The knocker boys were probably the first criminally minded modern-day chancers to get rich in the city, but many have followed in their footsteps.

David Henty and Clifford Wake could never be accused of being small-time crooks. Friends from school, they had a hunger that burned inside them. Their desire to accumulate colossal wealth was matched only by their antipathy to taxes. They felt that faceless government bureaucrats had no right to fritter away the money they earned through the sweat of their brows. No, only they should decide how their profits should be spent.

Both in their early thirties, Henty and Wake had served long and mainly successful apprenticeships climbing the greasy pole of Brighton's criminal underclass. Henty had been brought up in Moulsecoomb, a compact council estate, developed after the First World War as a site for 'Homes Fit for Heroes'. It is a warren of narrow streets with rows of small semis crammed along its pavements. Henty used to be sent out from there by his father on burgling errands. He learned to trust no-one, though, as even his own dad would short-change him.

They would try any scam from antique theft, stealing and selling on cars to manufacturing forged vehicle documents. They knew how to spot the chance to make a fast buck. Henty came from a family who were well known in the antique and art world, hence his expertise and reputation preceded him.

Both, though, were only too aware that rivalries, capture and incarceration were all occupational hazards.

But beneath all this, they were businessmen. They carefully weighed up the risks, forecast their turnover and took their decisions based on cold, calculated assessment. Was the gain worth the pain?

Grace has to deal with people from across the sociological spectrum. In *Looking Good Dead*, he considers the various layers – mainly defined by wealth – that make up the diverse bulk of the city. He reflects on the contrast between the genteel retired set whiling their days away watching Sussex play cricket at the County Ground to those of a similar age who by day beg for their next meal, and by night bed down in windswept seafront shelters. He has also been around long enough to know that the criminal classes range from subsistence thieves who melt into the background at the first sign of a police car to the ones at the top of their game living a life of faux respectability in their mansions behind security gates and high-walled perimeters in the Dyke Road Avenue area. Henty and Wake made it their life's ambition to claw their way up this ladder, and no law was going to stop them.

In the early 1990s, the UK was at the tail end of a property boom. Vendors were still making silly money on get-rich-quick schemes buying and selling houses. Mortgage companies couldn't keep up with business and no-one looked too carefully at how credit-worthy applicants actually were. The risks were low for financiers as, if the borrowers failed to pay, the property in question would have soared in value and they would be quids in.

David Henty had never earned an honest buck in his life. He certainly didn't have payslips or audited accounts to prove his income. That did not seem to matter to the bank manager who chose to lend him £175k – 100 per cent of the purchase price – to buy the prestigious 1 Wykeham Terrace. Providing Henty could make the monthly payments, cash of course, and the property continued its meteoric rise in value, how could he lose?

Many of Brighton's villains live in swanky mock-Tudor houses in Hove – on streets such as Dyke Road Avenue and Shirley Drive, which Glenn Branson in *Dead Man's Time* nicknamed 'Nob Hill'. Grace, in *Dead Like You*, shares Branson's skewed opinion of its residents, musing that while most were squeaky-clean its garish opulence also attracted some of the city's wealthy ne'er-do-wells.

However with Henty's artistic taste, which he would exploit later in his career as a successful art forger, he chose this delightful and grand period terraced house just yards from Brighton's Clock Tower, adjacent to the 900-year-old mother church of the city, St Nicholas of Myra, and on the doorstep of the Western Road shopping centre. This was one of the best located and most well appointed homes in the county.

Like Steven Klinger in *Dead Man's Footsteps*, Henty's steady, suspicious accumulation of wealth had awarded him the police status of 'person of interest' some time ago.

I had joined CID from uniform about six months previously and was revelling in rising to the challenge my new Detective Inspector had set me when I joined.

DI Malcolm 'Streaky' Bacon was a dapper and immaculately groomed gent. His pencil-thin moustache and ramrod posture gave the false impression he'd been a Regimental Sergeant Major in a previous life. He could easily have been a batman to Brigadier Neville Andrew, the Bursar at the Cloisters school in *You Are Dead*.

'We want young blood in the office, Graham, but you will work harder than you ever have before and you will be judged on results,' was Streaky's greeting to me on day one.

Julie and I had just bought our first house together and had become engaged to be married. She knew what CID would mean. Long hours of hard work. She was no stranger to that herself, however. She had become a check-in supervisor at Gatwick Airport. A sixteen-hour shift dealing with multiple flights, anxious passengers, long delays and stressed staff was a normal day at the office for her. On the plus side, it meant that short, last-minute holidays to anywhere in the world were there for the taking. She gave me so much support and encouragement while keeping me grounded at home. I landed one in a million with her.

Just as well. I was working like a trouper.

The networks and characters behind the crimes I was looking into were fascinating. While in uniform I'd had little insight into the machinations of the city's underworld. The work there was very reactive. Here as a detective I was paid to get under the skin of every criminal and see what I could unearth.

I was surrounded and supported by colleagues who had for decades been trawling the gutters of the city's criminal networks and I was absorbing everything I could from them. In the few snatched hours each day that Julie and I had together in our new two-up, two-down starter home, I would regale her with tales of derring-do, of how we had busted this scam or tracked down that villain. I was relishing this new life.

We had been paying more and more attention to Henty. So, when he bought his new pad we started to look even harder, just as he knew we would. Police scrutiny was expected in his world. It was always safer for him to assume that the police were watching and listening, rather than not. For his own sanity he had to balance this with not becoming paranoid. With this attitude, he was able to have some fun in his predicament.

David and Cliff used to meet in a lovely little cafe in Stanmer. This tiny, beautiful village comprises a farm, a dozen cottages, a church and a manor house in stunning parkland to the north east of the city.

Soon aware the police were observing them regularly and suspecting that surveillance officers were hiding up in a barn opposite their meeting place, they took to donning crash helmets as they arrived and then spending hours sipping coffee, soaking up the heat of the roaring fireplace that was the centre-piece of the coffee shop. They did not have that much to say to one another, but they delighted in the thought of the cops freezing their extremities off in the dung-infested cowshed over the road, while they nestled in the warmth.

One of their scams around this time was the forgery and distribution of MOT vehicle roadworthiness certificates and car tax discs. Through their network of printers and 'fencers' they had practically saturated the city with these fake documents. In the days before any databases or electronic detection devices, police officers had to rely on a keen eye and their own judgement when assessing the validity of any documents. Henty and Wake's products were of fine quality and rarely, if ever, called into question.

Word got round that they had a talent for making very passable official papers and soon a prominent London-based gangland villain nicknamed Lenny the Shadow got to hear of them. He had earned this sobriquet due to his seemingly mystical ability to appear and disappear in the blink of an eye.

Like the evil Marlene Hartman, who sourced street children and sold them for the price of their organs in *Dead Tomorrow*, Lenny had a criminal network with tentacles that spread across the world. He dealt, not in thousands, but in millions of pounds.

Around this time the province of Hong Kong was just a few years away from being handed back to the Chinese. As the 1997 deadline drew closer, its citizens were starting to panic, many unwilling to surrender their Western lifestyle. Consequently the region was experiencing a feverish rush for British passports. Residents wanted to claim UK identity to preserve the freedoms they had become so accustomed to. As with any surge in demand, the opportunities to make a quick buck were tantalizing.

Lenny saw the gap in the market almost immediately and looked round for a reliable network of forgers who were up to the challenge of making 3,000 UK passports for onward sale in Hong Kong. They had to be available quickly and to a standard that would pass inspection by seasoned immigration officials. He estimated that he could market them for £1,000 each making this a £3-million operation. Half of that would be his, half the forgers'.

David and Cliff were immediately shortlisted for the job. They had proven their worth in all the selection criteria. Cliff was known for his work ethic. If he took on a job, he worked at it slavishly and expected all around him to do likewise. David knew this serious-minded approach would ensure the seemingly impossible timescales would be met. This was business and a lot of money and their reputations were at stake.

They worked out that to provide the passports to the desired quality and in time, they would need three others to assist them. Their cut of £1.5 million would still be very attractive at £300k each, and David was already spending his share in his head.

He had been offered the opportunity to buy a Scottish castle for £1 million with a down-payment of just £100k. The remainder of the money, financed through yet another dodgy mortgage, would be paid back by filling the place with fake antiques and selling them to unwitting rich American tourists. The passport income would solve his headache of coming up with the deposit.

He knew the stakes were high. No government warms to anyone who fakes their passports, especially as part of a get-rich-quick scheme. Both David and Cliff had young families and commitments that lengthy periods in prison would render them unable to meet. They had to consider carefully whether the risks were worth taking.

As any wise businessman would do when faced with such a decision, David sat down and talked it through with his wife. It would be her who bore the burden of supporting the family should it all go wrong. For his part, Cliff needed no second opinion. This was a golden opportunity and there was no way his wife, Jan, would be given the chance to persuade him otherwise.

Having carefully weighed it all up, both David and Cliff made the call to Lenny.

'We're in!'

There followed a frenzied period where the pair sought out the skills and materials to create 3,000 passports so perfect that, even under the closest scrutiny, they would be indistinguishable from the genuine article.

They needed the correct paper, identical rexine (the leather-like material used for the distinctive dark blue cover), the right inks and a high-quality gold foil for the coat of arms. Photos would be added later, but creating these little booklets would be no mean feat.

It so happened that Cliff, who had a more modest taste in houses but whose flamboyance came out in his choice of cars, lived in the nearby suburb of Peacehaven, next door to a printer, Barry Cheriton. Unlike the rest of the team, Barry had never once had so much as a parking ticket. His credentials were simply the skills of his trade, and that he got on well with his felonious neighbour.

Cliff went to great, but subtle, lengths to dazzle him by flaunting his glamorous lifestyle. He reassured him of the rewards, should he take up his offer to 'just do a bit of printing for us' and minimized the risks by maintaining that Barry would be only a bit player in whom no-one would be interested. It worked a treat; Barry could not resist.

Barry was like a gangly love-struck teenager in this new underworld. He would do anything to impress Cliff and David. They treated him like the liability he was. His blundering ways together with his habitual tendency to lie his way out of any corner meant that he needed watching closely.

To produce 3,000 fake passports Barry could hardly use his

employer's presses, so they had to find a safe place for him to work that had all the right machinery and where no-one would ask questions.

Wilson Press, in nearby Uckfield, was well known as the place where many extreme right-wing publications were printed. Owned by Holocaust denier Anthony Hancock, it was no stranger to clandestine printing runs, nor to police surveillance. The day staff had long since learned to ask no questions. It was the ideal place to rent overnight for Barry to print a few passports. None of the team particularly liked Hancock, but this was business and they knew they needed him. A few thousand pounds would be enough to buy his silence, an essential guarantee when working a scam on this scale.

The irony was lost on no-one that a place so accustomed to promoting racism and intolerance was to be used to enable 3,000 people to enter and reside illegally in the UK.

When they needed to, David and Cliff claimed that their materials were to help them manufacture personal organizers. It was enough to satisfy even the most curious.

While this lucrative new project was taking shape, they were starting yet another scam. Music cassettes, even then, could cost up to £6 a throw. They worked out that if they could find a way of producing counterfeit versions for a fraction of that, they could put on a decent mark-up, yet still retail them for far less than the High Street.

Having procured a copying machine that could create duplicates to industry standards and hundreds of thousands of blank tapes, all they needed, once more, was a printer and a press for the labels and inserts. The timing was perfect. It transpired that Barry could churn out very passable artwork. He and Hancock's machines had never worked harder in their lives, all under Cliff's unrelenting supervision.

Soon box-loads of crystal-clear chart-topping cassettes were on the streets, changing hands for £1 each or £3 for five. Given that they only cost 50p to make, the profit margins were impressive.

Henty and Wake could not believe the demand. They had staff employed on shifts each running off hundreds of copies a day. It was netting them £1,500 per week.

However, selling such huge quantities of counterfeit goods at markets and car-boot sales is not the best way of staying below the police radar. It was this that flagged up that Henty and Wake had engineered this new racket. We knew nothing yet of the passports.

Police surveillance showed them dashing around the city stashing boxes at various garages and houses. What did not seem to fit were the trips to London to faux-leather factories and the purchase of yards of gold foil. No-one had seen a tape decorated with either of these. Clearly there was some multi-tasking going on.

By researching possible uses for those materials, supported by intelligence coming in, we became aware of their passport project. At first we thought that they were just trying their hand at making a few to see what they turned out like. Never in a million years did we think that they stood to make nearly £300k each, nor did we realize the connection to Lenny.

As we were trying to fathom out exactly what was going on, 1 Wykeham Terrace was playing host to a thriving cottage industry in counterfeiting. The kitchen had been taken over for the shaping and cutting of rexine, the bath was filled deep with dye to achieve just the right hue for the covers. Other rooms were used for the drying, stitching, quality control and packing operations. They were certainly working hard for their money.

Their business brains ensured they adopted a creative approach to any problem that threatened to derail their production. Old-style passports had two elongated ovals cut into the front cover. One would reveal the holder's name, the other the document number. They wrestled with how to recreate these shapes in a way that would look like the real deal.

When they were forging car tax discs, they faced the same quandary in replicating the perforated circular circumference. In that case, they found that a metal pastry cutter hammered onto the paper did the trick perfectly. Applying the same principle, they carefully manufactured a razor-sharp steel die to strike down on the cover. They were delighted with the results.

When the pages arrived from the printers, David spotted a problem. The background on any official document is always, deliberately, incredibly busy. On a passport, however, it is overlaid with the multicoloured image of a complex crest. Barry had not spotted this. Its omission was an error that could fatally scupper the whole project.

David and Cliff were furious. How could Barry have been so stupid? They needed a solution and needed it quickly. It would ruin all the pages to run them through the printer again. This could set them back weeks.

Barry had a suggestion. 'I could design a template to match the genuine one and build up the colours using screen-printing.'

'What, on every page of every passport?' asked an incredulous David.

'It's the only way. We've come too far and I'll work night and day. It'll take some time but it's do-able.'

'OK. It had bloody better be. We've got one and half million quid and a reputation to protect,' threatened Cliff.

The date was soon set for David and Cliff to travel to London and show Lenny the samples of their handiwork. Barry had to sweat blood to rectify his schoolboy error in time. The others took deliveries of the freshly corrected pages on a daily basis and with care and precision stitched them together into more than acceptable imitations of UK passports.

As the day loomed, the counterfeiters were exhausted. They

had known that to earn a prize of this size they would have to graft, but this had taken even Cliff's industrious nature to new levels.

A sense of achievement and impending prosperity prompted David to treat his wife to an intimate dinner at the world-famous English's Restaurant and Oyster Bar in Brighton's Lanes. Generally acknowledged as the city's oldest and finest seafood restaurant, over the years it has hosted the rich and famous, such as Charlie Chaplin, Dame Judi Dench and, of course, Peter James.

There, they excitedly planned their future with riches that just months ago would have been beyond their wildest dreams. Castles, holidays, fast cars; nothing was beyond their reach.

The following day, Cliff had to pop out to sort out some problems with the tape production leaving David, Barry and one of their helpers putting the finishing touches to the samples before the trip to London later in the day.

As with several large-scale police operations in those days, the investigative arm of CID knew little of the hundreds of hours of surveillance or the huge intelligence case being built by those in covert roles. We only found out about what had been happening on the day itself. This was all to do with operational security – the need-to-know principle that ensured the risk of leaks was kept to an absolute minimum. The downside was that we had to play catch-up. To keep an operation secret the painstaking evidence-gathering often had to wait until after the arrests had been made. This meant taking statements and securing exhibits relating to events that had long since passed.

As every Grace novel reminds us, briefings are the centre-piece of any investigation. They are the place where information is shared, snippets of intelligence checked out, updates given and priorities set. Roy Grace is deft at ensuring that during his, there is control and structure yet even the most junior officer feels able to speak up; it is often they who have the nugget that all the others have been waiting for.

I did just that myself once when I plucked up the courage to suggest Ian McLaughlin as a suspect for a homophobic murder. It was him. It turned out he had killed before and did so again while on day release from prison in 2013. He will now die in prison.

This one, however, was really more of a chat. The venue was the nicotine-stained, threadbare-carpeted CID office that had the appearance of having been equipped at a car boot sale; each battered and bruised piece of furniture was different from its neighbour. Each workstation, however, was the nerve centre of dozens of investigations into man's appalling inhumanity to man. As Grace reflected in *Dead Simple* when revisiting that self-same office, each desk appeared as if 'the occupant had abandoned it in haste and would return shortly.'

The information was a tad light on detail. All we knew was that we were going to storm 1 Wykeham Terrace, and a few garages dotted around the city. There was only sporadic mention of tapes, printers and passports. All I picked up was that 'stuff had been happening' and we needed to crash through Henty's door to find out exactly what.

I was still working with DC Dave Swainston and I felt incredibly privileged to be learning from such a seasoned master; he relished the most complex and arduous investigations and what he didn't know wasn't worth knowing.

On hearing of hundreds of thousands of tapes, and a hint of the counterfeiting of passports, Dave volunteered to run the investigation, as it would be something different to get his teeth into. I knew, given how closely we worked, if Dave took this job on then so would I. I couldn't wait.

This was long before the days of Local Support Teams who now would crash open doors and secure premises needing to be searched. This raid was down to us suits.

Off we went, crammed into our oh-so-identifiable unmarked CID cars. Anyone watching us screech, in convoy, up the traffic-choked North Street towards the Clock Tower would have wondered what on earth was going on. So did I.

It really wasn't essential to race to the target address. The only point at which it becomes necessary to go hell-for-leather is when you risk being seen by your quarry. Frankly, tearing up the road was nothing more than ego-boosting, adrenaline-pumping fun.

As we cleared the Clock Tower, the cars juddered in unison to a halt opposite the ivy-clad, stone-arched entrance that provided Wykeham Terrace with privacy from the outside world. Today it worked to screen us as we squeezed out of our three-door saloons, allowing us a few more seconds of surprise.

Eight of us raced up the flint steps into the courtyard in front of the imposing Tudor-Gothic facade of the terrace. Now was the time to rush.

We sprinted out of the shadows and leapt up the steps leading to house number 1. DS Don Welch, a rugby-playing, marathon-running giant, booted open the huge front door.

As we raced in creating an ear-splitting din with our shouts of 'police', 'stay where you are', and 'nobody move', we heard pounding footsteps and shouts above us. A door banged and it became clear that whoever we had disturbed didn't want to hang around to say hello. Dave and I raced up the stairs, knowing that whatever their intentions, the architecture of the building would make any escape attempt futile.

Behind Wykeham Terrace sits Queen Square. Between the two is a ten-foot-wide void that drops four storeys from the roof-top. Only the bravest free-runner would have any hope of leaping across and we, of course, had officers watching and waiting on the other side.

As we reached the first landing, I was distracted by a terrify-ing scream followed by a thud then further shrieking coming from outside. Dave and I turned and found a doorway to a narrow balcony overlooking the backs of the houses. My gaze turned towards the sickening cries coming from the depths below. I could just make out in the shadows a crumpled figure writhing around.

'Help me. Help me.'

'It's OK,' I said, 'we're coming to get you. Where does it hurt?'

'I've bust my ankle.'

'OK, OK, we'll get help.' I shouted to the stricken fugitive. 'Well, he's going nowhere,' I quipped to Dave.

At that moment, I heard more shouting above.

'Come down now. You're going to kill yourself,' yelled a detective hidden from our view.

'What of it,' came the reply, 'I'm stuffed.'

I gazed up into the afternoon sunlight and saw David Henty teetering precariously on the rooftop. With nowhere to go, he was stranded, and seemed frozen with fear, looking desperately around for an escape route. Then he peered down into the void, apparently weighing up his options. The sight of his crippled comrade writhing in agony below discouraged him from any attempt to leap.

As Cleo points out to Grace in *Dead Man's Grip* after learning that he had been scaling huge chimney stacks, many cops are terrified of heights. I am a proud member of that club. I was petrified that, as the new boy, I would be sent up after Henty.

Lots of voices were pleading for him to come down safely and I was relieved to see him being skilfully coaxed into the arms of waiting police officers. Probably the promise of having a moment to say goodbye to his wife, coupled with the agonizing cries of his companion below reminding him that it would bloody hurt if he jumped, had something to do with it.

Other officers came to guard our crippled fugitive, waiting for the Fire and Ambulance Services to extract him from his impossible position while Dave Swainston and I went back into the house to join our colleagues, assessing the scene.

With time now to survey what we had, I couldn't believe what I saw. Our timing had been perfect. We had literally burst in mid-production. The kitchen worktops were littered with passport components: offcuts of rexine, strips of gold foil, fake immigration stamps alongside inkpads and odd-looking oval-shaped metal templates. It was the counterfeiting equivalent of a smoking gun.

Only one person, Stephen Tully, a well-known armed robber, had bothered to stay behind and welcome us and, despite his assertions that he had only popped in to see his god-daughter, he was led off in handcuffs.

Cliff Wake, oblivious to what had been going on and having dealt with the tape issue, walked blindly into the gardens at the front of Wykeham Terrace. He was quickly pounced on, cuffed and taken into custody before he knew what was happening.

The search of the house then commenced in earnest. First, though, the SOCOs photographed the damning kitchen scenes. It was vital to capture a record of how we found the house – a factory in full production.

Unlike Grace we did not have the benefit of a POLSA (Police Search Advisor). However, we did go through the house with a fine-tooth comb. We even sent specialists down the chimney of a neighbouring house, as Henty had been seen stuffing something into it, from where they recovered passport remnants.

Henty, years later, would insist that we missed a box full of the finished product hidden in the house, and another in a car parked nearby. He said that he quickly had them recovered and burned while in custody. We never did find very many, a surprise given that the passports were due to be delivered to Lenny, so perhaps he was right.

The man crushed by his fall was quickly identified as Barry Cheriton. As someone unfamiliar with police investigations, we hoped that he would prove the weak link and open up the secrets of this intriguing crime. However, he had more pressing priorities to attend to, like having his wrecked foot and ankle repaired.

As the evening went on, we searched the plethora of houses, garages and printing works identified throughout the weeks of surveillance.

One particular garage was rammed to the rooftop with scores of boxes containing thousands of cassette tapes. Elsewhere was the tape copying machine, pages of inserts, a foil embossing device, tapes ready for sale and reams of paper and rexine. All had to be seized, documented and their movement accounted for from now until the trial. Early in *Dead Simple* Grace faces the consequences of being unable to explain the chain of the continuity of an exhibit while under cross examination at Lewes Crown Court. This is territory defence barristers invariably attempt to exploit when faced with a damning case against them – like this one.

Dave and I went across to Peacehaven with a photographer to search Cheriton's house. It had been a long day but one full of surprises and successes. We were running on adrenaline. As we heaved open the up-and-over garage door we revealed a huge tangerine-coloured four-armed screen printer sitting centre stage on the concrete floor. Surrounding this cumbersome contraption were pages and pages to be used in fake passports. A stencil replicating the crest that appeared on each page sat on a table nearby.

'Bloody hell!' Dave and I gasped in unison. Having had the whole set-up photographed, we started the painstaking search.

As I glanced at one of the pages, something caught my eye.

'Dave, how do you spell Britannic, one N or two?'

'Two, isn't it? Why?'

'What about Majesty? J or a G?'

'J. What are you doing, some kind of crossword?'

'Thought so. Come and look at this,' I said.

Dave wandered over and chuckled as he looked at the page that had sparked my curiosity.

The well-known passage on the inside of each British passport proudly proclaims that *'Her Britannic Majesty's Secretary of State requests and requires in the name of Her Majesty all those whom it may concern to allow the bearer to pass freely without let or hindrance, and to afford the bearer such assistance and protection as may be necessary.'*

The Henty/Wake/Cheriton version, however, started *'Her Britanic Magesty's Secretary of State requests and requires . . .'*

'The proofreader wants shooting,' said Dave.

We wondered whether the whole batch would have been rejected on this basis by whoever had ordered them.

Having gathered up all the evidence in this anonymous makeshift print factory, we headed back to the nick. Little did I know that over the next sixteen months I would become a master at dismantling and re-assembling this ancient press, as we had to produce it to countless prosecutors, defence lawyers and courts.

Henty and Wake knew their number was up. All their dreams had been shattered. There would be no Scottish castles and no £300k windfall to fund a new life of luxury. They decided to give us one last snub. Normally, reticent villains will at least sit in an interview room even if they ignore every question. It gives them relief from looking at the walls in their six by eight-foot police cells.

David and Cliff, on the other hand, decided that they would not even do that. When asked to step out for questioning they just sat and stared, moving not a muscle. In an irritating act of defiance, they had resolved not to give us an inch.

Based on the evidence that had been amassed in the preceding months, together with the damning scene we had gatecrashed, Henty, Wake and, eventually, Cheriton were charged with counterfeiting passports and music tapes. Tully was lucky, he walked away scot-free.

On being remanded in custody, Wake and Henty had engineered it so they could share a cell in Lewes Prison. True businessmen that they were, they spent their time not lamenting their predicament, but planning their next scam. They needed to cut their losses and find the next opportunity. They plotted and schemed, even though they didn't know when they would be free to put their plans into action.

Surprisingly, they only remained in custody for three weeks before a bail application was granted. In the next year and a quarter of unexpected liberty, while awaiting trial, they stumbled across a fabulously simple, yet lucrative, scheme involving stolen cars from the Republic of Ireland.

Henty was stopped, late one night, driving an Irish car. The officers, convinced it was stolen, struggled to confirm that fact. David overheard a radio message explaining that there was no protocol with Ireland that would help quickly identify questionable cars.

Always alert to an opportunity, the germ of an idea took root. If that was the case then surely he could import stolen cars on an industrial scale from Ireland, give them new identities and sell them on. Using his trusted contacts, he worked the scheme for months, exploiting the naivety of the Driver and Vehicle Licensing Authority staff into believing his account of legal imports and lost documents, to persuade them to re-register the cars in the UK.

He was caught eventually but not until the scheme had provided a tidy nest egg for his family should he lose his impending trial.

As Grace grumbles in *Dead Tomorrow*, having inherited a new role that includes reviewing files for forthcoming trials, the bureaucracy of the criminal justice system is almost beyond belief.

The amount of evidence we had to gather over the months was colossal. We needed to source all the material, confirm all the surveillance sightings, cost everything and prove that all three were guilty as charged. One enquiry took us to Gatwick Airport, where a senior immigration officer told us that, aside from the spelling mistakes, these passports were the best forgeries he had come across.

When the trial finally took place, the defence did their best. They queried the exhibits, tried to convince the jury of a host of coincidences, sought to dissuade them from assumptions and attempted to place the whole scam at the door of some of the witnesses. They were hoping that they had sown just enough doubt to win a marginal acquittal. However, the surveillance evidence, the incriminating material we found on the raids and the painstaking tracing of all the passport and tape components, secured swift guilty verdicts.

The sentences were an eye-watering jolt for Henty and co. Five years apiece sent an unequivocal message to other would-be forgers. The spoils may be tantalizing but the penalties are severe even if, like Cheriton, you had a blameless past. As for Lenny the Shadow, he did what all shadows do when you try to shine a light on them. He disappeared.

We are all human and, like Grace when he saw Gavin Daly being led away for murder in *Dead Man's Time*, I felt a twinge of pity for the three as they were taken down to the cells. They deserved all they got, but they had taken a huge gamble, the loss of which they and their families would pay for dearly.

Even with the shock of such a long time away, David and Cliff still plotted and came up with projects for the future. Most, if not all, were on the right side of the law, including stocking vending machines in Cyprus, selling discarded plastic to the Chinese and marketing popular paintings online. Others, involving more stolen cars, won Henty nine months in a Spanish

prison and Wake later went back to prison for money launder-
ing.

The difference between them and many criminals today is
that despite their prolific offending they never bore any animosity towards the police and never complained about their
comeuppance. And, being businessmen, they had other people
and schemes in place to ensure that the money kept rolling in.

Twenty-five years on, Dave Swainston and I spent a very
pleasant morning with Henty reminiscing over the old days,
swapping war stories and musing about some of the 'what-ifs' of
those days when we were on opposite sides of the law.

He and Wake knew that all businesses have their ups and
downs, and our ups were their downs. They never failed to make
a buck even if sometimes they paid the price with their liberty.
That was the life they had chosen and custody provided a time
of reflection to brainstorm the next scam to help them up the
social ladder.

Henty proudly explained to Peter James and me on another
visit that he now produces paintings openly branded as fakes
and makes a pretty penny bringing masterpieces to the masses.
His new wife is insistent that his life must now be on the straight
and narrow and, so far, he has not let her down.

Wake, when we spoke with him, was looking forward to his
release from prison. When I asked him what he planned to do
he was quick to remind me, 'Graham, you know me, I'm never
going to be poor now, am I?'

I chose not to ask any more. Nowadays, ignorance can be
bliss.

6: HORROR AMONGST THIEVES

Everyone needs friends. People who stick by you through thick and thin. Grace and Branson have just that in each other: a life-long bond, underpinned by trust, tolerance and forgiveness. Sometimes it's only when these are tested to the limit that you can really be certain whether those around you are the real deal.

One middle-ranking villain made some huge assumptions about the bona fides of his mates. His wake-up call came in the most eye-wateringly brutal manner imaginable.

DC Andy Mays is a great friend of mine. We first worked together playing undercover cops in the banally labelled Plain Clothes Unit at Gatwick Airport in the late 1980s and his first wife worked with Julie. We socialized together often and Andy arranged my stag night before Julie and I jetted off to get married on a beautiful Seychelles island in 1992.

His career eventually moved into a world too secret for these pages but no less exciting for it. We are friends to this day.

We shared a good number of years too as DCs on Brighton CID and, during that time, Andy developed a phenomenal talent for getting villains to talk to him – not just because, being a lookalike of Phil Mitchell from *EastEnders*, he resembled most of them.

Policing is often very reactive. We think that we have our fingers on the pulse and that intelligence-led proactivity is how we get our best results. We flatter ourselves. Like the conse-quences of the crash that killed Tony Revere in *Dead Man's Grip*, the most serious jobs are the ones we often fail to see coming.

There does seem to be something about Sundays that causes them to generate the most intricate and intriguing policing challenges. The late shift on this particular winter's day in 1992 was no exception.

Andy was clearing an outrageous backlog of reports that his sergeant had been badgering him over, while willing the clock to tick round to 9 p.m. when, as was the custom, he could go to the pub. The phones rarely rang on a Sunday so when his did, he sensed his evening was about to be disrupted. With a sigh he reluctantly lifted the grey receiver.

'CID. DC Mays.'

'Oh, hi. It's the control room here. Response are at a job in the Rose Hill area where a chap has fallen out of an upper-floor window. The sergeant is saying he doesn't think the bloke is going to survive. He's in a really bad way. They've taken him to the hospital and they are asking for CID to meet them there.'

'Why do they want us? Do they suspect foul play?'

'They're not sure; there's just something they aren't happy about.'

'Jeez, they give these sergeants stripes for a reason,' Andy muttered. 'Why can't they make a bloody decision? Yes, OK on my way,' he continued, this time intending to be heard.

The cars we were forced to drive rudely quashed any credibility Brighton's finest detectives tried to purvey. As they were no doubt procured solely on the basis of price and economy, we never quite felt like the slick crimebusters we aspired to be as we rocked up in one of these rusting, pastel-coloured Mini Metros. Distinguished only by their whining engines and the fact they looked ridiculous with two hulking great detectives wedged into their tiny front seats, they were more suitable for a circus than the UK's second-busiest police station. Grace's sidekick, Branson, with his somewhat frighteningly advanced driving skills, wouldn't have been seen dead in one of these tin cans. Still, that was all we had so, having grabbed a set of keys, off Andy went.

The gridlock that irritates Mafia hit man Tooth after he has abducted Tyler Chase in *Dead Man's Grip* is omnipresent in Brighton. Sundays are no exception. If it isn't caused by the hordes of day-trippers clogging up the streets, it is the fanatics who insist on crawling from London to Brighton by various modes of transport ranging from veteran cars to historic lorries and good old-fashioned bicycles. Every weekend there are always people trying to make the fifty-five miles from capital to coast by one means or another, and they all seem to come to a standstill just by the police station.

Andy used his encyclopaedic knowledge of the city to snake through the backstreets, engine shrieking, to the Royal Sussex County Hospital.

On arrival he abandoned the car in a bay marked 'Taxis', slipped his Sussex Police log book – which serves as a 'park any-where' permit – behind the windscreen and marched into the Accident and Emergency Department.

Among the teams of doctors, nurses and paramedics, he located the sergeant who seemed unable to make a decision.

'Right, Sarge. What have we got, then?'

'Well. It's hard to say. It seems this chap has taken a tumble out of a small casement window. It's quite high up and we can't really work out how he's done it.'

'Are you saying he might have been pushed?' asked Andy, coaxing his senior colleague to express a view.

'That's the point,' said the sergeant. 'We've been up to the flat and it's a lounge window but a bit of a squeeze. Oh, and there seems to have been a bit of a disturbance in there.'

'Oh, right. And what's the deal with matey, then? I take it he's in resus? Who is he? What are his injuries?'

'Don't know who he is but some of the neighbours say

he's only been living there for the last couple of weeks. He's unconscious, which is definitely a bonus for him given the mess he's in. He seems to have fallen smack bang onto some spiked railings. One has impaled him, then his weight must have pulled him back as he has fallen off them, ripping his innards in the process.'

'Jesus,' winced Andy.

'What's more, his leg is in a right state. Looks like he's somehow got a horrendous break resulting in, well, put it this way, his knee is now fully double-jointed.'

'How's that happened if he's fallen out belly first, landed on the spikes then fallen off? How's he done his leg?'

'That, DC Mays, is why we called you all-seeing detectives,' the sarcastic sergeant replied, implying that Andy's muttered dissent earlier had not been as hushed as he intended and that his sentiments had been passed up the chain of command.

The problem with being a detective is that once you show a hint of interest in an incident, it's yours to keep. It's like a one-way game of Pass the Parcel – you never get to give it back.

Like so many of the calls Grace picks up, be it the disappearance of Michael Harrison in *Dead Simple* or the dredging of the first body in *Dead Tomorrow*, the full story is seldom evident straightaway; indeed some such incidents can be dismissed by indolent, less gifted cops, thereby denying justice to victims.

This was a dreadful fall, possibly a pretty serious suicide attempt, but something was not quite right. How does anyone actually *fall* out of such a small window? If the man did jump, why from there? What about that snapped leg? How did he do that at the same time as skewering himself on the ironwork below? These questions gnawed away at Andy.

Good cops don't ignore their niggles. The hair standing up on the back of the neck can be as good a clue as any at the outset of an enquiry. Good old copper's nose is something you learn to trust. Sometimes you just can't put your finger on why you feel suspicious but that is no reason to shrug off your hunches.

As I moved up the ranks, I was always sure to help junior officers listen to their inner feelings and encouraged them to follow lines of enquiry on the sole basis that 'something just didn't add up'. If it didn't feel right it probably wasn't; the trick was to find out why.

Andy waited at the hospital, working the phones in an attempt to find out more about this mystery man and how he ended up fighting for his life.

Having been told the ward where he had been taken, Andy emerged from the groaning lift at Level 7 of the hospital's Thomas Kemp Tower, and quickly orientated himself while absorbing the distinctive 'Eau de Hospital', an aroma of disinfectant and disease combined with death.

Quite miraculously, after just a few hours and against the odds, the casualty, his body wrecked and saturated with morphine, regained consciousness. Despite his best efforts Andy still had little to go on other than it all seemed a bit odd. He therefore charmed his way through the medics to see him.

Breezing past the maelstrom of activity at the nurses' station with a quick flash of his warrant card, it didn't take his years of detective training to locate his man. Mummified neck to toe in plaster and bandages, the victim was wired up to the same squawking machines and slowly bubbling drips that shocked Ashley in *Dead Simple*, when she visited the same hospital to see the aftermath of her fiancé's disastrous stag night.

An unannounced visit from the CID often provokes a prickly reception. This can be rooted in curiosity, guilt or just plain irritation. The reaction Andy received was no exception but he was accustomed to frostiness.

'Hello, mate,' he said. 'I'm DC Andy Mays. Looks like you've had better days.'

'Piss off,' grunted the stricken man.

'Now let's not be like that. I don't do pissing off when people are lying half dead in hospital beds and in your state you're stuck with me. Why don't we start by you telling me who you are and see where we go from there?'

'Fuck, well, I suppose you will find out eventually. I'm Angus Sherry, that's all I'm telling you.'

'That's better. Look, you're not in trouble, Angus, not with us anyway, but it would be nice to know how you managed to take the dive out of the window today.'

'I just fell out. I was taking some air and I fell.'

'Look, mate, you and I both know that's a load of old bollocks. No-one falls out of windows like that, let alone big blokes like you. Just tell me what happened, I can go and satisfy my bosses everything is OK and, tough as it may be, we won't need to see each other again,' suggested Andy.

At this, a nurse entered the ward wheeling an aged payphone on a trolley.

'Angus, there's a friend of yours on the phone. Would you like to take it now or shall I get them to call back?' she chirped.

Andy gave a nod of permission and settled back in the chair as she plugged the phone wire in. Angus lifted the receiver, struggling with pain.

His face took on a deathly pallor. His eyes widened to the size of saucers as he listened intently, spluttering to get a word in. Andy could hear shouting coming through the earpiece.

Eventually Angus managed to speak.

'You fucking leave her out of this. Fucking touch her and I'll rip your fucking head off. Do what you want to me but I'm fucking warning you. Harm one hair on her head and you are dead,' he ranted as Andy sat up, riveted by this angry call.

A short pause, then, 'I fucking told you yesterday. It's safe but now you've done this to me it's going to take a bit fucking

longer.' Angus slammed the phone down as the other incredulous patients stared on, fascinated by this dramatic interruption
to their tedium.

Recognizing that his intuition had, as usual, proved right,
Andy swiftly arranged for Angus to be moved to a side room and
made a flurry of calls to get some uniform back-up at the hospital in case it all kicked off. Once the emergency actions had
been put in train, he returned to get to the truth.

'Right, Angus. Shall we stop pissing around now? Something's
going on. Someone has hurt you and, unless you co-operate,
sounds like someone very close to you is going to be in the next
bed or even the morgue. Start talking and make it quick.'

'First things first, get someone round my girlfriend's house in
Kemp Town and get her out of there. They are going to kill her
and, as you can see, this lot don't fuck about.'

He gave a name and address, which Andy scribbled down,
before dashing out to the nurses' station to put in the call that
would send a marked police car straight round to protect her.

He slid back into Angus's room and quietly clicked the door
shut.

'Right. She will be safe. Now everything, please.'

'Well, I'm not a grass so you ain't getting everything, but as
you will have worked out, I'm in a bit of shit. I'm no angel and
I've fallen out with some very bad people.'

'Well, that was a bit careless,' quipped Andy.

'Yeah, right. Anyway, I've pissed them off big time.'

'Right, I want to know how much shit you are in and what we
need to do. No doubt we will need to speak to you later in more
detail about what you've done but for now let's just see if we can
keep you and your girlfriend alive, shall we? What happened
today for you to end up in here?'

'Well, I had a visit. They've been after me for a couple of
weeks. They reckon I'm trying to cut them out of a deal. Anyway,
they were in a bad, bad mood. They came down to beat the crap

out of me until I gave them what they wanted. When I wouldn't play ball the three of them started on me. First it was just a few slaps, then they got more and more angry. Kidney punches, cigarette burns, knives at my bollocks, the whole lot.'

'So what happened then?'

'They could see that I was holding out and they were livid. They knocked me around so much I was just a heap on the floor. Then they rolled me on my back, held me down, and put my leg up on a chair. I couldn't move. My leg was completely locked out. I had one bloke holding me down and another sitting on my foot; I was trapped. I couldn't work out what was going to happen. Then the third bloke climbed onto the table just by my side. The penny still didn't drop. Then the bloke on my foot yelled, "One more chance 'cos this will fucking hurt." I stared back at him and told him to fuck off.

'He then just nodded to the bloke on the table who jumped in the air and, with both feet, crashed down onto my leg, crunching right through my kneecap. The last thing I remember was a crack like a gun going off and seeing my foot flipping up towards my face. I was in fucking agony; it shot through my whole body. They knew they had gone too far, as I was screaming my head off. They needed to shut me up. The next thing, I was being grabbed, the lounge window was opened and they carried me over to it. Thank God I can't remember being chucked out or landing on the railings. They wanted to kill me. They will next time.'

'Jesus,' muttered a stunned Andy, 'who did that and why?'

'I can't tell you. You just need to protect me and my girl-friend. They will kill us if you don't help.'

Three uniformed PCs arrived and Andy told them to take positions outside the room to prevent anyone dodgy getting near Angus. He briefed the hospital staff, informed hospital security and did his best to ensure no-one had a second go at punishing this mysterious villain. After all, the windows here were significantly higher than the last one he had been thrown out of.

Everything in place, Andy phoned his DI, John Grant, and asked to meet him back at the police station. John abandoned his plans for a night in front of the telly, made his excuses to his wife and rushed back to the nick to run his own real-life drama.

They needed to find out who was behind all of this. With Angus disinclined to further endanger his precarious future by naming names, the only hope was Jenny, the girlfriend.

Andy briefed John while they headed off to find the tiny Kemp Town flat. It was relatively easy – the marked police car guarding her door was a bit of a giveaway.

Kemp Town features heavily in Peter James' novels due to its quirky multiple characteristics. It is described in *Looking Good Dead* as having evolved from a posh Regency enclave to one that has 'the same seedy tatty aura that has corroded the rest of Brighton'. Logan Somerville in *You Are Dead* was kidnapped in that neighbourhood and an officer met a fiery death there in *Want You Dead*.

Playing good cop, bad cop, Andy and John pumped Jenny for information, Andy using his matey charm in an effort to persuade her to see the sense of spilling the beans and his boss adopting a less compromising style. The combination soon drew from her what they wanted.

She knew that Angus had been in deep trouble for a few weeks. It was all down to some money that three blokes accused him of stealing. As the phone calls had become increasingly menacing, so he had been getting more and more scared. She insisted that she did not know their names or what it was all about, but she gave enough to set the police on the trail.

'Right, love, where are you going to stay tonight?' demanded John.

'Well, er, here, can't I?' she asked, glancing from one officer to the other, seeking reassurance.

'No you can't,' replied John. 'I'm not giving you a twenty-four-hour guard. You need to find someone who can put you up where these delightful people can't find you. Once you have found somewhere, give the details to your babysitter here,' pointing to the bored-looking police constable, 'and we will get there like yesterday.'

On the short drive back to the police station, at around 2 a.m., they agreed that Andy would need to turn the screw on Angus. The time for pussy-footing around had come to an end. Others would be following up the scant leads they had picked up so far, but Angus needed to fill in the gaps.

As Andy slipped into the side ward shortly after 7 a.m., an almost indiscernible flick of his head gave the uniformed guard the clear message that he was not welcome for the moment. He stepped outside.

Angus tried to sit up, momentarily forgetting in his trepidation the extent of his massive injuries. He was convinced that Andy was bearing bad news. Sensing his anxiety Andy quietly reassured him, 'Jenny's fine, Angus.'

Visible relief washed through him.

'Jenny is safe, out of the way, but you and me are going to have a chat.'

'I've told you all I can,' Sherry replied.

A common tactic when trying to get someone to do or say something they would rather not is to blame an uncompromising higher authority.

'Listen, Angus,' urged Andy, 'my boss is getting very pissed off. When you see Jenny, ask her how he spoke to her. He can't stand what he calls "tossers like this" upsetting his city. He doesn't much care what you do to each other, but it never looks good with people flying out of windows on a Sunday evening and then us having to tie up our scarce cops sorting it all out and protecting people like you.'

Before Angus could argue Andy held up a hand. 'His words

not mine. So. Let's have it. Everything. No more bullshit. No more misguided loyalty to blokes who use kneecaps as trampolines. I want everything and I want it now or else, the mood my governor's in, the next time you see me I could be wearing a hospital gown identical to yours.'

Silence is a powerful tool. People hate it. The power lies with the person who left it; the person whose turn it is to speak feels an almost irresistible urge to fill the gap.

Andy just sat there; nothing but the whirr of machines and the distant chatter of nurses punctuated the hush. He simply stared at the man in plaster. He knew he would give in first. They always did.

'Shit, I've never been a grass before.'

Bingo. Works every time. Now for a little encouragement.

'You're not grassing, Angus. You'll be saving your life and Jenny's. It doesn't get much bigger than that. Tell it from the beginning and we can stop all this.' *Keep it all positive. Emphasize the benefits, don't mention the risks.*

Criminals would have you believe that they subscribe to some Mafia-like code of *omertà* – or not informing to the police. Unlike in Sicily, most UK villains are more fickle in its application. Darren Spicer, the career burglar in *Not Dead Yet* and *Dead Like You*, is typical of many in being happy to play Judas when it suited him.

'What will happen when I've told you?' asked Sherry.

'We will look after you and Jenny will be safe, but we have to know. You have to trust us. We can't do this without you and, from where I'm sitting, you need all the help you can get right now.'

'What are my options?'

'You've run out of those.'

'Shit.' Angus closed his eyes. His fists clenched. He shook his head. Andy saw that he was in turmoil. He was weighing it all up. This was positive. So long as he was thinking about it, rather than telling Andy to go fuck himself, there was hope.

Silence again, then: 'Bollocks. Right, here goes.'

In the back of the net! Andy was all ears.

'You'll have worked out I'm no choirboy. You're right but, believe it or not, I have some honour. I never break my word, I am loyal to my mates and, until now, I've never grassed.'

Andy kept quiet; just a nod of the head encouraged Sherry to continue.

'Me and my mates, we've been very busy. You must have heard about what we have been up to but hopefully not who we are. All across the south of England, we've been robbing travel agents. Their security is a joke compared to banks or building societies but they all have thousands of pounds in traveller's cheques and foreign currency. I've got a mate who tells me which shops are having cheques delivered and when.'

Andy listened intently. He, along with just about every other detective south of Bedford, was well aware of this vicious spate of tie-up robberies.

We had all dealt with them. The calls always came in before the first coffee of the day had been drunk. The gang struck, seemingly at random, at small travel agents, in numerous towns and cities, just as they opened. Relying on a lack of customers, they would bundle the staff into a back room, force the shop keys from them, lock the door, tie them up and then, with threats of horrific violence, similar to those used on ninety-eight-year-old Aileen McWhirter in *Dead Man's Time*, demand the safe keys. They would grab as many traveller's cheques as they could in a minute or two and then scarper.

'We never hurt anyone. We only needed to scare the shit out of them. They were trained to sell holidays, not to protect the family silver, so we always got what we were after. What we nicked were worthless pieces of paper unless we could turn them into hard cash. As I've been living here and know a bloke who can deal with traveller's cheques, we decided to do a job in Brighton. It all went well and we got away with a few grand's worth. It was my job to convert them into cash quickly.

'So, I took the cheques and gave them to my contact. He said he could deal with them. Well, after a few days the lads started to ask questions. "Where's the money?" "When are you going to pay us?" "How well do you know this bloke?"

'I kept chasing him but it seems your lot were putting some pressure on his bloke up the chain so he couldn't shift them on. Well, we were all getting nervy and the others were getting suspicious. They started to accuse me of nicking all the money for myself. There was no way I was going to tell them who my contact was, so they thought I'd made it all up.

'They started to get nasty, threatening all sorts of things. I mean for Christ's sake, we have known each other for years. We've never let each other down but they were turning the heat up on me. I got scared so I stopped taking their calls, moved out of my flat and tried to lie low until I could get the cash. I was getting desperate and was begging my mate to get the money but he was in as much of a corner as me. I knew the others were trying to find me. I had to keep out of the way, but at the same time be around to make sure I was there to get the money when the cheques were fenced.'

This was all very interesting for Andy; it filled in some gaps, and was certainly going to be instrumental in dismantling this hitherto elusive gang. It did not, however, give many leads to help protect Angus and Jenny.

Andy's silence prompted Sherry to continue.

'So, eventually they tracked me down to the flat in Rose Hill. I've told you what they did to me there but it was basically torture. You know the score, tell them what they want and I would walk away. If I wouldn't, or in my case couldn't, I would never walk again. Thing was I had no way of conjuring up the money or knowing when they would get it, so they did what they did and here I am.'

Andy kept quiet.

'They are going to kill me unless I get the money. They were watching while I was scraped into the ambulance. They followed it to the hospital. You can't protect me unless I get the money to them and you ain't going to let me do that now. They said they've got guns and they are going to come here.'

'How have they told you all this?'

'They phoned me really early, before you got here today. Your guards just stepped out. I said it was my missus and they didn't question that.'

'For God's sake,' muttered Andy. 'OK, now tell me who they are, where they are, what they have said, what they are going to do. Every last detail, and now. I'll be the judge of what is and isn't relevant.'

Finally, like an opening lock gate, Angus gushed the details that Andy needed to piece the jigsaw together: the key to stopping a slaughter.

'Right, I'm just going outside to make a couple of calls.' He and the PC guard swapped places.

Time was against them. All the police knew was who they were looking for and in which town. Like the hunt for Bryce Laurent in Want You Dead, this was a life or death hunt for a needle in a haystack.

Nobody could be certain what the targets' movements would be, which of their threats were scare tactics and which were real. What was certain, however, was that if they attacked the hospital Andy and the unarmed uniformed guard would be woefully inadequate protection. Some serious firepower was called for.

Intelligence was now coming in thick and fast; the gang intended to take Angus out at the hospital. The impact of that would be devastating. It would inevitably result in a shoot-out or siege which, with hundreds of sick patients as potential hostages or secondary targets, had the potential of being catastrophic.

A ring of steel was thrown around the hospital and its numerous entrances. Armed officers were drafted in, forming concentric circles of protection around the stronghold containing Sherry.

One of the core values of the emergency services is courage – the willingness to put oneself in harm's way to protect others, whoever they are. Whether it is the firemen running towards the Twin Towers on 9/11 passing thousands sprinting away or Grace risking his life to save Pewe on the cliff top at Beachy Head, both depicted in *Dead Man's Footsteps*, extraordinary gallantry is a role requirement for officers. Andy knew he and others would need to draw on every ounce of theirs.

Meanwhile, surveillance officers were combing Hastings, thirty-five miles east of Brighton. Intelligence suggested that the gang were holed up in that area but were planning to make their way towards the city imminently. The pressure was on to get to them before they reached their quarry. And the odds were very much stacked against the police. They had no registration number, just a rough description of the gang and of the car they would use to travel on their brutal errand.

By an astonishing piece of skill, a sharp-eyed undercover detective spotted a car similar to the one being hunted, with out-of-town number plates, parked in a row of vehicles on a dimly lit backstreet in Hastings.

Recognizing the twitch of his 'copper's nose', he shouted for his colleague to stop the car; they watched and waited. A swift Police National Computer check on the car's registration plate confirmed their suspicions. Moments later he glimpsed three burly men furtively making their way towards it, jumping in and driving off.

They started to follow and it wasn't long before the car headed west towards Brighton.

This was it.

Providing the suspects did not get near the hospital, or Jenny's secret hideaway, the advantage had now switched to the police. The order to arrest would be finely timed to ensure the safety of all but at the point where enough evidence had been gathered to see the gang locked up and the key thrown away.

Thankfully, the journey from Hastings to Brighton can be slow and tortuous. Normally this is acutely irritating, but with a high-impact firearms operation to plan, the more time available the better.

Andy, still in the ward, felt his pulse racing as, together with the armed officers who had joined him, he planned the contingencies should the bandits evade the pursuing cops.

Would they get warning of an imminent attack? Where would they take cover? What about Sherry? How would they protect a man encased in plaster? *Please God, don't let them get through.*

The knowledge that there were several lines of defence that would have to be breached before their sanctuary was invaded did little to assuage their anxiety.

'I hope you lot know what you are doing,' Sherry remarked.

'You're bloody lucky,' replied PC Mick Richards, one of the firearms cops. 'If anything happens to me, just make sure Andy grabs my gun. I trained him at Gatwick and I tell you, he can shoot as straight as me.'

Despite his intentions, this quip did nothing to lighten the mood.

On the street, a plan was being hastily pulled together. These three men who had shown their propensity to inflict the most appalling violence were not going to come quietly. It required military tactics and an overwhelming show of force to make them realize there was no chance of escape and to shock them into submission.

You could have cut the atmosphere with a scalpel in the hospital room as the armed cops heard that the team had crossed the Brighton border. Their radios squawking into their earpieces, the firearms officers were privy to exactly what was happening and where. Andy could rely only on their body language and a few snatched code words that his previous firearms training had allowed him to grasp.

The grip on their weapons became tighter. Their features took on a tautness that betrayed the adrenaline coursing through their veins as they anticipated a kill-or-be-killed firefight. Their bodies tensed as they took up tactical positions to give them dominance, intended to overwhelm their targets the second they breached the doorway. They hoped beyond hope that, like with so many operations before, their precautions would prove unnecessary and they would not be forced to take a human life.

The four occupants of the side ward were bonded by a common silence, a shared fear. Only two knew exactly what was going on; the others tried to pick up and read any signs given away.

Suddenly, a stunning array of firepower and fast cars exploded onto Eastern Road, below them. From nowhere, three plain but high-powered police vehicles raced up to the bandit car. In a flash, twelve heavily armed police officers clad from head to toe in black surrounded the targets, their weapons a frightening reminder that they had not come in peace. With no choice but to surrender the villains clamped their hands on their heads, awaiting the ignominy of being dragged onto the cold tarmac, cuffed, searched and dragged off to custody. The meticulously planned and executed high-threat arrest had neutralized the suspects.

'Got 'em,' was all Mick Richards said. They could all unwind. Except Sherry, that is. His relief could only be temporary; he was now an even more marked man.

Other officers dealt with the aftermath of the arrests, the securing of evidence from the car and the searches of various properties long into the night.

The next day, as Andy arrived on the ward just as Sherry was being wheeled off for yet another operation, he found an argument going on between the patient and a porter.

'Tell him, Andy. I need my tissues with me,' demanded Angus, holding a box of man-sized Kleenex.

'Your tissues? What on earth do you want those for? You will be sparko. If your nose needs wiping, I'm sure the NHS can find someone to do that for you.'

'For Christ's sake. Well, you look like you need one. You've got a bogie.'

'What's all this about bloody tissues, Angus?' replied Andy, subconsciously wiping his nose.

'Just take the fucking tissues,' was the patient's last word as he was rolled from the ward.

Andy took the box from him and, still puzzled, casually glanced inside. Expecting to see a bed of snow-white paper handkerchiefs, he was perplexed when he tried to make out the strange objects wedged beneath a couple of tissues in the carton.

He probed in through the slot and pulled out half a dozen sealed bags, all containing paper bills.

'Good God,' was all he could mutter as he laid them out on the over-bed table. Each contained thousands of pounds of crisp, new, unsigned traveller's cheques.

How on earth did they get there?

Only one person could spill those beans and he was sleeping like a baby while the National Health Service's finest strived, once again, to fix his broken body.

Hours later, when Sherry returned from the operating room, Andy quizzed him on the miraculous appearance of the cheques.

It seemed that the guards posted on the room weren't up to much. When one had disappeared to answer a call of nature, a mysterious visitor – a local pub landlord – slipped in to see

Angus. In that short visit he brought him the box of tissues with its very valuable contents. As the officer returned he made polite excuses and scurried away.

He was a runner for the man Angus had entrusted with the cheques. Angus had previously lodged at his pub, hence police had spoken to the landlord soon after Angus took his tumble. He had denied all knowledge of anything but clearly alerted the handler who, while keen to get the cheques back to Sherry, was too scared to turn up at the hospital himself.

The plan was for Angus to hand over the cheques in exchange for his life if the gang made it to his bedside. As that clearly was not going to happen now, with great reluctance he made sure that they ended up in the safe hands of the police but trusted nobody except his new mate Andy to deal with them properly.

Following interviews of all four men – Angus's taking place in the hospital – they were charged with a string of robberies of travel agents across the south east of England.

In a bizarre twist, as yet another uniformed police guard became too confident that the patient's plaster casts would frustrate any escape attempts, Angus managed to disappear from under the officer's nose. Having arranged it through many unsupervised telephone calls, he fled not to evade justice but the consequences of being a grass.

He hobbled out of the ward on crutches, employing the ruse of needing the toilet. His accomplices were waiting and wheeled him right out of the hospital explaining, to the few who bothered to ask, that they were taking him out for a smoke.

There were countless red faces as we scoured the city, fearing the worst. As Andy wasn't available, I was charged with leading the hunt and, despite my very clear assertion on BBC TV News that a *uniformed* officer had been guarding him, most of my friends and colleagues preferred to believe that I was the clumsy cop. They saw no reason why the truth should ruin an opportunity for a wind-up.

A couple of days later I tracked Sherry down to an address close to the city centre.

'For Chrissake,' he said, disgusted, 'you're useless, you lot. How d'you let a cripple get away from you? I thought you were supposed to be looking after me!'

He had a point.

Such was the geographic span of their crimes, the gang eventually appeared for their trial at Luton Crown Court in Bedfordshire as that is where they had committed the most offences. Once again their spell in custody had been bungled as some bright spark had put them all in the same holding cell. The cuts and bruises that adorned their faces as they stepped into the well of the court were evidence that they still hadn't found it within themselves to kiss and make up.

Angus couldn't resist sly smiles in Andy's direction, nodding his head at his co-defendants, indicating his satisfaction at the revenge he had exacted. The swift convictions and heavy sentences that followed were as inevitable as they were celebrated.

Despite the months that had passed since they'd last spoken, Andy felt a trip to the Isle of Wight prison where Sherry was serving his time might prove fruitful in squeezing more intelligence from him.

As Angus was frogmarched into the dark prison interview room by two stern-looking warders, Andy stood up, his outstretched hand indicating that he had come on a friendly assignment. Sherry took it and shook it warmly. However, his opening statement made his intentions crystal clear.

'Andy. Thanks for coming to see me. Nice you should take the time. However, whatever you want you're going back empty-handed. I told you much, much more than I should have back then in the hospital. That was to save my life. No-one can protect me in here, not even these goons. I speak, I die. You are getting nothing from me. Not one more word. You've had a wasted trip. But, before you go, I don't think I ever thanked you for what you did back in Brighton. Despite all this, you saved my life.'

With that he stood up, turned round and disappeared into the greyness beyond, to a soundtrack of scraping locks and slamming steel doors.

Andy, feeling slightly melancholy, made his way back to the ferry port reflecting that the further intelligence that he sought would have been wonderful but was not to be.

However, he consoled himself with the knowledge that it was his copper's nose which had started all this that Sunday when he saw Sherry's broken body in the hospital. The events that followed were intense and sometimes scary. But with four extremely dangerous people being locked up, the recovery of thousands of pounds and countless cashiers saved from becoming future victims, he rightly felt very proud.

7: EVERY DETECTIVE'S NIGHTMARE

Crimes and tragedies don't always happen in office hours. For a detective, being on call means that at any moment during the day or night a phone call can come out of the blue that will require you to instantly drop all your plans for the following days and sometimes weeks – if not months. Some jobs crash into you with such devastating force they leave you damaged forever.

It was late 1995 and I had been promoted to DS about eighteen months previously. After a short stint in Child Protection I was back on CID, running a small team of detectives. Julie and I had just celebrated our third wedding anniversary and had moved into a spacious four-bedroom house in Burgess Hill, about thirty minutes from Brighton.

While life was good, my two great ambitions – further promotion and having children – were evading us. Julie was making a huge success of running the Gatwick to Scotland Air UK passenger service operations but we were rattling around in our new home. We craved the patter of tiny feet.

Beep beep beep: three sounds that at 4 a.m. one morning dragged me from sleep. *Wake up properly before you phone in, Graham, don't make a fool of yourself.*

Then there was the usual rummage to locate my grey message-pager under a pile of clothes in the inky-black bedroom. Pressing its button, I floodlit the room.

'Shit, sorry, Julie!' I muttered as she grabbed the duvet, flung herself over and burrowed under the bedclothes.

As usual, the message gave no clue. Just a bland 'Please call Control Room Ext 35280 re serial 76.' The messages never betrayed the waiting horror.

The polar opposite to Sandy Grace or Ari Branson, the police wives in the Roy Grace novels, Julie accepted much about my job. If a mould for the perfect policeman's wife was needed, Julie was it. My long days, the late-night and early-morning phone calls, cancelled days off, being on call, bringing rainforests of paperwork home: she took everything in her stride. She absorbed my moods, my stresses, and my tears; there were plenty of those. Cops are human. The horror, the helplessness mostly stays in the 'job' side of the brain but sometimes it breaks through the psychological shield into the 'home' side and that's when it hurts. Hurts like hell. Julie would rightly wonder why I put on such a cheery and brave face to friends and family when she knew that inside I was fighting demons. I could be so unfair to her.

Two things, however, she could not stand. First, if I tried to start a phone call before I had woken up properly – she had been known to grab the phone from me and tell the confused caller to whom I was talking nonsense, 'Graham will ring you back in five minutes'; second, if I used the bedroom phone to call in, unnecessarily waking her from an already disturbed sleep.

So, having safely navigated the stairs in the 4 a.m. half-light, I squinted at the telephone keypad and punched out the well-worn numbers that would connect me to some perky wide-awake controller.

'Hi, it's Graham Bartlett, someone paged me to ring in re serial 76.'

'Oh, morning, Graham. Serial 76, let me look, oh, right, that's a cot death, I'm afraid.' Otherwise known as Sudden Infant Death syndrome, it didn't get any worse.

Shit, shit, shit, shit. Get a grip, Graham, get a grip.

I'd been around a long time and had dealt with most things, but I hated, detested, anything connected with harm to children. I wasn't alone. The toughest cops in the world could turn into emotional wrecks or angry hulks at the very mention of child abuse or a youngster being injured or killed.

Odd, really, that early in my career I had been so keen to spend a short time as a Child Protection detective. Perhaps that was a professional reaction to my desire to wrap all children, anyone's children, in cotton wool. Whatever it was, the anger evoked in dealing with child abusers, violent parents and people who cared more about drugs and alcohol than their kids was offset by saving children from a catastrophic start in life.

A study in 2012 reported that 29 per cent of prisoners had experienced child abuse and 41 per cent had witnessed violence in the home. Not all abused children go on to offend just as not all criminals suffered abuse. However, the robbing of a child's innocence and safety by the very people who should be protecting them provides the worst possible start in life.

Around this time, however, my aversion to being called out to a hurt or dead child was particularly acute. My personal struggles risked overwhelming my professionalism. These battles were rising closer and closer to the surface every day.

I was a pretty typical uncle. Julie was a perfect aunt. Our nieces and nephews were, like Roy Grace's god-daughter Jaye, loved beyond words but nothing could be a substitute for children of our own. As with Roy and Sandy, years of trying had resulted in nothing. Month after month of tests, heartache, self-pity, angst and wondering 'why us' defined our lives and emotions. It was so hard to hide our jealousy and longing when we heard of others' good news. People close to us even delayed telling us of their impending new arrival to spare our tears. Often Julie and I would cling to each other in the small hours weeping and asking why we had been denied the gift of a child again this month. It really hurt and it started to creep into the job. When dealing with child abuse, an inner voice would bellow at me *why can they pop out children just to abuse and neglect when we can't have just one?* Personal feelings have to be ignored when work demands it; but it was a struggle.

Tragic as these cot death calls are, they are rarely more than that – a natural death, and a world-crushing tragedy for a family whose questions would never be answered but whose loss would be total. However, there was always the terrible possibility that one or both of the parents had murdered the baby. *Thinking the unthinkable*, that's what the police are for. We have to be suspicious. The ABC of crime investigation is never more relevant than when dealing with cases involving children.

Grace uses a phrase to lecture young or perfunctory detectives: 'Assumptions are the mother and father of all fuck-ups.' He's right. No-one sends a DS to a house in the middle of the night just to provide tea and sympathy. So while we have to provide pastoral care, we have to approach each home where a cot death has occurred as a potential crime scene. Not easy. There was no way I was putting on the white forensic suit and wrapping the place in blue and white 'Police' tape but I knew I might have to switch from good cop to bad cop in the blink of an eye. A tough stance to take but one I was prepared for. And all the more so in this instance as I knew the family, for all the wrong reasons. The father and mother being well-known receivers of stolen goods and occasional drug users, there was a rich history between them and the local Old Bill. To add to that, all the children were on the Child Protection Register as, despite loving them, the parents struggled to provide them the care and nurture they deserved.

Thankfully, their history gave me the excuse of calling a more senior officer, the duty DI, who would no doubt make my investigation easier as he would take all the hard decisions. This could have been one of four I worked with. I would have been happy for it to be any of them except one, Clive. Just my luck, it was him.

A big man in every way, Clive's entrance into any room was invariably preceded by a bellow, a guffaw or a crash of furniture. Sartorially he always looked as if he had dressed in the dark, but that just made everyone even fonder of this big friendly giant. His experience and wisdom made him the go-to DI for almost everything – except cot deaths. His closest friend had recently lost a child in this way and Clive had got very close to the tragedy by practically living with the family to support them in their darkest days.

I gave him a call. 'OK, Graham,' he said. 'You crack on. I'll get myself sorted and be with you soon.' No hint of when. I was sure I detected the faint sound of his heart breaking. Once he'd battled his own demons and steeled himself for the emotional tightrope he was about to walk, I knew he would join me.

Invincibility cloak on, I headed to the quiet semi on a sprawling council estate, feeling like a trespasser, as I always do when crossing the threshold of a house where death has visited. There are no words that can comfort a family who have been robbed of a child. This household knew me well. In different times, we were antagonists, but now we were on the same side – probably, possibly.

I went in alone. The shock and bewilderment hit me like a force field. Tears streamed down the ashen cheeks of the parents and their three surviving young children as they hunched on the tatty sofa in the smoke-filled lounge, looking lost and stunned. Furniture was sparse but I had to sit. At six foot tall I would often use my height to an advantage with seated suspects, but now I had to get down to their level, using body language to demonstrate our equality; my role here was to serve, not intimidate. Only the coffee table remained vacant so I took my chances. Thankfully it was sturdy.

The account they whispered out through the sobs was typical, if the unexplained death of a baby can ever be typical. Fed well in the small hours, cuddled to sleep, put in the cot and slept forever. No crying, no pain, no clue. Found a couple of hours later for no other reason than Dad's habitual check when he used the bathroom. Frantic attempts to revive, rushing to neighbours, panic, despair, and endless distress. Then the heartless system kicked in and took over.

'You know we have to do some extra checking, Mike, with, well you know, the kids and the Social Services and all that?' I explained. A reluctant but understanding nod was the affirmation I needed and all I knew I would get.

The worst part for me is seeing the body. Most deaths the police go to are tainted with blood or a dirty syringe but babies just go. Nothing helps you to rationalize their passing. Even Cleo, eventually Roy Grace's second wife, with all her years' experience in the mortuary, seeing the most terrible sights, never grew hardened to the death of a child; 'they got her every time'.

I see them as china dolls, but always hope they will suddenly open their eyes. But of course they never will. They look so precious and fragile and all the more disturbing because of it. This baby was lying just as he had been when put to bed, never to wake again. Kids are different. They really get to you.

The personal angst Julie and I were going through made the horror of attending a baby death even harder but I snapped out of it and regained my professional composure. We had to seize the bedding, bottles and clothing in case they held clues. I decided that we needed to check with the neighbours just in case they had heard or seen anything untoward. This last measure was unusual but, in my judgement, necessary given the previous concerns. Mike understood and wanted it all over and done with as soon as possible so that he and his family could try to reconstruct what was left of their wrecked lives. I was soon to regret this decision.

Having finished at the house, I sucked in the crisp morning air to flush my mind of the horror and grief. Just then my pager chirped. 'Graham, get back to the nick before you go to the mortuary. Clive,' the message read. There were no mobile phones back then, and Clive knew I had to accompany the baby's body to the morgue, so despite his message, I thought he would be happy to wait. Following the mortuary van through the streets of people waking to a new day, I wondered how many of the bleary-eyed souls we passed could ever guess the wretched cargo it carried.

After the little body had been booked in I phoned Clive, presuming he wanted an update. 'Since when did we do house-to-house enquiries for cot deaths? Might as well have arrested them for murder,' he yelled.

What had got to him, when he hadn't even had the balls to come to the scene? *Bite your tongue, Graham. Say nothing you'll regret.*

'Clive, I'm not having this conversation with you on the phone. This is hard enough. I've done what I've done and now I've got the post mortem from hell to watch.'

'Don't you know what these poor families go through? Well I do and it's agony. They don't need you trashing their lives further,' he shouted.

He wasn't bloody listening. Where was his heart? Oh yes, I'd heard it breaking when I called him earlier.

Seeing this as completely out of character, I finished by saying, 'You don't know what I know and feel. I'll see you later,' and hung up.

I knew what was behind his rant, but he didn't realize the personal battles I was fighting. Why should he? He was my boss though; I knew he wouldn't let me get away with talking to him like that, and I'd have to face the music when the time came. However, that was nothing compared to what awaited me in the next room.

Peter James describes, with eerie accuracy, what a mortuary feels like. In *Dead Simple* he writes: 'A post mortem was the ultimate degradation. A human being who had been walking, talking, reading, making love – or whatever – just a day or two earlier, being cut open and disembowelled like a pig on a butcher's slab.' Now replace those verbs with 'gurgling, crawling, giggling, suckling' and you start to get a picture of what it's like at the post mortem of a baby. Horrific, surreal, scarring but necessary.

As I was gowning up, my stomach heavy with dread, in walked Clive. 'Hi, Graham, thought I'd come down and give you some support.' His sudden change of mood stunned me.

'Clive, is this the right place for you to be? You don't have to stay, I'll be fine.'

'No, you can't do this alone.'

'It would be a lot easier if I did,' I muttered so he couldn't hear, fearing another Incredible Hulk moment.

I will never forget the tenderness of the pathologist as he dismembered that little boy. He was so gentle but seeing that delicate body cut up was the saddest, most solemn experience of my life. The only thing that helped me through was the knowledge of how much doctors learned from post mortems.

In the UK post mortem examinations, or autopsies, are carried out to determine how someone died. They happen where the death is unexpected, sudden or violent or, in some circumstances, to help medical researchers understand more about a particular illness or condition. One day, the opening up of the body of a barely cold baby might unlock the key to Sudden Infant Death Syndrome itself. Or, as sometimes happens, the pathologist might learn the cause of death was something much darker. I was here to ensure that, in that eventuality, the coroner and the criminal courts had the best evidence to help them reach the right decision. My personal demons were, for now, locked away.

When the autopsy came to an end neither Clive nor I fancied the traditional breakfast detectives indulge in when they have been called out early. Neither of us mentioned the slanging match from earlier either. Had he forgotten? Unlikely. Was he embarrassed? Probably.

Whatever we did and did not talk about, one thing is for sure; we should have got that morning out of our system, but in those days a stiff upper lip was the only acceptable response – unless the sun was over the yardarm, when it was all right to have a large whisky or two.

No suspicious circumstances were found, so my involvement should have ended that day. That was the plan.

Cops aren't made of stone though; we take this stuff home with us. We bury it while we can but it burns away from the inside. It hurts, it scars, it changes us. And what I had seen, smelt and experienced that morning would subsequently test my marriage to the limit.

The next day Julie and I were guests at a lavish wedding in one of the most affluent villages in rural Surrey. Our good friends were tying the knot in a beautiful church on the green and we were to celebrate afterwards at a stunning country manor hidden miles from the beaten track. The wedding saw the usual nerves, tears, compromised guest lists and a pushy photographer who always wanted 'just one more' to keep us from our drinks.

Arriving at the reception something triggered the memories, emotions and feelings of seeing that little boy, naked and cold, on the slab. Every piece of china reminded me of his delicate skin; every child playing led me to reflect how he would never do that; the cutlery, to me, became the pathologist's tools of disfigurement.

I needed to get away but was trapped, forced to join in the celebrations and pretend to be happy. I sought solace in the help at hand: beer, red wine, white wine, anything to blot out my nightmare. I don't remember the speeches, I was there only in body – but finally the baby under the knife, and everything else, had been blotted out in a haze of alcohol. The next thing I remember it was dark, I was cold and I was being violently shaken. Somehow I had found my way to the car and sunk into a drunken stupor in the passenger seat. Julie was shouting at me.

'Where the hell have you been? I've been looking for you everywhere, everyone has for hours.' She threw herself into the driving seat and we sped off into the night. Our journey home was silent and, from what I can remember of it, mainly involved me dropping off to sleep and only stirring when the car was thrown around a roundabout or as we ground to a halt at traffic lights.

The second post mortem within forty-eight hours was my own.

The next morning Julie demanded, and deserved, answers, despite me suffering the hangover from hell. For the first time all my weaknesses and insecurities poured out. I told her about my fears for our future, my terror of losing my professionalism, my helplessness with the family, the horror of the post mortem. Everything. She was furious that I hadn't opened up to her before, hadn't told her everything, hadn't allowed her to hold me and help my pain subside. She hugged me. I wept.

Normally we cope. The training kicks in and we switch on the work filter. But sometimes, that filter is not strong enough and everything comes crashing through. I was lucky, I picked myself up and many of my ex-colleagues still don't know this story.

Policing is hard. The physical traumas can be dreadful but so too can those inside your mind, the ones that no-one can see. Not until they erupt, leaving your loved ones to pick up the pieces. My rock, Julie, did that time and time again and to her I owe everything.

8: WALLS HAVE EARS

'Respect your elders', they would have been told. 'Don't shit on your own doorstep' would be another code ingrained into them from their formative years. Well, life moves on. That sentimental nonsense counts for nothing any more.

In late 1995 the name of Bloomstein was synonymous with the highly respected jewellery trade that jostled for primacy with the shady knocker boys who shared The Lanes in Brighton.

Michael Bloomstein was a proud professional. His reputation was everything and his bank balance illustrated his success. He knew that he was not going to live forever so he prepared his young son, Charles, from an early age to take over the family business when the time came. Privately educated at the outstanding Brighton College, young Charlie had it all.

Nothing was too much for the apple of Michael's eye. He ensured that Charlie was looked after, nurtured and educated so that soon he would have the skills, the passion and the savvy to become a worthy heir.

Charlie, though, had different ideas. The money, the flash cars and his waterside bachelor flat at Brighton Marina gave him status. He had the kudos, the girls, and the respect; at barely twenty-one, he had the world at his feet.

Mal, the father of the tragic Caitlin in *Dead Tomorrow*, considers Brighton as a fusion of city and village, big and bustling but not somewhere to keep a secret – everyone knows each other's business. So Charlie's flamboyant lifestyle and wealthy friends soon drew the attention of a band of thugs who saw a once-in-a-lifetime opportunity to get very rich, very quick.

Daryl Aldridge, Justin Bishop and Andrew Barratt were sadistic, brutal and greedy as well as scheming and highly professional. They were like early-day Terry Biglows who, in *Dead Like You*, Grace recalls had his heyday when adversaries were branded with razors or acid. They could also, in the blink of an eye, turn on the charm when needed. And with Charlie they knew a subtle approach was required.

They made it their business to befriend him, and Charlie quite liked the attention. He was attracted to their edginess. He knew they had criminal records going back years but they were cool and dangerous, not like the cultured types he had endured at school. He rather enjoyed the world they introduced him to. His three new friends were clearly bad boys but, hey, didn't everyone have a dark side? What is more, they obviously liked him. Loved his flat, flirted with his girls, laughed at his jokes. Charlie revelled in their tales of night-time raids on the wealthy and the quick bucks made from drug deals. He matched their boasts with some of his own. He waxed lyrical about who he knew, how rich they were and how well he was trusted.

He was sleepwalking into their trap.

Charlie was being made to believe these three men just wanted to be friends, just loved being around him. After all, they told him all their murky secrets. That's what only true friends do.

It had not occurred to him that he was being targeted for a reason. Charlie knew people. He was liked and trusted. Unbeknown to him, he was being set up as the inside man for one of the most wicked and violent robberies that Sussex had ever seen. In Charlie Bloomstein, Aldridge, Bishop and Barratt had found an important but as yet unwitting ally.

Sometimes, when a piece of intelligence comes to the police, the first reaction is a sceptical 'Really? I don't think so!' People tell the police all sorts of things for all sorts of reasons. To curry favour, to wreak revenge, to distract the Old Bill; all are motivations for criminals to break their so-called sacred code of silence. The police, therefore, have to make a judgement. *Why are we being told this? How does it fit in with what else we know? How reliable has this person been before*? Also plain gut feeling can't be ignored. *Does this seem right?*

Many informants, like Darren Spicer in *Not Dead Yet*, straddle the line between good and bad. Like Darren, most only give tip-offs if there is something in it for them, not out of some deep altruistic streak.

In the years after apartheid ended in South Africa, it was rare to come across any examples of that country's coveted and rare yellow diamonds in the UK. In 1995 wealth did not move freely between the Rainbow Nation and Europe. Word that such a gem was being offered around the dealers of Brighton was therefore taken with more than a pinch of salt. Surely this was just another chancer trying to big himself up in the eyes of the police.

Expertise on diamonds in general was in short supply within police circles so, to learn more, DC Nigel Kelly from the Antiques Squad visited a well-known diamond expert. He revealed to Nigel that he too had heard tales of such a gem being touted and that, if it was as described, it was worth tens of thousands of pounds. On this basis, Nigel started to get interested, but not yet excited.

It wasn't until other intelligence started to drip in that the Antiques Squad gave the tip-off more credence. People were saying that an old lady had been robbed of a yellow diamond right there in Brighton. Word was that it was the hottest property around and it was in high demand.

The head of the squad, DS Don Welch, started to get curious. Surely they would have heard if an old lady had been attacked in her own home. There was no way a theft of this magnitude could have slipped under the radar.

There is little that angers cops more than crimes that target the elderly and vulnerable. Roy Grace is typical in his hatred of that genre of villain, never more so than towards those who attacked Aileen McWhirter in *Dead Man's Time*. Little did he know that was the work of another wealthy boy turned bad: her own great-nephew.

In the 1990s, a search of the crime records meant just that. No clicking of a few keys in the hope that the answer would immediately flash up on the screen. No neatly indexed database that could be analysed from the comfort of the office. In those days, searching records meant donning boiler suits and risking life and limb going down the perilous stone stairway into the dark of the grimy, dusty, rat-infested police station basement. There, it could take days to sift through the dozens of racks of long-forgotten files hoping that whoever had catalogued them had done so carefully, in case one day someone just might want to retrieve them.

Having unsuccessfully searched the recent crime reports, more conveniently held on the same floor as his office, Don grabbed Nigel and together they reluctantly descended into the bowels of the station. After a mere three hours, they struck gold. Nestled between dozens of other unsolved robberies they found the scrunched-up buff crime report they were looking for. Old lady, robbery, own home, four men, yellow diamond – it was all there. So why were the Squad not aware of it when it happened a few months ago? Why had it not been splashed all over the local paper, the *Argus*? Why was it lying here forgotten and uninvestigated?

On reading it, Don realized that the officers who had been sent on the day had decided the robbery had probably not happened. They thought the old lady, Alice, was not quite with it. She was losing her marbles. She was confused. She must have imagined it. Their justification for 'sleeving' this evil crime was shameful.

Don decided to pay her a visit.

She was confused for sure. There was a good reason for that; she was terrified. She explained what had happened.

A few months ago she had met four nice young men at the Co-op supermarket round the corner. They were so kind in offering to carry her shopping home. Chatting freely with them, her faith in the youth of today had been restored, especially when they helped her open her front door and asked if she would like a hand indoors with her bags. Then, out of the blue, these nice young men hurled her to the floor, held her down, threatened her with all kinds of harm and then wrenched her beautiful sapphire and yellow diamond rings off her frail wrinkled fingers before making off.

Don realized that Alice had been targeted by a novel yet callous method. Her grip on the supermarket trolley showcased her glistening rings for all to see.

She may have been duped but this old lady was no shrinking violet. Don decided that his team would pick up where their colleagues had left off. First of all, he wanted to find out a bit more about this plucky victim.

Alice and her husband had lived most of their lives in colonial southern Africa, moving around Commonwealth countries enjoying a very comfortable yet discreet lifestyle. She was used to having staff at her beck and call. She was to the manor born.

Don established that her yellow diamond ring had been a gift from her late husband and its sentimental value greatly surpassed its monetary worth. Alice gave a detailed description, backed up by a crystal-clear photograph on the mantelpiece depicting her wearing it. If only the previous officers had bothered to look.

Don and Nigel grew very fond of Alice and she was delighted that those lovely people at the police station had sent that nice sergeant and constable to help her.

A few days after that first visit, they dropped back round to tie up some loose ends. No sooner had they wiped their feet on the doormat than it became apparent that the class system was alive and kicking in central Brighton.

'Yes, I know you have to talk to me about all this nonsense with my rings but, Mr Welch, be a dear and pop to the shops to fetch me a few things. Here, take this list, it's all there and hurry back now,' she commanded.

Another day, the request was, 'DS Welch. My car needs one of those wretched MOT tests. Be a good chap and pop it to the garage for me. I've told them to expect you.'

How could they refuse?

Having given way to her eccentric demands, Don and Nigel worked hard to get to the bottom of this intriguing case. Rumours were reaching them that young Charlie Bloomstein had flown out to Switzerland with a yellow diamond. Bona fide dealers require a certificate of authenticity to accompany high-value stones. At the time, these could only be obtained in New York, Amsterdam or Switzerland. Eager to find out what had happened, Don flew out to Geneva and confirmed that Charlie had indeed made the trip. At any other time, it would have been an unremarkable visit but now it raised the stakes.

Accepting that confronting Charlie with this information or even obtaining search warrants would serve little purpose other than spooking him and pushing him and the elusive diamond further underground, Don opted for a more covert approach.

This seemed like the job of a lifetime for the surveillance unit. They were used to being given good quality intelligence packages from the Antiques Squad – after all Don had once served with them – so they knew what bait the undercover boys would go for.

This job had it all. A rich playboy, high-value jewellery and, if they were lucky, trips abroad. Clearly, with the timely trip to Switzerland, Charlie was up to something, but exactly what was still a mystery. Twenty-four-hour surveillance on him started to fill in the gaps.

The emerging association between Bloomstein, Aldridge, Barratt and Bishop astounded Don. They had never predicted such an alliance nor the incredibly suspicious behaviour they were observing on a daily basis.

One of the first signs that gangs are plotting a crime is their obsessive use of counter-surveillance tactics. Driving 360 degrees round a roundabout to see who did the same, heading down dead ends and driving at excessive speeds are all ways by which the guilty try to identify or shake off a tail. This quartet thought they were masters at it. The cops, thankfully, had seen it all before.

In fairness, these were the days when technical surveillance was in its infancy. Naively the gang assumed that covert policing was limited to cops tearing around in unmarked cars, watching from a neighbour's window and staying ten paces behind the target on a busy shopping street.

One of the challenges for Don was that all four suspects lived in different towns and used various means of travel. Despite the huge number of officers Don had at his disposal, there was a limit to how thin they could be spread before they started to be recognized. The same car containing the same two dark-haired, thirty-something blokes parked outside the same house each morning was eventually going to stand out. The police needed to up their game.

Through the use of various covert technical tactics, such as tapping into their message pagers, and bugging their houses, it became apparent that the gang were meeting up on a regular basis and in a variety of places. They used predictable venues, such as Aldridge's house in nearby Peacehaven and Charlie's luxury pad at the Marina. But, thinking they were being clever, at the drop of a hat they would arrange to meet at randomly coded rendezvous points paged to all members of the group.

However, through painstaking detective work and a process of elimination, Don and the team were able to crack the code.

They were now on the front foot and there was little the gang could do without the cops knowing. At home or at large their every movement was being tracked and their every conversation eavesdropped on. The police were building a cast-iron case of association to deflect any future defence of being arrested at a 'chance meeting'.

It was not long before the gang started to boast of their villainy. They thought they could take on the world. In their minds they were invincible. They felt they had the perfect combination of inside information and an inclination to inflict extreme violence on anyone who dared resist.

Most of the detailed plotting took place in either Aldridge's or Charlie's home. Even though they assumed they hadn't been rumbled, they still used code words for most of their planning. Intelligence indicated that one of their tricks was to dress in police uniforms, follow people home and flash forged search warrants to force their way in. Once inside, they would tie the unfortunate victim to a radiator and, with the persuasive power of guns and knives, elicit the whereabouts of their most valuable possessions. The uniforms themselves were coded the 'Armani suits'.

More and more Don's team heard them talk about a forthcoming robbery, referring to it as the 'Tom job'. They didn't give away much more to narrow it down. However the team assumed it probably involved jewellery, or 'Tom Foolery' in rhyming slang. But there were hundreds of jewellers. Which one?

As the weeks went on it became clear that the 'Tom job' was clearly a big one. It was to involve the Armani suits, handcuffs and, terrifyingly, firearms. But where was it? Who was the target? Unusually, none of the codes the police had cracked previously were now being used. It was causing Don a real headache.

As with any investigation, motivation and energy ebbed and flowed. As the senior officer he needed to keep the whole team motivated – but it was a struggle. The gang weren't doing much and the surveillance was becoming tedious.

'Barratt keeps walking past Magpie Jewellers,' came a crackled radio message from the surveillance officer watching the gang meandering around the narrow confines of The Lanes one morning. 'Might be nothing but he's paying a lot of attention to it.'

'That's Tommy Preisler's shop,' Nigel reflected. 'He's a good friend of Michael Bloomstein.'

It hit him like a bolt of lightning. Grace's love of Occam's Razor, the simplest solution usually being the right one, would prove true yet again.

'We've got this all wrong. Get me the logs from the listening devices!' Nigel demanded.

He grabbed them from Carol, the dutiful Antiques Squad administrator. Scouring the pages in a wild frenzy as his incredulous colleagues watched on.

'Yes, that's it. I've got it,' he shrieked.

'Got what?' asked Don.

'The "Tom job". We've been looking at it all wrong. We've over-complicated it. It's not slang at all. It's not jewellery. Tom is a person, Tommy Preisler. Read the conversations from the log and it's clear. They are talking about Tommy Preisler.'

Shell-shocked and red-faced they realized that they had been looking in the wrong place. Don grabbed the logs, determined to see for himself.

'Bloody hell, you're right. They are using Charlie to select the targets. It's going to be Preisler.'

Now with an identified victim to protect, Don felt he still owed it to Alice to find her jewellery. The squad had a tip-off that a yellow diamond had been sold by Charlie Bloomstein to a dealer in Bond Street, London.

Unlike popping into a local high street jeweller, Don and Nigel had to pre-arrange their visit, provide descriptions of themselves, set out their enquiry and, of course, arrive with bundles of identification. The henchmen outside made up for in muscle what they lacked in social graces. Eventually the two detectives persuaded the monosyllabic guards that they were who they said they were.

Whisked off the street, they were prodded down a darkened stairway into a musty strongroom beneath ground level. The room, similar in appearance to where Gavin Daly emasculated Eamonn Pollack with his ninety-year-old handgun in *Dead Man's Time*, took their breath away. The walls were almost entirely made up of Perspex cases containing hundreds of thousands of pounds' worth of priceless watches and diamonds.

A portly, gracious gentleman, who was the antithesis of the goons who provided his front of house service, emerged from a door they had not spotted.

'Officers, I am Edwin Hanson, how can I help you?' he enquired softly.

'Well, as we said on the phone, this needs to be in the strictest confidence,' explained Don.

'Of course, of course,' Hanson reassured them. 'Discretion is my middle name.'

'Thank you. We believe a dealer by the name of Bloomstein from Brighton sold you a yellow diamond we are interested in,' continued Don.

'I see. Interested in what way?' replied Hanson, feigning genuine concern.

'Well, stolen,' interjected Nigel, 'but you wouldn't have known that of course.'

'Of course,' confirmed Hanson, clearly grateful for the get-out clause Nigel had suggested. 'Yes, I do remember being sold a yellow diamond by a chap from Brighton. I am quite a specialist in these rare stones, you know.'

'Do you still have it by chance?' asked Nigel, more in hope than expectation.

'Yes, of course, I am collecting yellow diamonds to make a bracelet for a particularly affluent Saudi gentleman,' he boasted.

'That's fabulous,' said Don, in a rare display of excitement. They were on the verge of tying Bloomstein into the robbery and Alice was going to get her heirloom back.

Hanson moved to the corner of the room and unlocked a small wall safe. He stepped back to the table carrying a tiny chamois pouch in his right hand.

'Now, let me see,' muttered the jeweller, building up to something.

Like a magician fanning a deck of cards, Hanson flicked the bag. From it, the most stunning and blinding array of yellow stones sprayed across the baize table top.

'Gentlemen. Just tell me which of these is the stone you are after and it's yours to take away,' he promised with a glibness that revealed why he had been so helpful. They all knew that there was no hope of picking out the right gem from this glittering pile.

Dejected and empty-handed they were gently escorted from the subterranean goldmine. Don and Nigel knew there was now no hope of finding Alice's treasured diamond but were even more determined than ever to see her robbers locked up.

The big 'Tom job' was getting closer and closer. Almost daily, cars were turning up at the house in Arundel Road, Peacehaven, that doubled as Aldridge's home and robbery HQ. Number plates would be switched and the cars driven off. They were being hidden in various anonymous car parks and streets in central Brighton, readied for a complex getaway.

The Armani suits had been sorted, a fake search warrant prepared, pistols sourced, and restraints all in place. A very good friend of Charlie's family was about to realize that, in the world of crime and greed, there is no such thing as friendship, only opportunities.

As happened in those days, when the arrests drew closer an

investigative team were briefed to take the job over. This was to be led by a long-standing colleague and good friend of mine, DS Russ Whitfield. Russ was a dyed-in-the-wool detective, who had graduated from policing Whitehawk into CID and then been promoted.

We had been made Detective Sergeant at the same time but our paths then diverged. He had been given the job of setting up the first Divisional Intelligence Unit in the city while I moved to Child Protection. Not long after, however, I had transferred again to lead a team of detectives in nearby Haywards Heath CID. While rural policing had its own challenges, lack of staff being one of them, I still looked longingly at what was going on in Brighton. Six months of crime and excitement in Haywards Heath could be crammed into a week in the city I loved.

Russ was steely, intelligent and a stickler for detail. He worked cheek by jowl with Don to get up to speed on what had now been named Operation Dresden. So far the focus had been predominantly on gathering intelligence. Its success relied on that intelligence being turned into evidence. That was Russ's job.

He ploughed through the volumes of reports, the ninety-five surveillance logs, the hundreds of files on all the covert activity. His job was to draw out what would be admissible in court and fill any gaps. He approached his task with dogged determination, sharing Don's resolve to get this gang locked up for a very long time. He knew Barratt of old, having previously arrested him for a string of burglaries.

Within a few days the planning had intensified and, after some false starts when members of the gang had overslept, it seemed the day of the robbery had arrived.

Before dawn, cops secreted themselves around Magpie Jewellers and the getaway cars, providing an all-seeing yet invisible ring of steel. Given the intelligence that the gang would be armed, the elite Tactical Firearms Unit had replaced the detectives to carry out any arrests. That meant that this potentially lethal phase of the operation was now out of Russ and Don's hands and under a whole new command.

Where shooting, riots or disaster are likely the police put in place a very clear structure – Gold, Silver, Bronze. It's deliberately hierarchical with the Gold (or strategic) commander giving the orders *what* the police should seek to achieve, the Silver (or tactical) commander determining *how* that should happen and the Bronze (or operational) commander having to *make it* happen.

The detectives wanted the raid to be allowed to run to the point where they had their evidence; the firearms commanders were only interested in safety. And safety always came first.

Thankfully the firearms Silver commander was a gutsy type. He knew that if this lot weren't nicked for something decent, he would be running this job again somewhere else in the future. People like them do not go straight that easily.

Everything was looking promising. The gang had made their way over to The Lanes. Their anticipated counter-surveillance phase was under way – driving cars in and out of dead ends, their occupants scouring the rooftops and windows for giveaway signs that they had been found out.

All it needed was for the police to stay out of sight, letting everything appear normal, then, in the split second when the robbers were just about to attack but before anyone got harmed, they were to break cover in an awesome and overwhelming show of force, paralysing the would-be robbers into submission.

'Bloody hell, they are leaving,' came the incredulous comment from the officer closest to the targeted premises.

A scurry of activity confirmed their fears. Not wanting to show their hand, all the officers stayed put but it soon became clear that the gang, for no apparent reason, had all returned to their cars and headed back to Peacehaven.

The easy thing to do would be to stand down and regroup

another day, but the cops had the time and the manpower to be patient.

'Stick with it,' barked Silver, guessing this was the gang being even more careful than usual.

Sure enough, after a short break at Aldridge's house, the targets headed back. But in the meantime they had been plotting. Russ carried out yet another review of the intelligence and called a confidential meeting with the Silver commander.

'I think we've got enough to nick them now,' declared Russ. 'That activity we have just seen, with everything else, gives us a cast-iron case against all four for conspiracy to rob. I am sure we will find more evidence in the car. But I don't think we need to let them get near the shop and the public.'

'That's music to my ears,' replied the Silver commander. 'So you are happy for us to intercept them on the way into the city?'

'For sure, but tell your lot that the forensic integrity of the prisoners and anything they find is paramount.'

'After safety of course,' corrected the Silver commander with a wink.

'Of course,' confirmed Russ.

That agreed, Silver snapped out his plan to the firearms teams.

As the car containing Aldridge and Bishop headed west towards the city centre they were tracked by armed police. Close to Roedean School, which sits on the hillside above Brighton Marina, the command came for them to be stopped.

From nowhere raced four nondescript high-performance saloons, which surrounded the stunned villains. Their shocked faces, as they took in the horror they were about to confront, told the heavily armed car crews that surrender was inevitable.

Taking no chances however, and in textbook fashion, each car slammed into the target vehicle: the perfect Tactical Pursuit and Contact (TPAC) manoeuvre that Grace considered using to stop the car that he thought contained the kidnapped Tyler in *Dead Man's Grip*.

Half a dozen scruffily dressed yet heavily armed hulks sprang from the cars, their tell-tale 'Police' baseball caps giving away their mission.

Shouts of 'Stop, armed police' echoed off the cliffs as the officers thrust their deadly Heckler and Koch machine guns towards the defeated duo inside the trapped car.

'Get your hands on the dashboard *now*,' continued the command. No chance to flee, no choice but to conform.

Dragged out onto the roadway and handcuffed where they lay, the two men knew the game was up. The automatic pistol, the twenty-eight rounds of ammunition, the rope and handcuffs in the footwell ensured that. Bishop and Aldridge were well and truly bang to rights. Bloomstein and Barratt were apprehended elsewhere, with identical tactics which also scared them into submission.

This was just the start of the hard work. Many think arrests are the end of an investigation. Far from it. Making an arrest, while sometimes momentous, guarantees nothing. Arrests are made on 'reasonable suspicion', convictions secured on evidence 'beyond reasonable doubt': two legal tests that are poles apart. A justifiable hunch is enough to 'feel a collar'. The toil to convert that into the absolute certainty the courts demand can feel like climbing Mount Everest in a deep-sea diving suit.

None of the suspects was inclined to help the police. Even Bloomstein had adopted the professional's stance – sit and say nothing; let them prove it. The defence lawyers love this approach.

It must be very hard to defend people who are caught in such compromising circumstances and with such a weight of evidence against them. The temptation must be to urge them to plead guilty. However, there is always another way. If the evidence is damning then the only hope remains in trying to find chinks in the way it was gathered.

The Crown Prosecution Service instructed John Tanzer, now a respected judge, as prosecuting counsel. This was a smart move given that he was more than capable of handling a major conspiracy such as this. However, faced with a leading and junior barrister per defendant, he, the police and the CPS were quickly swamped with the multifarious demands for additional information and evidence all designed to overwhelm them.

During the six weeks of legal argument and voir dire – a trial without the jury to determine the admissibility of evidence – the prosecution found that they could not even say that an officer was on duty on a particular day without being challenged. The defence demanded independent proof of the fact. Despite the hundreds of hours spent observing the defendants, each surveillance officer had to prove the identity of the person they had been watching. Barratt's counsel relied heavily on the stunning similarity his client bore to his equally errant brother. One cop became so confused that even the judge wondered whether he was telling the truth and warned him accordingly.

Russ had to arrange for the voices heard through the surveillance bugs to be forensically compared with samples of the defendants' voices. They even had to prove that a dustcart that coincidentally arrived at one of the places being watched wasn't staffed by undercover cops.

The days in court were the easy bit. However, once the judge rose, Russ and the team would burn the midnight oil dealing with the multitude of bizarre defence requests. He recalls, to this day, sitting at his dining-room table late into one evening, using his daughter's crayons to create multicoloured analytical charts showing the defendants' phone calls, to head off another off-the-wall demand.

Finally, a full two years after the arrests and with all the legal issues settled, Bloomstein and Aldridge unexpectedly pleaded guilty and, after a trial, Barratt and Bishop were found guilty by a jury at Lewes Crown Court.

Don and Russ finally felt vindicated. Their hard work had paid off. Their professionalism had defeated the shenanigans the defence had engaged in. Despite those attacks on police integrity, justice had prevailed. Now they waited to revel in the length of the sentences.

It was a stunning victory when the judge sent the four to prison for a total of forty-three years. No-one had expected them to get this long. Nigel couldn't resist the temptation to turn to the dock to savour the moment the defendants were led away to serve their time. Barratt, Bishop and Aldridge had been through it before but Charlie Bloomstein looked devastated that his charmed life had come to this.

However, the last words the court heard were yelled by Barratt as the length of his sentence sunk in.

'Fourteen years, fourteen fucking years! You're having a fucking laugh!'

His Honour Judge Coltart wasn't but, despite not seeing justice for herself, when that nice Mr Welch popped round to break the good news Alice managed a wry smile. A very wry smile indeed.

9: DEATH COMES KNOCKING

The one good thing about a belly punch from Mike Tyson is that eventually you recover. Two solemn cops, however, wearing white hats, and one gleaming, chequered BMW blocking your drive and you just know it's not going to end well. After this, nothing will ever be the same again; there will be no recovery. We call it delivering the *death message*.

Few people like late-night callers. Someone raps on the door the wrong side of midnight disturbing your deepest sleep. It takes some moments to become compos mentis. The kids are in bed; the last thing they need is to be woken. You grab a dressing gown, hoping it's yours. Anger mellows to curiosity then ferments to trepidation. The hazy silhouette of those figures through the glass will sap any remaining hope as your realization of their terrible task overwhelms you.

Thank goodness for police training, you think. For the hours they must spend rehearsing for this most dreadful duty. For all the scenarios they are taught: kids, mums, granddads, crashes, murders, suicides. Thank goodness too for the counselling they get, for this must be awful for them. Thank goodness.

Thank goodness, then, that you don't know they aren't trained in this at all, and counselling? Forget it. We just have to get on with it, learning as we go along, and we all do it differently. And none of us has ever found the perfect way, because that does not exist. Why? Because no death is the same, no family like another.

I remember hearing of a lady who lived in a basement flat in central Brighton. Her son was in the Army in Afghanistan and she knew that the strict military protocol following the death or injury of a soldier was that a senior officer would deliver the terrible news. She was petrified that each day death would come knocking. Therefore she developed the habit, whenever she saw a pair of shiny shoes descending the steps to her front door, of rushing to the back of the flat and refusing to come out of hiding in case it was the Casualty Notification Officer with the news she dreaded. She did this for months and missed many a caller as a consequence. Eventually her son returned unharmed.

As a fresh-faced eighteen-year-old recruit I remember a wily old training sergeant drumming into me and my fellow rookies that, where possible, when making an unannounced visit the first sentence must go something like, 'Hello, it's the police, there's nothing to worry about.' Privately, and definitely out of the fearsome trainer's earshot, we used to scoff at this advice. It seemed so unnecessary.

Once out on the streets and assuming that nothing we learned about street craft at training college would survive contact with the public, I spurned that nonsense.

Not long after being unleashed on the public of Bognor Regis, I attended a burglary and needed to search the neighbours' gardens for the fleeing offender. It was around midnight and I thought it would only be polite to knock and ask permission to check the back of one particular house. There were lights on, what could go wrong?

My sharp rap on the door while updating the control room through the ancient Burndept personal radio affixed to my lapel launched a lifelong lesson for me.

'Who is it?' a croaky voice demanded.

'It's the police,' I proudly announced.

'What do you want?' – the voice now quiet and shaky.

'Please open the door, madam. I need to speak to you,' I said.

The door rattled as the locks and chains were released. The

shard of light between door and frame slowly widened to reveal a very frightened-looking middle-aged lady.

She was tiny. A pink candlewick dressing gown enveloped her pencil-thin frame. Her eyes were bloodshot and her straggly blonde and grey hair was matted to her scalp. Her cheeks were rosy, not through drink or healthy glow but worry and dread.

'No. Oh God, please no!' she cried.

Baffled, I spun around to see what had provoked this outburst.

'No, oh God, I knew when he didn't phone something had happened. Oh no, what am I going to do? How am I going to carry on?'

By now curtains were twitching, lights were coming on and an impromptu drama was unfolding in which I was the villain.

'I'm sorry, madam,' I blurted out, raising my hand to try and quieten her. 'What are you saying? What's happened?' Not realizing that it was me who had lit her fuse.

'My husband said he'd call when he got to Manchester. That should have been hours ago. What's happened to him? Is he dead? Please say he's not. Please say he's alive,' she begged.

'I am sure he is, madam – alive that is,' was my attempt at reassurance. 'I just want to look in your garden if that's OK.'

'You bastard!' Her worry and angst had morphed into rage and was aimed squarely at me. 'Why didn't you say? Have you no idea? I was convinced you'd come about Doug. Don't they teach you anything at training school?' she yelled.

All I could mutter as I made my exit was a pathetic 'Sorry', omitting to add that they actually did teach me lots but this one lesson I chose to ignore. We never did find the burglar, and from that day the phrase 'there's nothing to worry about' never left my lexicon.

As I matured I realized that telling people of the demise of their loved one is a huge responsibility. Of all the tasks that befall the police this one just *had* to be done right. No second chances, no retakes. Every word mattered, every gesture counted. The grieving process could hinge on how well or clumsily that dreadful message was delivered.

There is something very sobering in standing outside someone's house late at night, seeing their shadow behind the curtains, knowing you are just about to rip the heart out of their lives forever.

It's bad enough to see a wretched body surrounded by scorched foil or needles, vomit, mucus and the detritus of a life given over to heroin. Horrible to find what a few minutes previously was a laughing, joking, and loving young person, mangled within the wreckage of a hatchback, itself concertinaed into a sturdy oak tree. Tragic to hold a dying lad whose ill-judged retort to an aggressive drunk drew the single punch that crushed his eggshell skull. All are terrible things that police officers have to face.

For me, though, the death message was worse than any of those. In *Dead Simple* as Grace goes to see Phil Wheeler, whose son had just been killed thanks to his ambition to become a hero, he reflects that talking to the recently bereaved is the single worst aspect of police work. I couldn't agree more.

Many of the grisly aspects of the job can at least be lightened by gallows humour. A traffic officer once ambled into the station kitchen, looked at my spaghetti bolognese, and demanded to know how I had managed to so quickly recover the human remains of the fatal crash he had just come from. Death messages are the exception. No-one makes light of them. It's as if prolonging the solemnity is a mark of respect – like sharing the pain for someone you never knew.

The palpable trepidation in the car as PCs Omotoso and Upperton make their way to break the dreadful news of Tony Revere's death to his girlfriend in *Dead Man's Grip* is something all cops relate to. Their careful but clear approach in giving the awful message is drawn from experience and natural humanity, not training. The real, and now very sadly deceased, Tony Omotoso insisted on getting the word *dead* out as quickly as he sensed the situation allowed. Others ensure that the grieving relative actually says the 'D' word themselves to help them understand. Everyone has their own style. However it's done, it's an awful job.

You go through the words in your mind – never string it out because as soon as they see you they know; whatever they do and say, they know. You try to predict the response – impossible. Remember you may be investigating a crime but most of all remember that you are about to wreck their world.

'You're lying', 'you're wrong', 'he doesn't touch drugs', 'he can't be dead, he called me earlier', 'you bastards': I have faced all of these reactions when giving the news everyone dreads. Disbelief, blame, anger, all aimed at you, the messenger. All regretted later on but all quite normal. You have to take it on the chin.

I was on the wrong end of horrendous abuse and vitriol about 3 a.m. one summer morning. I had come from the mortuary and tried to tell a hysterical mum that her son had died of a drugs overdose. She howled. She shouted. She swore. She tried to throw me out, wanting to believe that if I weren't there her son would still be alive. After she'd used up every ounce of emotional energy, I persuaded her to get her other son round to be with her. She reluctantly allowed me to remain until he arrived. He wasn't much better, aggravated by the fact that he was a police officer from another force. Bizarrely, instead of comforting his mum he started by questioning my investigation and trying to give me advice. I had to take it all in my stride, seeing it as a reaction to something I never wanted to experience. As the hours went by my presence was accepted even if my news wasn't. I hope that in time the pain eased.

Another evening, a car full of teenagers had plummeted off the cliffs at Brighton onto the Marina Village. Two of the lads inside died but miraculously not all were killed. I hadn't been to the accident but was tasked with visiting the family of one of the survivors to break the news. All of the occupants had grown up together and the tragedy had been due to a simple lapse of judgement. A community was about to be devastated. There is no instruction book for how you tell a mum that while her son was alive – critically injured and on life support, but alive – that his best friends had died a horrible death plunging over a hundred-foot cliff to the ground below.

It was a long, hard evening with that family, trying to keep up with them on their rollercoaster of emotions: relief, guilt, grief, hope and despair. I will never know whether my approach, along the lines of 'this is really awful but try to cling on to hope and the fact that he is alive and in the very best hands', worked, but it was all I could think of. Sometimes gut instinct, common sense and humanity are all you have to fall back on; you have to hope they get you through.

Occasionally you have to adopt a parental role towards those whose world you have just destroyed.

Following yet another young life being snuffed out decades before its time by drugs, it fell to me to break the news to the young man's parents. It was the middle of the day and they were hard to find, but death is notoriously disrespectful of convenience.

I eventually tracked the father down to his small shop close to Brighton's border with Hove. Thankfully the lunchtime rush had yet to materialize so the shop was empty.

'Good afternoon, Mr Murphy. I'm from the police. Do you mind just shutting the shop for a while as I need to talk to you?'

'Yes, of course, Officer, what's the problem?' he chirped. Only I knew that would be his last cheery word for years.

Having secured our privacy, I went through the basics of quickly checking his identity, as you *never* want to give a death message to the wrong person, confirmed who his son was, and then I told him.

'I am very sorry to tell you that we have found your son dead in his flat this morning. We are sure it's him and the early indications are that he died of a drugs overdose.'

He stared at me in frozen shock. No emotion.

'I have to tell Pam, my ex-wife, his mother. I suppose I should do that after I close up tonight.'

'No, that needs to happen now. How would you like to do that?'

'Well, she ought to be told but I can't close the shop.'

'Really, you can. You must. You can't stay at work. It probably hasn't sunk in yet but this is going to hit you very hard.'

'Do you think so? I mean, do you think I should shut up the shop?'

'Yes, absolutely. Please do it. How would you like Pam told? Shall we do it?'

'No. I must. Can you come with me though?'

'Of course.'

After what seemed like an age I helped Mr Murphy towards my waiting unmarked car. He had not yet broken down, he had not yet asked the thousands of questions I knew would come; he had gone onto autopilot.

As we drove the short distance to Pam's office in the centre of Hove we agreed that we would ask for her to be fetched and that I would request a quiet room. He would then break the terrible news and I would support him by answering any questions and helping with any arrangements.

I took the liberty of parking directly outside, placing the Police Vehicle Log Book on the dashboard to ward off any over-zealous traffic warden. We climbed the narrow stairway to the office reception. We introduced ourselves and I persuaded them to give us the privacy we needed.

(*From left to right*)
Dad, me and
Uncle Gordon
in our uniforms.
I idolized
them both.

Enjoying firearms training during my time
policing Gatwick airport.

Tim Phillips
receiving aid from
the emergency
services after
being shot and
kidnapped by
Dew and Cooke.

The Lighthouse Club, owned by George Teed.

Police searching Shoreham Harbour for evidence following the Lighthouse Club triple murder.

George and Hilda Teed.

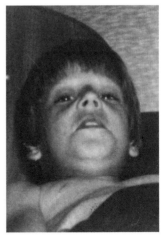

David Teed.

Paul Teed.

Paul Teed (*left*) with Peter James.

(*From left to right*)
Peter James,
David Henty
and me.

On the steps of Henty and Wake's passport factory following
their arrest, with printer Barry Cheriton behind.

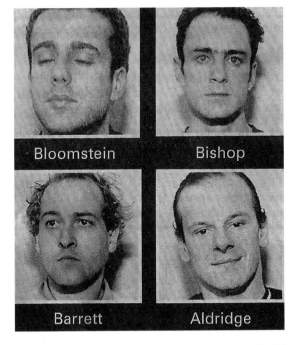

Charlie Bloomstein, Justin Bishop, Andrew Barratt and Daryl Aldridge.

Bloomstein

Bishop

Barrett

Aldridge

The pistol and ammunition found in the gang's possession.

Anthony Robinson's VW camper van being towed following the discovery of his body.

The ruthless Denis Mulder.

With Russell Brand filming a BBC TV documentary exploring drug rehabilitation in Brighton.

Career criminal Michael Fitzpatrick, who was shot by police.

The scene at Rock Place following the Fitzpatrick shooting.

Peter and I with the first 'Peter James car' that he sponsored for Sussex Police.

Activists besiege the EDO MBM factory – a carefully planned police operation ensured public safety.

My family at my retirement party in 2013.

So far so good. I would stay in the background while the tragedy unfolded between the bereaved parents.

In walked Pam. It seemed she had been told nothing, still less that her ex was with a police officer.

'Hello, I am DS Bartlett,' was all I said before the man beside me wailed like a banshee.

'What? What's going on? What's happened? Will someone please tell me?' Pam demanded.

The stoic determination Mr Murphy had shown earlier had crumbled at the critical moment. There was no way this poor lady was going to hear the terrible news from him. We should have agreed a plan B but I knew I needed to step in and fast.

'I am afraid to tell you that your son has been found dead this morning. He was in his flat and we think he died of a drugs overdose,' I said gently, for the second time within an hour.

Now I had two banshees. The screams must have been heard right through the adjacent offices. I had to get these two out of here quickly.

Bombarded with questions, denials, more questions and waterfalls of tears I managed to extricate the two devastated parents from the building, into the car and away to nearby relatives. There I went through the announcement for the third time, before leaving the mum and dad in the care of someone they loved.

I have no doubt they weep to this day. No-one should have to bury their offspring. As Grace says in *Dead Tomorrow* when explaining to Cleo why Lynn Beckett went to such lengths to save her daughter Caitlin's life: 'The gods have no greater torment than for a mother to outlive her child.'

There are lots of aspects of the job that don't necessarily fit in with the idea that the police's role is to cut crime. Giving death messages is an obvious one. Just as Grace applies Locard's principle of 'every contact leaves a trace' to the forensic quandaries facing him with the recovered bodies in *Dead Tomorrow* so it applies to the personal contacts the police have with ordinary people. The way officers speak to and treat those they are telling of an unexpected death will mark those people for life. All personal baggage must be left at the door. Be it the fight they have just been to, the tray full of reports waiting for them, the grief from home for being late off duty, nothing must interfere with that moment.

Bad enough that the bereaved have been visited by the angel of death, but to taint that further with arrogance, insensitivity or clumsiness would be criminal. Thankfully officers acting in such a way tend to be confined to television fiction; in reality they are invariably all you would hope them to be.

I pray you never have to find out for yourselves.

10: BLINDED IN THE NIGHT

That couple of months between Christmas and the first daffodils of spring can be a great time for the police. Less partying means fewer people inflicting unspeakable evil on each other; a welcome breather for beleaguered cops. The year of 1998 was the exception that proves the rule. We'd had the calm, now followed the storm.

This was a time of new beginnings for me. Fifteen months previously, after five years of trying, Julie had finally fallen pregnant – with triplets. Going from the despair of childlessness to hitting the triple jackpot on our first IVF attempt was as wondrous as it was exhausting. We had never predicted that we would have a complete family delivered in one go.

Julie had selflessly taken voluntary redundancy from her career at Gatwick Airport to fund and prepare for the fertility treatment. She put heart and soul into trying everything to conceive, including some incredibly painful and intrusive operations. We were both heading towards our mid-thirties and were worrying whether we would ever have the family we so craved.

The IVF had gone as well as such a physically and emotionally draining procedure could. The first pregnancy test in mid-December 1996 had us leaping, gently, around the Christmas tree – Julie would not get to use the new squash racket I had bought her as a present that day for some years.

A very nervous and edgy few weeks of the New Year ended with a scan in early February, which diagnosed twins, but the hesitancy in the obstetrician's poorly hidden reaction scared us.

Four weeks later, this time at a different hospital, the crowd of doctors and midwives that the sonographer called in again did nothing to relieve our fears.

A hushed pow-wow around the screen ended with the announcement, 'Mr and Mrs Bartlett, you are pregnant with triplets.'

Our reflex was just to burst into laughter and query, 'Are you sure there are no more?'

'No, just the three. Congratulations.'

Our euphoria was short-lived, however. As soon as we left the ultrasound room the consultant obstetrician called us in.

'You do realize we don't advise that triplet pregnancies are viable. You run a huge risk to all the babies if you continue with it. I strongly recommend that you reduce the pregnancy.'

'What do you mean?' I asked.

'You should only look to carry two of the babies.'

'What do you mean?'

'A simple injection into one of the babies will terminate it, leaving you with a more optimistic prognosis.'

'So kill a healthy baby. That's what you're saying?' Julie asked through her tears.

'Well, that's a harsh way to put it.'

'But that's what it boils down to,' she wailed.

She and I looked at each other for no more than a second. Words between us were not necessary.

'No way,' insisted Julie. 'If this pregnancy is meant to be then we will give all our babies a chance. How can you suggest killing one?'

'Well,' the pompous cold doctor continued, 'they will be premature and we won't have room for them here so they will be farmed out to other hospitals.'

'How dare you,' I snarled. 'This is our dream and you are *not* going to wreck it.'

We stormed out, marched to the car and held each other laughing and crying for the next twenty minutes.

Thankfully, the doctor who had carried out the IVF and first spotted two babies was more sympathetic. He was the clinical director at another hospital and took us under his care, saw us every two weeks and admitted Julie as an inpatient for ten weeks until Conall George, Niamh Sarah and Deaglan John, three healthy babies, were delivered at thirty-four weeks.

Julie's pregnancy had gone swimmingly and the triplets have grown into wonderful, intelligent, loving and healthy young adults. Thankfully I have never met that miserable consultant obstetrician since, but in some ways I would love to and show him the results of us dismissing his cruel advice.

By February 1998 Conall, Niamh and Deaglan were at that dangerous crawling stage where everything that was in reach was subjected to either the mouth or the drop test. As with the fictional DC Nick Nicholl, sleep was just a pipe dream. I'd recently returned, as a DS, to the city I loved. I had previously been posted from Haywards Heath to work at Headquarters for an Assistant Chief Constable – thankfully quite unlike Grace's nemesis ACC Vosper – but now I was back.

The country was mourning the death of Princess Diana, the Japanese Winter Olympics were about to start and President Bill Clinton had just asserted his undying fidelity to wife Hillary in a national address. The twenty-first century was now within touching distance and people were pondering whether Armageddon would strike when the planet's computers went into meltdown, unable to cope with eight-figure date formats: the millennium bug that fortunately never was.

It was always a relief for Glynn Morgan when he could finally lock up his cramped pizza takeaway restaurant squeezed among a row of shops on Church Road, Hove. A twelve-hour day getting deliveries out on time, serving the passing trade of ravenous drunks and managing unreliable employees could take its toll.

Lucky for Glynn that his partner and soulmate Fiona Perry was always there to help ease the burden and lift his spirits.

Glynn and Fiona lived in a compact mid-terrace flat in central Hove just a stone's throw from the scene of the crash that killed Tony Revere and set in train the most ruthless campaign of revenge in *Dead Man's Grip*. The roads in that area are narrow, giving a feeling of a close community who look out for each other. People were friendly, which was just as well as parking was a nightmare. Tolerance was essential in avoiding road rage.

Being with each other and scraping a living out of their franchised takeaway pizza business kept Glynn and Fiona busy and contented. They drove a clapped-out Austin Ambassador car which limped from one annual MOT to another. Affectionately naming it Anna ('Anna nother thing wrong with her!') they had no need for anything more ostentatious, which was just as well given they lived from hand to mouth.

Staff turnover was high. People did not view riding a Perfect Pizza-liveried moped around the city distributing boxes of Meat Feasts and garlic bread as a long-term career. Many treated it as a stopgap between other jobs or a short-term way of boosting their income.

Glynn was grateful when David McLellan had been transferred from another branch a few years previously. He knew the ropes already and didn't need training. When he left around 1996 he had been with them longer than most.

For Glynn and Fiona it was like any other Saturday night in winter; steady but not rushed off their feet. Trade petered out naturally by the midnight closing time so they were able to clean and cash up before the shutters came down, meaning a swift getaway. Never in their wildest dreams did they imagine what was about to happen. Never did they realize that their every thought, word and act that followed would be delicately drawn out of them by detectives and savagely scrutinized by a sterile justice system.

The safe locked, the ovens off and the mopeds crammed into the shop, they secured the doors, jumped into Anna and made their way the short distance home.

'One day we'll actually find a space outside,' complained a frustrated Glynn as the car crawled along the crammed street where they lived.

'Why don't you drop me off at the flat and I'll go and put the kettle on while you find somewhere to park?' suggested Fiona.

'OK. I won't be long. See you in a minute,' replied Glynn as he stopped in the road by their front door.

He would never see her again.

As Glynn inched the car round the corner Fiona noticed a man walking briskly past her. She immediately realized it was David McLellan, and it struck her as odd him being in Hove as he lived on the other side of the city. Despite being almost certain that he had not noticed her, she took the precaution of pretending to search for her keys so he would not spot which house was theirs. At that moment she became aware of a second figure pass her by. She glanced up and saw him join McLellan near the junction at which Glynn had just turned. They disappeared from sight.

Not expecting Glynn to be long, she ambled up the steps to the front door when suddenly the roar of a racing engine and the squeal of tyres grabbed her attention. Startled, she turned to see Anna racing and weaving away from her, the rear passenger door being slammed shut as it went.

She couldn't believe that someone had had the audacity to steal Anna so brazenly with Glynn being right there. How could he allow that to happen?

She walked to the corner, expecting Glynn to emerge from a shadow, clueless, wondering what was going on. As the minutes passed by so her fears soared.

Where was he? What was happening? She was right to be worried.

Glynn had found a perfect parking space just around the corner. Normally it would be, at most, a five-minute walk back from where he managed to squeeze his oversized car into the gap.

As he switched off the engine, he flung open the driver's door and swung his legs out. He wearily stretched as he stood on the deserted pavement, tired from his long day.

As he was closing the door, he saw McLellan walking straight at him. A second man was closing in from behind. The man behind grabbed Glynn's keys, forced him into the front of the car, pushed him across to the passenger side and jumped into the driver's seat next to him. At the same time McLellan leapt in the back behind Glynn.

The driver seemed flustered and couldn't get the keys in the ignition.

'You do it,' he ordered.

Confused, Glynn did as he was told and leant over and started the car. As it raced off and around the corner, he came to his senses. He spun sideways and tried to kick the door open, intending to throw himself out, but it held fast.

McLellan grabbed him from behind and he felt cold steel being pressed against his throat. The threat of the knife told him this was about more than Anna. Terrified, he sensed they were making their way northwards out of town. The last thing he recalls is the driver demanding, 'Have you got the shop keys?'

His memory of that night, and the next three months, finishes there. The brain is a wonderful thing. It can blot out forever the most horrific events, saving its host from a lifetime of flashbacks and nightmares.

Fiona frantically dashed to find a working telephone box. After hitting 999 she asked for the police. 'My boyfriend's been kidnapped. They've driven him off in our car. Please help me.'

Officers were dispatched immediately and, returning late from another enquiry, DC Mick Burkinshaw headed straight for

Fiona. Doing his best to reassure her, he coaxed her into his car and drove around the local area hoping to glimpse Glynn or Anna. More cops saturated the neighbourhood and beyond, desperate to find him, hoping that he would have been dumped and that it was just the worthless car that was the robbers' target.

PCs Richard Jarvis and Jo Nutter were conscientious and intelligent young officers. Regularly crewing together, they were a good team. Richard, despite his youth, had a dour demeanour that belied his dry sense of humour. Jo was the opposite. Irrepressibly bubbly and chatty, she was a perfect foil for Richard. They played to their differences expertly with the public, adopting good cop, bad cop roles when needed.

Knowing the patch well, they were familiar with the sites where stolen cars were dumped. Sometimes they were easy to find as the flames the thieves had ignited lit up the night sky. They made their way slowly northwards to Devil's Dyke, making sure they clocked every car, moving or stationary, on the way.

Roy Grace used to visit Devils Dyke with his wife Sandy. They liked to park at the top of this 2,000-acre beauty spot and walk across the fields, taking in the panoramic views of the city and the patchwork of the mid-Sussex farmland to its north. So named because, legend has it, the magnificent downland valley was dug by the Devil to flood the local churches.

There are a number of small stopping points along the meandering road that leads to the top; some are just passing places, some bus stops and some, like Poor Man's Corner, handy little car parks that serve as viewpoints.

As that particular car park came into view, it seemed empty, with not even a carload of teenagers sharing a crafty joint. Ever professional, Jo turned the car towards the narrow entrance as a movement caught her eye.

She made out a jerky figure desperately yet pathetically trying to lift an arm in a plea for help. Crunching the car to a sudden halt, Richard and Jo jumped out and rushed towards the blindly stumbling form, and leant the poor soul up against the car, unable to determine if they were dealing with a man or a woman. If you stretched your imagination you would possibly have recognized a mutilated shape that might be a head. You might just have been able to work out the facial features. If you'd thought about it, the gurgling spluttering groans *could* have been an attempt at speech.

Were it not for the fact that this horror had been discovered in a rural car park way off the beaten track, you could easily have assumed that the devastating injuries had been the result of a collision with a 70mph truck. It wasn't. This was pure evil, plain and simple. This poor soul had been beaten and kicked almost to death. Every single facial bone had been broken, probably by repeated stamping, as if crushing a tin can. Richard and Jo knew that he had been left to die, and he certainly would if they didn't act swiftly. From the description of his clothing, Jo and Richard established this was indeed Glynn Morgan. However, his own mother wouldn't have recognized him.

Roy Grace, in retribution for damage to Cleo's car, dumped the hateful Amis Smallbone in the same area in *Not Dead Yet*. We know from Smallbone's whingeing to his fellow villain Henry Tilney the physical toll the five-mile walk back had on him, a reasonably healthy yet odious specimen. No chance then that a man with his head and face completely staved in would survive it. He wasn't meant to.

The paramedics worked miracles, stabilizing and treating him on the gravel and grit of the rough car park. They knew that time was running out. The temperature was close to freezing. It was a balance between getting him to the specialists he would need, but not killing him in the process. Eventually they were able to gingerly lift him and glide their way to the hospital, knowing that every pothole could be a killer. The staff at the

Royal Sussex County Hospital worked against all the odds in trying to save his life.

As the duty DS, it was my turn to have my sleep disturbed. Once again my mobile phone chirped at me in the small hours. As soon as I was a safe distance from the sleeping Julie and our beautiful babies – my life would not be worth living if I woke them up – I listened to Mick Burkinshaw's staccato briefing, trying to comprehend not only what had happened but why.

Motive is all-important in such cases. Sometimes the hypotheses are hard to swallow. Crime investigation is intrusive. It strips away all privacy and dignity. Branson and Grace brought this into sharp relief when divulging to the father of Janie Stretton, shortly after her murder in *Looking Good Dead*, that she had been a high-class hooker. No secret is safe.

Roy Grace, at the start of every murder enquiry, refers to the *Murder Investigation Manual*. The route to his favoured MIR-1 – Major Incident Room One – is adorned with checklists from it. However experienced, we all need reminders.

This was not yet a murder, but I was sure it would be. Why would anyone want to kidnap someone off the street, steal their car, crush their head and leave them on a hillside to die? The manual offers possible reasons people kill, including gain, jealousy, revenge, elimination, thrill, hate, to name but a few. To get to the bottom of this I had to find the 'why' as well as the 'what'. That might involve asking difficult questions of Glynn, if he survived, Fiona and all who knew them. One thing I was sure of – you don't kill someone for an old rust heap of a car.

Later, we would need to broach the delicate subject of the relationship between Fiona and Glynn and whether there were skeletons in any cupboards, but now I needed to think like the attackers. Why Glynn? Why take him from the street? Why drive him away? Why so brutally attack him? Why focus the battering on his head? Where was the car? What was the big idea?

As I danced around the gloomy spare bedroom trying to get my trousers on and hoping the jacket I'd grabbed was from the same suit, I was making call after whispered call getting facts, triggering fast-track actions, pulling a team together.

Apologetic yet assertive was the style I used to call teams out, just as Roy did when Stuart Ferguson's lorry was recovered in *Dead Man's Grip* and on many other occasions. I needed who I needed. Apologize for disrupting their plans, yes; accepting no for an answer – never.

From the dearth of clear information I had to plump for a plausible scenario. It could have been many things but I tried to eliminate what I could. I had to strip away the unlikely to see the obvious. I needed to see what was in front of me and understand what it was telling me.

Having gently kissed Julie and our three miracles goodbye, as I was leaving the house I was told that Fiona had mentioned that she had seen a previous employee, McLellan, just before the attack. Was that relevant?

Thoughts were racing through my head as I rushed into work. McLellan might know where the takings were kept and how much there could be. Glynn himself was in no fit state to speak but Fiona had revealed that he had the shop keys with him. Surely McLellan would know that. Was that it? Was this an over-the-top burglary? Where were the keys now? I was soon at Hove Police Station and in Senior Investigating Officer mode.

The grisly task of searching the blood-soaked clothing the hospital staff had cut off the pitiful victim was one I delegated to the PC on guard. I needed to know if the keys were still with him. I sent officers to the shop to check for any sign of a break-in. Both enquires were negative; no keys, no sign of a forced entry.

No sign of a burglary, but why would there be if they had used the keys and been tidy when they went in? One of my first instructions from home had been for the nearest CCTV camera, which was on a lamppost fifty yards down the road, to be pointed towards the shop. I'd asked for it to be watched in case anyone went there after the attack. The second part of my message didn't get passed on. I was livid about that. In those days you couldn't review CCTV quickly. It all needed downloading onto VHS tape. I'd wanted someone monitoring it in live time. I'd been let down and someone would pay, but there was no time for that now.

Only one thing for it. I phoned Mick. 'We need to get Fiona to tell us if there are spare keys to the shop. If there are we need to get in there now and check to see if anyone's been in.'

'Just in time. We were about to take her up to the hospital.'

The phone went quiet. I'd been put on mute. Was he setting me up as the bad cop to get what we wanted, even though it delayed her seeing Glynn? Click. 'Good news, Graham, she's got a set with her. Do you want us to go down there?'

'Yes, but keep that shop watched while you are on your way. I need to know if anyone's been in there since lock-up. Get a SOCO to meet you there. One who hasn't been near Glynn or the Dyke. I'm not losing this job on cross-contamination.'

Fifteen minutes later Fiona, Mick and a PC huddled in the narrow doorway of Perfect Pizza, waiting for the SOCO, Dean O'Hara. When he arrived, he and Mick went in. Assured it was empty, and getting the forensic OK from Dean, he called Fiona through.

Still shaking with fear and worry, she checked the till. Fine. Then looked down at the safe. Open. Crouched down. Empty.

'It's gone, they've got all the money.'

'How much?'

'Only today's takings. We used to have up to about £5,000 on a Saturday as we paid the wages on a Sunday, but not any more. There was probably only £600 or £700 tonight.'

Mick was straight on the phone. That was it. I was going after McLellan. He was right there when Glynn was snatched, he probably knew the old banking procedures and had assumed they were still the same, and he would certainly know where the money was kept. I needed more, but Mr McLellan and I were going to have a chat. He had a lot of questions to answer and, if my hunch was right, he or his clothes would be covered in blood.

Dawn was breaking and we were already beyond the Golden Hour. The Grace novels mention this period of sixty minutes following a crime, and it is critical: the immediate aftermath of discovering a crime or victim provides the best chance of finding forensic evidence, witnesses and getting the truth out of people. So time was now against us. My team knew this. On days like this we worked like Trojans for as long as it took. No-one was waiting in the wings to take this over from us so everything was put on hold from now until we could come up for air.

We had the scene at Poor Man's Corner taped off and being searched. While not quite on the scale of the chicken farm in *Not Dead Yet*, it was a large windswept area that, being Sunday, ramblers would want to reclaim.

We needed the CCTV footage from all the shops near Perfect Pizza as well as our own. We needed to speak to anyone who might have seen the car being driven off. We needed intelligence on McLellan; was he capable of this and who did he knock around with?

I needed everything to be done in parallel but McLellan was my priority. With those of my team who had not been near Glynn, the Dyke and now the pizza shop, I went in pursuit of our man armed with a search warrant. We were surprised when McLellan, who was five foot ten and athletic, coolly let us in.

He denied leaving Moulsecoomb, claiming to have been watching MTV with his soon-to-be brother-in-law, Phillip Hurley. He seemed plausible. Hurley, a gangly six foot four bus driver, gave the same account. My team searched both McLellan's and Hurley's houses. We found nothing in Hurley's. But in McLellan's we recovered what appeared to be some stained black jeans and a grubby dark jacket. We couldn't work out whether it was blood or grime but I decided the suspicious clothing should be seized and McLellan arrested. We needed more on Hurley, so left him.

Having booked our man into custody, we had a series of lucky breaks that normally only occur in the movies. Mick Burkinshaw had relayed to the CCTV staff my wrath that no-one had bothered to watch the camera in live time. This persuaded them to get the tapes copied quicker than normal.

'Get over here, Graham,' he said as I walked into the bustling CID office, 'and tell me who you think this is.'

On the flickering screen in front of him was a CCTV image of two men side by side, who were dead ringers for McLellan and Hurley. Mick paused the tape. 'Now watch.' He pressed 'play'.

There before my eyes were the same men darting into the doorway of Perfect Pizza. Nothing happened for a couple of minutes then, bold as brass, out they came, this time face to camera. I needed no more convincing. 'Well done, Mick. You've cracked it'

'It gets better.' Amazingly they ambled into a taxi office a few doors down then, a minute or so later, came out, got into a cab and were driven away.

We had got them.

'Get out and nick Hurley,' I instructed DC Lee Taylor.

'No need,' said DC Steve Flay as he replaced the telephone receiver. 'The idiot's just turned up at the front desk with some fags for McLellan!' Lucky break number two.

'Well, get down there and nick him for attempted murder then!'

Our two suspects locked up, and having arranged for full forensic searches of their houses, I turned my attention to poor Glynn. Things weren't looking good. He was in Intensive Care but barely alive, wired up to machines that were performing every function his body couldn't.

Like Nat Cooper who was devastatingly injured in a motor-bike crash in *Dead Tomorrow*, he'd had emergency surgery to ensure he could breathe, but his brain was so badly injured it was swelling dangerously. Fiona wouldn't leave his side. We needed to speak to her but that could wait. He was going to die – I was sure of that – and her place was with him.

Normally, a Detective Superintendent would have taken on this enquiry. Just my luck, none were available. There were no dedicated Major Crime Teams in those days so, unless Glynn died, it was down to me to lead the investigation. As Grace was taught in his training, J Edgar Hoover once asserted that 'no greater honor or duty is bestowed on an officer than to investigate the death of another human being.' I felt both honour and duty even though Glynn was not dead yet.

As suspects, McLellan and Hurley did their best, sticking to the story that they had been in all night. They dismissed the evidence of the female bus driver we found, who knew Hurley well, who said she had taken them from Moulsecoomb to Hove. They scoffed at the taxi driver we identified who took them home again just as the CCTV had shown. They denied we'd find any forensics on their clothes. The ID parades, CCTV evidence, their discredited account and the blood they must have known we would find didn't shake their resolve.

We plugged on for days. Home became a distant memory for most of us: just a place to snatch a couple of hours' sleep, a quick cuddle with our loved ones and a change of clothes.

We were still looking for Glynn's car, still sifting witness statements and CCTV footage. We had daily late-night and early-morning meetings with the Crown Prosecution Service. The pager was always by my side waiting for the inevitable message that Glynn had died. During a custody extension hearing at Brighton Magistrates' Court, I was poised to whisper to the prosecutor that we were now dealing with a murder.

Amazingly that message never came. Call it a miracle, call

it the wonders of medical science, but Glynn gradually started to rally. First came small signs, just a tiny response to stimulus, then minute, almost imperceptible movements, followed by months of the very best care and rehabilitation the National Health Service could provide. His optic nerve, however, had been severed and he would be blind for life. His face needed a complete rebuild, his memory was a total blank, but he survived. The skill of the surgeons and the love of Fiona gave him a second chance.

As for McLellan and Hurley, they were charged with attempted murder and remanded in custody to await trial. Tough for Hurley who had no previous convictions but absolutely right nonetheless.

We soldiered on after the charge. As Grace reflects in *Dead Man's Grip*, that's when the real work begins. Convictions don't happen by themselves. We found the car, not far from Perfect Pizza. Inside was a balaclava that contained one of Glynn's hairs. Glynn had never owned such a garment so had it been put on him to stop him recognizing McLellan? The icing on the cake came when the brilliant forensic scientists found a significant amount of Glynn's DNA in the blood on the clothing of both suspects.

What had started as a hunch became a cast-iron case. Even arrogant pleas of not guilty, allegations of police corruption and an attempt to ban the blinded victim from the courtroom 'in case it swayed the jury' didn't pull the wool over anyone's eyes. Both men were convicted and imprisoned for a staggering thirty-seven years between them.

Glynn got a life sentence of blindness however. He was forced to rebuild his life and try to make sense of why he was so nearly killed for a paltry £620. He and Fiona made a new but quiet life for themselves, refusing to be bitter, refusing to hate.

My final memory of the trial was an indication of how some in the criminal justice system refuse or are unable to see the horror of what is at the root of their profession. We all experience it; to some it's a sick, heartless game.

Having spent hours in the witness box being accused of planting what must have been about a pint of blood on the clothes of both defendants from the vial of a few millilitres we had for testing, I bumped into one of the defence legal team outside the Old Bailey after the verdicts. He tapped me on the shoulder and glibly remarked, 'Well done, Graham, old boy. Good case and right result. Sorry about all that nonsense regarding the blood. When one has one's instructions one has to try, you understand.'

Understand? How dare he? How dare he try to minimize the horrors inflicted by his client by downgrading the trial to a debating society joust? That was typical of some. Never mind the rights and wrongs, never mind searching for the truth, never mind the victim. Throw some mud where you can and hope you get enough jurors to doubt for a moment. Do what it takes, and see if you get one up on justice and let the guilty walk free. How do they sleep?

11: THE SILENT ASSASSIN

As Peter James notes in *You are Dead*, never say the word 'q**et' to a police officer. It's like mentioning the Scottish play to an actor. It's a sure way to bring down the wrath of the gods. 'Q' is as far as you dare go in describing the kind of day you are having or hoping for. Complete the word and you are doomed! Some joker must have bellowed it from the rooftops one unseasonably bright October morning in the late nineties.

Sundays were never ordinary. As the duty DS at Hove I worked every other weekend, which could be gruelling, but never dull. Sundays could start in a myriad of ways. It might be clearing up the many and varied prisoners from the excesses of the night before, waking up the 'never at home' suspects with a very early morning knock (never rely on a Sunday lie-in if you are wanted by the police) or using a rare lull in demand to plough through mountains of tedious paperwork accumulated during more frantic weeks. Sundays were never a day of rest.

This particular one started with all the signs of being an opportunity to clear the decks so, in true CID style, I took my team for breakfast to the ever-popular Carats Cafe at Shoreham Harbour. This jewel of a diner is hidden from the rest of the world by Shoreham Power Station and the lock gates, the place where, in *Dead Man's Grip*, young Tyler nearly met a very grisly end and through which Tooth executed his Houdini-like escape.

Carats doesn't do mediocre, either in quality or quantity. Neither do detectives with a rare hour away from the grind, so we gorged ourselves on a gut-busting full English before making our way back for our Q day. Some hope.

Having abandoned the rusty CID car in the last free parking bay in the police station back yard I was met by Sergeant Russ Bagley who was just on his way out.

'Don't go far, Graham, I may need you.'

'Oh no! You dare ruin my plans for the day!' I threatened. 'What have you got?'

'My lot have just found a body in a camper van. Seems the poor fella's dog had been pining outside.'

Russ was a recently promoted patrol sergeant but had previously been an experienced DC. As described at the discovery of Ralph Meeks' corpse in *Dead Man's Time*, policy was that if a death was potentially suspicious, then a DS had to attend and 'call' it as such. I trusted that Russ would only ask for me if genuinely needed although I never minded helping even the more cautious sergeants.

It's very lonely being the one who has to decide whether or not a death is natural. The relatives expect us to get it right. If we are suspicious then the balloon goes up and a whole machine akin to that described in all the Grace books kicks in. If not it's quite low-key. At times we all need a second opinion, and I would never deny that to a colleague. I came to wish that I had someone to consult that day.

I sloped back to the office, reluctant to settle in to anything that I couldn't drop. Something told me I would soon be back in the car again.

Sure enough the call came. 'Seems an odd one, Graham,' reported Russ. 'The van's all locked up. We had to force our way in. The poor chap appears to have fallen over but the bizarre thing is there's a small window that's broken but no glass around and we can't find the keys.'

'What about the window? Couldn't someone have got in through there?'

'Not unless they were an Oompa-Loompa. The window's too small and in the wrong place, also there's no sign of a disturbance. I'm just not happy with it. Can you pop down?'

Glad of any excuse to leave those reports for another day, DC Lee Taylor and I hopped back into the CID car and drove the short distance to First Avenue, which runs off Hove Seafront.

Parked at the back of the monolithic King's House, the HQ of Brighton and Hove City Council, the tatty VW camper van was guarded by uniformed officers and encircled by blue and white 'Police' tape. Other than its 'For Sale' sign in the window and the shattered pane there was nothing to set it apart from any other vehicle among those belonging to day trippers enjoying time at the beach.

Lee and I wasted no time in establishing the story. A whippet, whimpering around the van, had caused passers-by to become curious so they called the police. The first officers to arrive were sceptical that this was a police matter. Then their sixth sense caused them to agree with the concerned bystanders. There was more to this than a stray dog. They tried and failed to find a way into the van so, using their batons, they forced an entry. Inside was a sight they had hoped they wouldn't see.

Slumped in the cramped floor space was a shabbily dressed man, probably in his early sixties. His head was resting against a blue body board. There was no doubt he was dead, but his eyes held a startled expression. A closer examination revealed the faintest abrasion on his left temple but no other obvious signs of injury. Unusually, there was no sign of alcohol or drug misuse and the putrid aroma of decomposition was yet to arrive. As Russ indicated, even from the broken window there was no internal or external debris and the van was tidy. This was a really tricky scene to read.

Sadly it's not uncommon to find people having died alone and in squalid circumstances – but this one didn't seem right. I couldn't put my finger on it. There was no sign of a fight or broken glass from the shattered window; the van was locked but the keys could not be found. All these facts, singly and collectively, were calling out their importance as I tried to fathom out what they were telling me.

Recognizing that this might indeed be suspicious, I gave the order to seal off the street and treat the immediate area as a crime scene. Never an easy decision given the chaos that causes, but necessary under such circumstances. The impact on the public of me shutting off a busy thoroughfare, and on police in tying up scarce officers to protect the area, meant that I was probably the least popular person in Hove that morning.

I called out the duty Senior SOCO and Police Surgeon. They were with me in no time. Dressed head-to-toe in white forensic paper suits, together we gingerly ventured further into the van. We took in what we saw, considered its meaning and tried to understand what it was telling us.

There is no perfect checklist for suspicious deaths, so experience, judgement and hope supplement knowledge.

After as much examination as we dared in such an open setting, we were still unable to determine what had happened. We needed more. Surely the body itself and any minute forensic traces in the van would unlock the story for us?

I summoned the mortuary team to take the body away, and the low loader to remove the van to a forensically secure yard. I called a POLSA to start a fingertip search of the immediate area and arranged for an early post mortem. In the meantime our reflective Sunday changed tack and pace and my team and I slogged on to identify and understand our tragic victim.

We quickly worked out who he was. Anthony Robinson was a local man, a popular chap, who was well known in the close-knit community around the chic Norfolk Square in central Brighton. Once a cheap rental area, described by Grace in *Not Dead Enough* as the abode of students, transients, hookers and the impoverished elderly, this part of the city had undergone a transformation. Anthony was the proprietor of the successful Spectrum Copy Shop and known for being always cheery and on hand to help local people and businesses with that last-minute printing or typesetting.

Home was a well-appointed flat a couple of miles away on the blustery Hove seafront, which he shared with his faithful whippet Bonzo. He loved surfing and would regularly pack himself and Bonzo off to Devon and ride the West Country waves. His VW camper van, while entirely in tune with his surfing lifestyle, was getting old and tired and he needed to sell it. It had attracted little interest and he was apparently getting concerned he would be stuck with it.

Nothing we unearthed that day gave any clue to how and why he died. And in hindsight neither could it have. You couldn't make up what really happened – unless your name is Peter James.

It was only at the post mortem at Cleo's Brighton and Hove Mortuary the following day that the truth started to emerge. The slight abrasion we had all seen was, unbelievably, an exit wound from a tiny .22 bullet, its track through his head only shown up by X-ray. This stunned everyone. No-one had spotted the even smaller entry wound on the opposite side of his head under the hairline.

All my firearms training at Gatwick Airport had taught me that gunshot wounds were visible on entry and catastrophic on exit. This is graphically described following the shooting of Marla in *Not Dead Yet*. The bullet pushes flesh, muscle, sinew and bone ahead of it and out of the body. A gaping mush of death. This was nothing like that: a barely perceptible entry and a tiny exit. I beat myself up for months after. How did I miss that?

The nature of police humour being what it is, my supportive colleagues never missed an opportunity to recall the time I missed a gunshot wound. Plenty of DS Norman Pottings came out of the woodwork reminding me of this oversight. The real Tom Martinson, Chief Constable Martin Richards QPM, even made mention of it in my retirement speech some fifteen years on! The truth, and the nature of .22 injuries, would never be sufficient to defend me from the ribbing. That's coppers for you.

From the outset this was not only a baffling whodunnit but, to complicate matters, became a where, when and why dunnit, a real quandary. However the answer to the who became apparent as a result of the tenacious nature of my partner in crime DS Bill Warner. Bill, once again, was interfering in matters that simply did not concern him.

He was trawling the force incident logs for his daily adrenaline rush: what could he meddle with in other parts of the county that had absolutely nothing to do with him? It didn't take him long to find something. Little did we know though that, for once, his inability to keep his nose out of other people's business would be of some use.

The title of the incident serial leapt off the screen: 'Armed Kidnap'. What followed was fascinating. A terrified middle-aged couple, Mr and Mrs Purnell, had been kidnapped at gunpoint twenty-five miles away in Eastbourne and forced to drive north, snatched while trying to sell their camper van. A man had produced a gun and pointed it at Mrs Purnell's head. He ordered Mr Purnell to drive to London. On reaching the M23 he then demanded to be driven to Gatwick. He clearly did not appreciate that they had just entered the place with the most armed police and CCTV outside London. It also had plenty of convenient dead ends.

On arrival, with breathtaking courage, Mr Purnell told his wife to get out and the gunman either to shoot him or get out too. Amazingly the man chose the latter and ran into the heaving South Terminal.

The terrified hostages raised the alarm and were able to help police swiftly locate their assailant. His arrest by heavily armed officers was both rapid and decisive. It was only at this point that the story of a mad five days of drug trafficking, deception, theft, kidnapping and murder started to emerge.

South African Denis Mulder knew little of Brighton. It's unlikely that he ever intended to visit the UK, let alone this quirky city. However when you are dealt cruel cards you never know where it will end.

He had been a highly successful, multilingual entrepreneur. He owned a swimming-pool business in his homeland but wanderlust got to him. A fanatical sailor, he acquired a number of yachts around the Caribbean and enjoyed a healthy income chartering them to wealthy businessmen. He too enjoyed the seafaring life but one day suffered a massive stroke while offshore. This left him partially paralysed and needing to relearn to speak. Without health insurance he found the treatment costs as crippling as his illness and had to sell his boats and business to settle his medical debts.

Once back on his feet, he moved to Europe and acquired a franchise selling rooftop tents for cars. According to intelligence, recognizing that this wasn't going to keep him in the style to which he had become accustomed, he diversified into the seemingly lucrative business of cannabis trafficking. Expecting a quick buck, he smuggled a large quantity of weed into England in his highly conspicuous Renault estate complete with rooftop tent.

More by luck than judgement he evaded the attention of Her Majesty's Customs and somehow ended up in Brighton. There, in the beachfront Volks Tavern bar, he naively approached two potential buyers of his stash. Seizing an opportunity exposed by his criminal and geographical ignorance, they hoodwinked Mulder into driving the 160 miles to Bristol to sell to a Mr Big, promising a handsome return on his investment. Of course no such person existed and inevitably they stole his drugs and he returned penniless.

Broke, cold and in a strange country, Mulder decided he needed a camper van as a warmer alternative to his canvas-topped station wagon. All he had to his name were his wits and the .22 pistol he had carried undetected for years.

A few days prior to the kidnapping of the sharp-witted couple, he had seen an advert in a window of a van parked close to Hove seafront. He rang the number scribbled on the notice and agreed to meet the vendor for a test drive. This would turn out to be the last thing Anthony Robinson would ever do.

Painstaking detective work eventually helped piece together the brutal events on that fateful drive. Through the jigsaw of testimony that emerged it became clear that the two had driven the van eastwards on the A27 to Lewes and then retraced their journey west towards the scene of the *Dead Simple* dramatic car chase close to Shoreham Airport and the River Adur.

For reasons known only to Mulder, the van pulled over in a layby just east of Southwick Tunnel. We could only guess what happened there between the two, possibly a dispute over the price, possibly an attempt to steal the van, but whatever it was, all the evidence points to that short stop being the scene of the execution.

One shot to the head with a .22 pistol was all it took to end the life of this hugely popular and fun-loving surfer, who was probably in the back of the van while Mulder stood outside. The bullet was never recovered, having presumably broken the window on its way out of the van, hence there was no shattered glass when we found the body. Mulder must have driven the van back into the city, body in the back, parked it and dutifully locked it up, before leaving it where it was found. We don't know if Bonzo witnessed the murder of his master. Being a dog lover, I sincerely hope not.

Curiously, during the interviews that followed Mulder's arrest, he provided a full picture of the kidnapping, yet casually and callously made only passing mention of 'killing the guy in

Brighton'. We brought in the most able and tenacious interviewers but they could elicit no more than an unequivocal yet bland admission that he had shot Robinson in cold blood.

The full story is really known only to Mulder, as he has never yet had the humanity to tell it.

Imagine being one of Mr Robinson's nearest and dearest. Imagine not knowing how and why your loved one died. Cruel enough to rob someone of their life, but it rubs salt in the wounds of those left behind to tantalize them with an admission, but not the courtesy of an explanation.

Mulder was not a clever killer but his ruthlessness made up for that. There seems little doubt that were it not for the brave evasive action taken by his hostages at Gatwick he would have gone on to kill again. He had brushed with death through his stroke and it seemed that his survival instinct was so strong that, in his mind, it overrode everyone else's right to life.

Some might regard it as fanciful if Peter James were to link such a complex and contradictory character to this kind of violence but, as is ever the case, nothing is too bizarre or inexplicable to happen in Brighton.

A life sentence was the least Mulder deserved but he remains one of the hardest men to fathom. His guilty plea meant the facts couldn't be explored, so only he knows what turned this previously successful, sick, failed drug dealer into an executioner of the type thankfully we rarely see.

12: THE BODY BUTCHER

Dogs love bones. It's in their nature. All bones, any bone. They just love them.

There is something heart-warming when a faithful hound sprints back to its owner with a gift in its mouth, found while rummaging through the undergrowth. A bouncy ball, maybe even a gnarled branch from a nearby oak – the look of triumph on the mutt's face warms the cockles of your heart.

Late one balmy evening in July 1999, that joy was tarnished for a middle-aged lady as she called her dogs in for the night near a pig farm in Bexhill, East Sussex. She crouched down, her arms out wide, as her dog bounded towards her with an object protruding either side of his salivating mouth. *Strange-shaped stick*, she thought, *strange colour too. A bit bigger than his usual find.* As the distance between them narrowed so her curiosity heightened. *Not another mangy rabbit?*

With a proud flourish he dropped it in front of her.

It took her a moment before the horrific truth hit her. A severed human hand, riddled with maggots and emitting the pungent stench of death and decay, lay festering at her feet.

Two and a half weeks earlier, I was enjoying a weekend off, leaving Bill Warner at the helm of Hove CID as duty DS. Julie and I had spent the Saturday afternoon with Conall, Niamh and Deaglan at their friend's second birthday party near Gatwick. The summer sun provided the first outing in shorts, tee-shirts and flip-flops, and brought a wave of optimism that there would be balmy days ahead.

Julie and I spent most of the time counting in threes to make sure we could track all of our children and checking that they were not damaging themselves or wandering off. As was the way in those days our conversations with others were invariably centred around the kids with answers such as, 'No, we feel blessed, not burdened', 'Yes, it was hard in the early days but we both mucked in', 'Yes, we know it will be expensive when they go to uni'.

'They are very natural babies, if that's what you mean,' was a retort we used to rebuff one of the more intrusive questions people would ask.

As the party drew to a close we said our goodbyes and clipped our exhausted trio into their car seats across the back of our huge Volvo estate car. As if waiting for a lull in the child-shepherding, my phone started to buzz.

'You're not on call, are you?' enquired Julie, knowing the answer but fearing the worst.

'No,' I said as I looked at the display. A sense of relief washed through me as I saw who was ringing. 'It's only Bill,' I said. 'He will only want to moan or brag about something. I'll answer it then he can leave me be.'

Julie took the driver's seat and I answered the call.

'Hi, mate,' I chirped. 'What have you done this time?'

'Ah, Graham,' Bill droned in a manner that invariably pre-ceded some bombshell he was waiting to drop. '*Were* you having a nice weekend?'

'I still am, mate, unless you have finally come to accept what I have said all along – that you can't cope without me there to guide you.' I glanced at Julie as she drove and detected a faint sign of exasperation on her face as she sensed this would be a long call of banter and brickbats being exchanged.

'Very funny,' muttered Bill, 'at least I can recognize a gunshot wound when I see it.'

'Out of order,' I declared. 'What is it? I am enjoying some time with the ones I love and you come nowhere near that classification.'

'We think we've got a murder.'

'You think? And there were you questioning my crime scene analysis skills. What do you mean, think?'

'Well. We are pretty sure but we haven't got a body. David Gaylor is here and is asking if you can come in.' My heart sank. Weekends at home were precious, not least because they gave me an opportunity to take over the childcare, allowing Julie to catch up with friends and sleep. I knew if this was a murder, home would become nothing more than a staging post and dressing room for me for the next month or so. I loved investigating homicides but I adored my new family and these conflicting demands tore me up. I knew I would have to go in.

'I suppose David wants me there to ensure that you don't stand officers down just before the suspect walks through the door. Am I right?'

'*Touché*,' Bill replied.

As I finished the call, I looked across at Julie. She knew what was coming.

'Babes. I've got to go in. They think they have a murder but no body and they need me there.'

'How can you have a murder with no body?' she asked, as ever not revealing the disappointment and frustration she must have been feeling.

'It's not common but sometimes the facts point towards a crime but the body has been disposed of or hidden. Could be a long job.'

'OK,' she said. 'Can you give me a hand settling the kids when we get home before you shoot off? At least we have had a nice afternoon.'

I leant across the gearshift and kissed her on the cheek as we finally left the motorway for the homeward stretch.

'I must have been very good in a past life to have deserved you,' I remarked.

'Yes, you must, but I am sure you'll pay me back with your bodyweight in flowers and chocolates,' she replied, a resigned smile spreading across her face.

She pulled up outside our house and I started heaving pushchairs and babies out of the car as my mind raced with scenarios that might be awaiting me. Getting out and about with the kids in those days was a logistical nightmare that needed to be approached like a military operation. Julie was the commander-in-chief and I was the quartermaster. Everything had to be counted out and then counted back, into its designated storage. We had recently returned from our first foreign holiday with the babies and planned our stores so precisely that after a week we had just one out of ninety-six nappies unused.

Kit stowed and children settled, I quickly transformed myself from casual barbecue bum to professional detective, ensuring that I did not commit the cardinal sin of combining a spotted tie with a striped shirt.

As I dashed down the stairs, Julie was already serving up rations of meatballs, mashed potatoes and peas to three gurgling, chuckling, hungry mouths. With a quick kiss for each and a sincere but feeble apology, I jumped into the car and headed south.

As I squeezed the car between two people-carriers in a far corner of Hove Police Station car park around 5 p.m. it became clear that I was not the only one whose weekend plans had been dashed.

I climbed the two storeys to the CID floor and as I walked briskly along the corridor, the excited mumble of speculation and one-sided phone calls that define the early hours of any murder enquiry grew louder.

I stepped through the DCs' office door, to be greeted by Mick Burkinshaw. 'Eh up, Graham. Don't worry, we've got an overtime code.' This was one of the more typical concerns at the outset of any enquiry.

The issue of such a code meant a separate budget and this often was seen by some as being handed carte blanche to work as long as it took to finish the job, sure that they would be handsomely recompensed. Overtime was seen as a great perk and made up for the personal disruption murder enquiries brought.

I remember, some years after Giles York, who later became Chief Constable, being at a briefing I was holding for a major public order event. We provided the hundreds of officers with a bewildering catalogue of details about what was anticipated, what their job was, where the threats might come from, their meal arrangements and the overtime code. Giles pulled me to one side at the end and remarked, 'What is it about cops, Graham? You can give them all the information they will ever need to do their job and keep themselves safe, but it's only when you tell them the overtime code that any of them get their pens out.'

I walked into DCI David Gaylor's office, where Bill had already taken root.

'Ah, Graham. Thanks so much for popping in,' joked Bill.

David was in his familiar focused murder mode. He was our boss, but was also a hugely experienced detective with a rapier mind. His hypotheses and orders would come thick and fast when he was in this zone and woe betide us if we missed anything.

'Thanks, Graham. I think the best thing is to get Mick Burkinshaw and Dave Corcoran in here to bring us up to speed first hand rather than me tell you,' he said.

I still had only the very basics that Bill had delighted in passing on in that phone call, which now seemed hours ago.

'Burky, Corky, DCI's office now,' bellowed Bill with a feigned military bark.

David and I looked at each other and lifted our eyebrows,

recognizing we were in the presence of a troublesome child who was beyond help. Burky's jocular response was less restrained, typical of the Yorkshireman.

'Fuck off, Bill. You are nothing without us. In fact you are nothing full stop and the boss only called Graham in because he wanted some brains at DS level.'

As Bill was about to counter, David raised his hand and reminded us, 'Gents, there will be plenty of time for Bill-bashing later. For now we have a body to find and a murder to solve. Now go through for Graham's benefit what has happened this after-noon.'

Mick and Dave were two of the most experienced detectives we had. DC Dave Corcoran was a loveable rugged Irishman whose life revolved around greyhounds, Guinness and horse racing.

The pair couldn't have been better chosen to start this enquiry. Both detectives had good old-fashioned copper's noses, enabling them to read people and situations as if words on a page. Grace uses body language to detect liars. The eyes go left or right when a person lies. It's not conclusive but it is a good signal that something is amiss. Spotting and taking notice of anomalies is an essential ability for detectives. As Grace grapples with a long-running enquiry in *Dead Man's Grip*, Sir Arthur Conan Doyle's quote is foremost in his thoughts: 'A precise and intelligent recognition of minor differences is what is required of a good detective.' Mick and Dave were good detectives.

I had worked with them for a couple of years and felt privi-leged and reassured in equal measures that it was they who were about to brief me.

'Now then,' started Mick. 'About one thirty today a local drunk by the name of Jeff Mighell called the switchboard and told the operator he had some information about a body. He was a bit pissed and slurring but thank God the call taker stuck with him. He said that the other day, he couldn't be sure when, he was chatting to a girl called Jenny Shaw. She's seventeen and lives with her boyfriend Reg Connolly in a flat at the top end of Hove. I take it you know these three?'

We all nodded. None of us was surprised that this mystery had a cast of very familiar characters.

Jeff was typical of so many in Brighton and Hove and could often be found in our cells sobering up. He was a sorry character who was a bit of a joke in the area.

The city had a huge problem with alcohol. It's a tourist destination, a stag and hen party favourite, and had a disproportionate number of pubs and off-licences together with a hard core of street drinkers. Alcohol-related deaths of men in the city were running at about 22 per 100,000 people, which was almost twice the rate for the whole of England, and nearly two and a half times the south-east average. That's a lot of lives lost to booze. Add to that the 32 per 100,000 lost to drugs in the city and the problem with substance misuse starts to become clear.

Drunks were part of the landscape, whether they are begging, fighting or collapsed in the street. Like so many, though, in his more lucid moments Jeff had a heart of gold and hated himself for his drunken lifestyle.

Reg was a drunk too, but with a nasty streak. Odd, as he came from a very close and proud family. He'd migrated to the city from the north west of England and was into drugs, petty crime and beating up his young girlfriend. Reg stole and scammed his way through life and heaven help anyone, including the police, who tried to stop him.

Jenny, on the other hand, was a vulnerable young girl who, despite coming from a big and equally close local family, had been allowed to make her own decisions, her own way in life, far too soon. Poorly educated and with no effective role models, she moved in with her thug of a boyfriend with all the danger that entailed.

The police had been called to their flat several times following disputes between the two but rarely were we able to persuade Jenny to end their relationship or to keep Reg away for anything more than a few days.

'They were by the shops just round the corner,' Burky continued. 'Jeff said that she was really upset. Not unusual apparently as it's common knowledge that Reg knocks her about but this seemed worse. He says she burst into tears and threw her arms round him.'

'Bloody hell, she must have been desperate from what I can remember of Jeff,' interjected Bill.

Ignoring him, Burky continued. 'So he asked her what's up and she said, "Come round to the flat. I'll show you." As they arrived Jeff asked her if Reg would mind, as he had beaten him up before. Jenny just stayed silent as she opened the door. She didn't go in but pointed to the cupboard just to the left. He squeezed past her and peered in.

'Well, there slumped inside with a gaping hole in his chest, blood crusting all around it, was Reg. Lifeless. Jeff couldn't work out how long he might have been there but he knew he was dead. He says there were blood and drag marks all around and down the hallway towards the lounge. He says he was too scared to go in any further.

'He said he gagged, turned to Jenny and said, "What the fuck?" She apparently was shaking and bawling her eyes out but managed to blurt out, "I'd had enough of his beatings, Jeff. He was going to kill me. I stabbed him when he was asleep. I had to but I am so scared. I'm going to go to prison, aren't I?" So, helpful as ever, Jeff just told her he wanted nothing to do with it and turned and ran. He has been thinking of nothing else since so he decided eventually he had to call us.'

We were all hooked, listening intently and scratching all the gory details in our blue A4 investigators' notebooks. None of us wanted to be the one to forget a critical nugget.

Dave Corcoran took up the story. 'So, thanks to the experience and judgement of the call handler, she didn't dismiss Jeff as some rambling drunk. She had a gut feeling that there was something in this so she called the CID office and Burky and I went out to find Jeff. It wasn't hard. We got him out of the pub and sat him in the car. He was pissed but basically repeated what he had told the operator. So we brought him back here for a statement and went straight up to Jenny's.'

Between them Burky and Corky described what they found.

As Jenny opened the door she'd had the look of the frightened little girl she was. Without naming their source, they gently explained what they had been told. She said nothing but meekly allowed them in.

The flat was filthy – the sort of place, we say, where you need to wipe your feet on the way out. However, a wall of bleach fumes hit them The surgical cleanliness of the cupboard was in stark contrast to the rest of the squalor. They noticed a body-shaped outline on the floor. That, together with the absence of a bed convinced them Jeff was right. The missing piece, however, was a body.

A dead body with a knife in its chest is pretty easy to call as a murder. You know what you've got and there is an obvious starting point. No body, a silent, frightened girl and the word of a drunk makes that decision less clear-cut. However, Burky and Corky both knew you can always step back from declaring an incident a murder but you can rarely make up ground if you don't.

They arrested Jenny for murder, called for back-up to seal off the house and summoned the cavalry.

Since then David, as SIO, had already called in the teams he needed, and now started to allocate the roles. I was to run the incident room, and Bill the outside enquiry team: the detectives who would be talking to witnesses, taking statements and hopefully solving the case.

In those first few hours we interviewed Jenny's family, traced her handful of friends and sought to find out whether Reg was alive or dead. We tracked down some terrified youngsters who, like Jeff, had been shown the grisly body but sworn to silence by Jenny. Their relief at being finally permitted to unburden themselves of their macabre secret was immense. For us it was critical corroboration.

However, the top priority was finding Reg, one way or another.

We had exclusive use of the same Specialist Search Unit that Grace relies on so often. From searching Brighton and Hove's various waste disposal tips to rummaging through a container of rotting animal carcasses, they followed every lead. In our desperation, there was nowhere we wouldn't ask them to look.

We'd been running the enquiry for what seemed like an age but were missing this essential ingredient. We had the murder scene, we had some damning evidence, we had a pitiful suspect. As far as we could we had shown there was no trace of Reg since the time Jeff saw him dead in the bath. At a stretch, that would probably be enough to go to trial but we knew the defence would insist that he had just moved on and that Jeff and the others were deluded. We needed the clues the corpse would hold. The pressure was on.

Despite the training and experience Police Search Advisors amass throughout their careers they will concede they are no match for the combination of warm weather and inquisitive dogs. It's not that POLSAs don't solve crimes, it's just that when you are looking for a body that has been missing for weeks you can't beat the canine nose. We were clinging to the hope that the current heat wave would work its magic.

In hindsight, the recovery of the body was inevitable but when it came it was a huge relief. As with Hilary Dupont, when her dog unearthed Janie Stretton's human remains in *Looking Good Dead*, the day for our dog owner was unremarkable. Little did she know that it would end with her dog subjected to the ignominy of being forensically combed and plucked of human blood and sinew and she herself having to provide a bewilderingly detailed witness statement describing what she saw, when, how and where.

For Grace the finding of the butchered remains was the first piece in the jigsaw; for us it was almost the last.

Once Reg's first hand had been retrieved, we had a focus. Finally we knew where to look. Our search parameters had been set by a dog and we used him again to lead us to the remaining body parts. Our operation moved from Hove to Bexhill and for a short while life was on hold for the residents in the lanes around the find, as the police Major Incident Vehicle, countless Scenes of Crime and dog vans and a fleet of personnel carriers gridlocked the narrow country roads.

Open-ground searching takes lots of cops. Lots of cops mean a huge support structure. It's like the circus coming to town. As with the recovery of the first body from the storm drain in *Dead Man's Footsteps* every expert known to man turns up at a deposition site. All hoping theirs is the 'ology' that will crack the case.

Eventually, Connolly's severed head with its startled staring eyes, two blackening legs and his other arm were found scattered close to the farm.

This time we were able to accurately mark their position, photograph them from all angles, recover them carefully and fingertip search the immediate surroundings. Grateful as we were to the dog for giving us the tip-off, he selfishly didn't think about the evidential trail when he found the first limb.

As each body part was recovered it was carefully moved to the mortuary for examination.

It's no coincidence that Roy Grace spends so much time there and it's certainly not all to do with it being Cleo's place of work. Dead bodies hold secrets. In the days of Agatha Christie and Arthur Conan Doyle, the crime scene was the centre of the investigation. While still important, many crimes are now solved in the mortuary or forensic labs. The absence of a body deprives the SIO of vital clues.

I went to numerous post mortems in Cleo's Brighton and Hove Mortuary as each body part was found. Always a soulless place, it is accurately described in *Not Dead Enough* as being 'a crucible in which human beings are deconstructed back to their base elements'. Its ethereal grey, which Peter James captures superbly, soaks every wall, surface and cadaver. It is a dire place that most visit only when they absolutely need to. But you have to find something to make the awfulness a little more bearable. One strategy is another use of gallows humour such as the term shared between police and morticians to describe a body mid-post mortem: 'canoe'. Why so? Well, that is what a human body resembles when it's been slit from neck to groin and all its internal organs removed.

With the various post-mortems Reg was becoming blacker and blacker as the cycle of freezing and defrosting restarted the inevitable decomposition. I hate post mortems at the best of times. Despite the efforts to retain his dignity, this appeared to be a prolonged ghoulish jigsaw puzzle being played out over many days. The picture that emerged was that he had been precisely and expertly dismembered.

Symmetrical amputations with striation marks gave away the use of professional razor-sharp high-powered instruments. This told us that whatever Jenny had done she had surely been helped by someone who knew what they were about.

We had the killer but it seemed Brighton and Hove was home to a butcher for hire. We had to find out where and by whom Reg had been chopped up.

We searched a local butcher's shop as we had intelligence that was where the deed was done – it wasn't. There were parallels with *Dead Tomorrow* in which people with surgical skills were evidently involved in the death of the unwitting organ donors. Whoever dismembered Reg remained a worrying mystery. Was there a market in hacking up bodies that we were unaware of? Was there someone out there prepared to capitalize on that? If there was, we never found out who.

It was another five months, the day before Christmas Eve, that a shocked council workman clearing gullies some thirteen miles away in Hailsham unearthed in the bucket of his digger the final piece of the jigsaw. Among the decaying vegetation and sodden soil, up came Reg Connolly's rotting, putrefied torso with the tell-tale stab wound still just visible. We had no idea why this was separated from the rest of the body but it must have been deliberate.

For the police and Reg's family it started to bring some kind of grisly closure to what had been a bizarre and tragic case.

Why Reg was killed we will never truly know but Jenny was a young and vulnerable woman who was being regularly and horribly abused. Her plea of guilty to manslaughter on the grounds of diminished responsibility was accepted. The horrors she had faced in her own home and the mental strain and impairment that this had caused were enough to convince the court that she could not be held fully accountable for her actions. However, to add to the tragedy, she took her own life midway through her community sentence.

This was another violent death solved, though, one that would have been straightforward were it not for the expertise in the disposal of the body. It may be reassuring to know that the clear-up rate for murders in the UK is 93 per cent. This is not because these cases are easy, nor because villains give themselves up. No, they are solved because of the breathtaking skill and tenacity of people like Peter James' fictional Grace, Branson, Moy and even Potting or the real life Burky and Corky.

Those that aren't solved become cold cases, never forgotten, never given up on but constantly there, filling cabinets in Detective Superintendents' offices as a constant reminder of the grief and angst families still suffer waiting for closure, answers and justice.

13: WHEN GOOD COPS GO BAD

'Trust me, I'm a policeman!' has a reassuring ring to it. More so maybe than 'Trust me, I'm an MP/journalist/estate agent'.

You would expect me to be among those who *do* trust the police. However, that faith has been shaken many times over the years. I have seen a number of previously respected colleagues arrested and jailed for offences as diverse as downloading child abuse images, selling information, fraud and plain theft.

Brighton has an infamous history of corruption. In 1957 there was an institutional police culture of demanding back-handers and turning a blind eye to the fencing of stolen goods, blatant licensing breaches and even illegal abortions. The CID was divided into the *fors* and *againsts*. If you were *for*, you could expect to augment your paltry pay packet with gratuities from local villains and businessmen. The *againsts* were allowed to get on with the job with integrity, providing they kept their mouths shut.

It took some brave junior officers and the evidence of career criminals to disrupt this murky world. PC Frank Knight and DS Ray Hovey showed outstanding courage by breaking the code of silence that had protected corrupt practices for years.

The trial of Chief Constable Charles Ridge, DI John Hammersley and DS Trevor Heath shocked the country. PC Knight gave evidence that he was openly asked by Heath whether he would 'like to earn a tenner a week'. He turned the offer down flat but knew it was an attempt to co-opt him into the criminal cabal that prevailed in CID. DS Hovey corroborated this and said in court that he had not said anything before as he feared the consequences given the relationship between Heath and the Chief Constable.

The evidence showed that not only were there relatively junior officers prepared to openly take bribes to allow crime to flourish, but that it was sanctioned from the very top. Ridge's acquittal in light of the conviction and five-year sentences that his underlings received did not go without comment from the judge. His scathing indictment of the Chief Constable made it crystal clear that he thought Ridge was far from innocent and that without a change in the leadership of the force the judiciary would feel unable to believe any evidence proffered by Brighton police.

People think that cops are naturally suspicious, always looking for the chink in someone's armour, for their Achilles heel. We have all experienced it at parties when people trot out their tired old prejudices: 'Oh, you're in the police, are you? I bet you are sizing me up?' 'Nothing gets past you coppers, does it?' 'I'd better watch what I say.'

Cops need to read between the lines; interpret what people *really* mean. Healthy scepticism is a useful attribute in budding law enforcement officers. It's a bit different with colleagues though. The starting point with your mates is to presume honesty, dedication and selflessness. It hits hard, then, when you learn that someone you worked closely with, whom you actually quite liked and would certainly have laid down your life for, is no better than the people you have committed to lock up.

In December 2000 everything was looking good for me. I had just achieved my boyhood ambition by being promoted to DI at Brighton. I was immersed in my new job of setting up and running a hate crime unit. I handpicked a team of the best investigators to work with me and I was the deputy SIO on two murder enquiries. One was a horrific homophobic killing of a lonely gay man by two thugs who targeted him just for those reasons and the second a cold execution of an elderly man by his gay lover who sought to benefit from his recently rewritten will.

At home, we were living the dream. We had just squeezed in two holidays over the summer, one to Crete where our daily trip back from the beach involved a 200-foot climb up a sun-baked winding road, pushing a double and single pushchair. We got to know the owner of the bar half way up very well over the fortnight. The second was to Devon, which was lovely, but the constant calls of 'I need a wee' from the back seat as we meandered around the notoriously narrow country lanes with no stopping points or facilities in sight wore a little thin.

In the September, Conall, Niamh and Deaglan had just started play school and Julie was working tirelessly at home and at her part-time job to keep everything together.

It did not occur to me, however, that despite all of our struggles to have children, I was spending less and less time at home. I was no social animal – I had outgrown that – but I just loved my job and all the demands it put on me. Julie and I were becoming ships in the night. In hindsight, we were at risk of becoming another Roy and Sandy Grace or Glenn and Ari Branson where the job came first and everything else had to fit around it.

On one of my rare evenings off, just before Christmas, Deaglan complained of feeling unwell. I gently lifted him out of his junior bed and carried him downstairs so as not to wake Conall and Niamh. I held him and tried to get him to tell me, between his tears, what was wrong and where it hurt. Suddenly his eyes fixed and his face went ashen.

I sensed something was about to erupt so held his face away from me. With that, he promptly vomited what seemed like gallons of blood all over the lounge carpet.

'Julie, come in here. I need help,' I yelled. She dashed in from the kitchen.

'Oh my God,' she cried, 'what happened?'

'I don't know. He was grizzling and then this. What are we going to do?'

'Phone the out-of-hours doctor,' she commanded as she took our sick little boy from my arms.

We were terrified and after some frantic phone calls – including one to get DI Bill Warner to take my on-call and one summoning my dad and stepmum Sue to look after the other two – on the advice of the doctor we rushed Deaglan to the Royal Alexandra Children's Hospital in Brighton.

He was admitted immediately and Julie and I took it in turns to be at the hospital over the next few days. Conall and Niamh were sensing their brother's absence and our angst; they needed us to comfort them as much as Deaglan did.

I was too anxious to work but Bill and another DI, Vic Marshall, covered for me in the way I would have for them. Thankfully, after four frantic days of tests for various conditions including leukaemia, the cause of Deaglan's vomiting was discovered. He had idiopathic thrombocytopenic purpura (ITP), caused by a disorder that leads to excessive bruising and bleeding due to unusually low levels of platelets. His prognosis was excellent, he fully recovered, and was discharged in time for Christmas.

Knowing Julie was with the other two along with her sister Maureen, who had popped in to help, I called my dad to drive us home. True to form, he dropped everything and was with us in no time. He took care of the bags and I carried a very sleepy little boy to the car parked nearby. I settled Deaglan in the back with me and gently told him that we were off to see Mummy, Conall and Niamh. He grinned so broadly when I said that it was only three more sleeps until Father Christmas would be coming. He stretched up to kiss me, cuddled up and dropped off to sleep.

My memory stops there and doesn't restart for another twelve hours. For what followed next I had only my late father's account to hang on to.

As Dad drove off the A23 towards Burgess Hill on a country road, a car coming from the other direction suddenly veered into our path. It was heading straight for us. There seemed no escape. Mercifully, my dad's skill and lightning reactions meant that, instead of the 60mph crash being completely head on he was able to steer away slightly, reducing the final impact by a few per cent, doubtlessly saving our lives.

After being cut out of the car, we were all rushed to separate hospitals. My dad told me later that I kept pleading with the fire-fighters and paramedics to let me see Deaglan before I was taken off. Apparently I was inconsolable with worry.

My first memory was waking up the following morning in the Princess Royal Hospital in Haywards Heath unable to move, with the creeping foreboding that something awful had happened. In my state of amnesia I was convinced that Deaglan and Dad had been killed. No-one could tell me otherwise and my certainty that I was paralysed paled into insignificance. I was bereft at the thought I was the only survivor.

It seemed an age, but later that morning Julie arrived. (I learned later that Maureen and her brother John had taken over babysitting duties and she had been shuttling all night between my bedside and the Royal Alexandra Children's Hospital where Deaglan had been returned.) I was convinced that I was about to experience what it was like to be on the other side of a death message.

Relief flooded through my aching body when she announced that Deaglan and my dad had both been patched up and released. I was not paralysed, just very bruised, and was to be transferred to the specialist plastic surgery centre at the Queen Victoria Hospital in East Grinstead for my severe facial wounds to be fixed. This is where Dr Sir Archibald McIndoe pioneered the treatment of severely burned Second World War allied aircrew, the Guinea Pigs. It retains its reputation today as a world-class facility for reconstructive surgery.

Once released, on Christmas Eve, I was driven home by Maureen's husband Ted, and all at once it hit me what I had so very nearly lost. They say things happen for a reason and this crash was a savage wake-up call. It dawned on me that, while my job was very important, it was nothing compared with Julie and the children.

Their love and kindness coaxed me through a very difficult recovery period. I slowly became more able, my wounds started to heal and the realization of where my priorities should lie came into sharp focus.

My colleagues too were exceptionally supportive. From hospital and home visits to buying presents for the children, they never stopped thinking of me in the dark months that followed. One even came round on Christmas Day both to visit me and to give the children the treat of a drive out in his all-singing, all-dancing police car.

As well as the scars I still bear, I had sustained a significant brain injury that made simple cognitive activities such as reading, remembering, concentrating and staying awake a massive struggle. Julie had the patience of a saint as I inched towards recovery. Her love and that of the children made me resolute that I would now rebalance my life.

On my eventual return to work the following March, I tried to continue where I had left off but with renewed emphasis on my family. However, I was deluding myself that I had fully recovered.

I was really struggling and in October, having come home after a typically busy day in floods of tears, I realized I was defeated. I couldn't keep up the pace so had to give up my precious job and take a policy role at HQ. I was devastated.

I thrived on proper policing. It was what I lived for. I knew the back-room job was for my own good but I was starved of adrenaline. I was well supported but so bored by the nine-to-five lifestyle.

My boss, Detective Superintendent Dick Barton (that was his real name – perhaps his parents knew his destiny), wandered into my office one Tuesday morning in spring 2002.

'Graham, are you free next week?' he enquired.

'Yes, nothing I can't shift,' I confirmed.

'There's a confidential briefing at the National Criminal Intelligence Service, about a national computer job. I don't know much more but do you fancy going? Get you out of the office, eh?'

I needed no hard sell. Whatever it was, it was a day away and something that sounded vaguely interesting; certainly better than pushing paper around.

The room in the anonymous South London NCIS HQ was packed. Officers from across the country had accepted the invitation and descended to hear the unveiling of the organization's closely guarded secret. We all speculated what was about to unfold.

I had never met ACC Jim Gamble before. Never even heard of him. Little did he or anyone else know that he would later become one of the most authoritative voices in child protection and online safety. It was Jim who would go on to establish the world-renowned Child Exploitation and Online Protection Centre (CEOP).

When he stood up and his booming Northern Irish voice echoed around the room, no-one was left in any doubt that this was a big job.

The US Postal Inspection Service had raided Landslide Productions Inc, an online pornography portal run by Thomas and Janice Reedy. On searching their database the service had discovered thousands of people had bought access to hundreds of thousands of horrific child abuse images. A list of UK customers had been passed to Jim's officers and they, in turn, were handing that to us. This was to be known as Operation Ore; a title with, quite deliberately, no relevance to the job in hand.

We were under threat of dismissal should we prematurely reveal any details and told we were each about to receive a list of names, local to us, who must be arrested on a given day. We would all be provided a further list within the next month, which might run to hundreds of names. We could investigate those at our own speed and by our own methods but the protection of children must be the priority.

Clutching my secret package tight, I boarded the train back to Sussex. There were just five initial targets for us, among the most prolific users of the site and those who had accessed the most depraved images. That was manageable and with some disappointment, having briefed them on what was required, I handed over the suspects to the local divisions. They wasted no time in sweeping up these paedophiles and bringing them to justice. My return to operational policing had been sickeningly short.

If his name had been Robert Davies or John McDonald, I may not have spotted it as I scanned through the anticipated second list when it arrived three weeks later. There were over 200 names on the pages I was idly flicking through. Some names stand out and the name CJ Wratten certainly did to me.

Chris Wratten had been my sergeant when I was a PC at Brighton in 1989. He had known my dad too, when he was a Special at Hove. Chris was a rough and ready copper but a great bloke to have with you when things heated up. I remember the relief on seeing him arrive when I was single-handedly trying to control a massive fight at the bottom of Elm Grove in the city centre.

A few years later he was promoted to Inspector and transferred to Hastings. I knew he had moved house to nearby Bexhill and the address on the list was all the confirmation I needed that it was the same man.

'Dick,' I called to my boss. 'You might want to come and look at this.' He wandered through and looked over my shoulder.

'Recognize that name?'

'Shit,' he exclaimed.

'Best we look at the rest of the list in case there are any more coppers on it. In the meantime, are you happy I crack on with dealing with Chris? We can't send this name to the division as we did the others. He'll find out in no time.'

'Yes, if you are happy to. I'll see if Chief Inspector Steve Scott can support you so at least one of you has a rank advantage over him.'

'That would be great.' Steve had briefly been my acting Detective Superintendent when I moved from operational duties. He had just secured a permanent promotion to the same rank in Surrey and was awaiting a start date.

Sussex is not a big force; there were rarely more than three degrees of separation between any two officers. We had to keep the investigation tight, strictly need-to-know. We also had to write the rulebook for investigating offences of child abuse on the internet. I learned never to use the term 'child porn' as this gives it an air of grubby respectability. Kids being raped on camera is what it is and that should never be forgotten.

We soon became aware, through NCIS, that perverted cops had also been identified elsewhere. We made contact with those forces, sharing our thinking and developing our plans together.

A date was set to visit Chris. We planned it around his shifts and his likely sleep pattern. His wife also worked for us and we did not want her there, so we planned for that too.

He was not in when we arrived at his flat, nestled in a sleepy Bexhill street. We could have forced our way in but we decided to sit and wait. Ten minutes passed before I spotted Chris strutting up the road carrying a newspaper and carton of milk.

Steve and I got out of the car and ambled up to our colleague.

'Hi Graham, hi Steve. What are you doing out this way? Fancy a cup of tea?'

That must have been a reflex response. He couldn't have failed to notice four overalled officers alighting from the white lorry with 'Sussex Police Specialist Search Unit' emblazoned along its sides.

'Not really thanks, Chris, but we do need to talk. Inside might be best,' I said as I gently ushered him towards his block.

As we stepped through the door, I produced the search warrant. 'Chris, I have a warrant to search your flat for items connected with you buying child abuse images on the internet.' His faced drained of colour. He started to shake. I sat him down.

I told him what NCIS had found. I told him he was not, at that stage, under arrest and I cautioned him, explaining his rights.

We searched the flat from top to bottom. Everything that could possibly hold data was seized, all his credit card records too. We had intelligence only that he was buying pictures of child abuse. To prove an offence we had to find them in his possession. We couldn't do it there. We had to load up the lorry and get the techies in the Hi Tech Crime Unit to sift through everything, byte by byte.

Still not under arrest, he agreed to go to Police Headquarters to be interviewed – he was too well known for us to wander into a normal police station. That might come later.

His initial account was that he had accessed the Reedys' vile site but maintained he was undertaking his own private investigation. He said he had intended to tell his Chief Superintendent but simply had not got round to it. He assured us that he had not saved any pictures. This dancing around the law came as no surprise. I knew it was nonsense, just as I knew he was never likely to admit downloading or keeping illegal images. Effectively he was throwing down the gauntlet. Prove it.

Chris was suspended from duty while the brains in Hi Tech Crime scoured his computers and disks for any sign of child abuse images.

We hear of this unique department in *Looking Good Dead.* The fictional Operation Glasgow occupying the working lives of the eclectic collection of techies that comprise Hi Tech Crime is very similar to Ore. Hundreds of paedophiles being exposed by the wonder of the World Wide Web.

The staff could have come from central casting. The dapper, suited and booted boss; the pony-tailed, denim-clad loner; the loud, ex-military code cracker – they were all there. All very different; their workstations ranging from a bewildering chaos of computer components on a bed of spaghettied cabling to a neat display of hardware set at right angles against a pristine desktop at which no-one else dare sit – hallmarks of their tenants' natural working style.

Two things, however, this pot pourri of personalities had in common: an awe-inspiring ability to make the most complex and deeply encrypted computer give up its secrets and a phenomenal resilience to spending days examining and cataloguing the most horrific images of child abuse anyone could imagine.

Less than a month after the search, I received the call I was expecting.

'Graham, are you sitting down?' asked Sergeant Paul Hastings, the head of Hi Tech Crime.

'Go on,' I urged.

'I think Chris is going to prison.'

'Tell me more.'

He then itemized the most repulsive description of child sexual abuse images I had ever heard; they were all there hidden on his floppy disks. This was the evidence we needed to prove that he had been more than merely looking. He had deliberately saved these horrible pictures for his own future use. As we predicted, his unlikely assertion that he was doing some detective work would not save him. The next time we spoke to him it would be under arrest.

He was unable to come up with a more plausible excuse during further interviews – he knew there was none. He was eventually charged with downloading ninety-five child abuse images.

Strangely, throughout all his court appearances he was always very civil to me. My father was, at the time, seriously ill with prostate cancer and Chris had heard about this. Each time he saw me he was keen to find out how Dad was faring, offering him his best wishes.

He maintained his innocence until the first morning of the trial. He realized that his account of a supposed investigation that he had told no-one about would be exposed for what it was: nothing more than a pathetic attempt to avoid inevitable conviction and imprisonment.

A guilty plea was his only option in the end. It was a late attempt to retain his liberty in the wake of the demolition of his good character. All he could do now was hope. In a highly unusual move, Judge Richard Brown ordered that video screens be placed along the press benches so that the journalists could see the images while he was delivering sentence. It was obvious that he did not want them to minimize the depravity of Wratten's crime. It was a way of ensuring no titillating 'kiddie porn' headlines appeared in the next day's papers.

Chris's pleas for leniency were heartfelt. It emerged that he had made a serious suicide attempt while on bail and that he and his wife were both slipping into mental illness. He mustered thirty-three friends and colleagues to provide him with character testimonies.

However, Judge Brown was clear. This behaviour could never be condoned, especially from a serving senior police officer.

Whatever the effect on his health, however hard prison life would be for a paedophile ex-cop, to jail he must go. He was sentenced to six months and ordered to register as a sex offender for the next ten years.

Prison must have been hell on earth for him – nothing, however, compared with that endured by those poor children, images of whom he had bought and downloaded for his own perverted gratification. He was dismissed from the police, but due to his length of service kept his pension.

It might be thought that losing his job, reputation and liberty, and suffering as he must have in prison, surely would have been enough to steer him away from such disgusting crimes. However, ten years later he was caught for the same thing yet again. This time his sentence was doubled and he was reported to have finally accepted he had a problem. Time will tell if this realization will lead to him changing his ways.

This was not the first or last time I encountered bad apples within the ranks.

The first was in the late 1980s when I lived in a nineteenth-century stately home. Slaugham Manor accommodated around sixty single officers who worked at Gatwick Airport. A highly sociable environment, the Manor, in its idyllic rural location, was *the* place to live with its bars, swimming pool and regular parties. All for £2 per month to cover the cost of the newspapers.

I lived in an annexe called Ryders, a smaller house set slightly apart from the main building. One resident, who I will call Dan, worked a different shift pattern from most of us. Sandy-haired and stocky, at thirty he was older than most of us but fitted in well nonetheless. He would always have a tall story to tell, especially about some of his more outrageous antics in the Royal Navy, and he certainly liked a drink. I don't think we were meant to believe all of his tales but what they lacked in credibility they made up for in entertainment value. He was great to be around.

That was until one late shift at the airport. We heard rumours of a police officer having been arrested, following a chase and a struggle in nearby Crawley. Word was that the off-duty cop had been caught stealing a bottle of whisky from a town centre supermarket. As the gossip evolved into hard fact we discovered it was our housemate, Dan. We were told he had been interviewed, bailed and suspended from duty. Inevitably we were shocked and we presumed that would be the last we would see of him.

However when we arrived back at Ryders after work we were stunned to find him happily crashed out in the communal lounge watching TV.

'Er, Dan, are you supposed to be here?' enquired Benny, our burly spokesperson.

'Oh. You've heard, have you?' came the sheepish reply. 'Well, it's all a mistake, of course. I just forgot to pay.' Like we hadn't heard that one before. 'It'll all be sorted but, even though I'm suspended, they say I can carry on living here.'

'OK. How long for?' I asked.

'As long as it takes but don't worry, as I'm not working I'll make sure I keep the place clean for us. I can cook for you if you like. Hey, I can even go shopping for you.'

A babble of 'No, you're OK', 'Don't worry', and 'I don't think so' from us all, accompanied a hasty mass exit as we made our way to our respective rooms for an uncharacteristically early night.

Everyone ensured that all their stuff was locked up after that – just in case. While you start by trusting your colleagues, once they betray you that changes to instant and irrevocable suspicion.

Thankfully, justice was swift and it was only a few months before Dan was convicted, sacked and evicted, but the nasty taste of that experience remained for years.

Peter Salkeld was not always a high flyer. He blossomed relatively late. The ex-drugs squad PC had, like me, spent most of his early years honing his craft on the streets of Brighton; he was popular and effective. You had to be both back in the late eighties if you wanted to fit in. If you were good at your job, fearless and ready to watch your mates' backs then you were OK. Lack any of those attributes and, well, the Job Centre was only across the street from the nick.

In 1992 Peter and I both qualified to be Sergeants but his rise to Inspector was swifter than mine. Thereafter he found his niche. A short stint in the Organizational Development Department, effectively the workhorse of the Chief Officers, brought him to the attention of those who mattered. He worked hard, he was bright, loyal and exuded boundless confidence. The world was his oyster; he was the chosen one.

Change really started to affect the police service from the turn of the millennium. Inevitably, some departments were more ready than others. The world of criminal intelligence was altering, with geographic borders becoming no more than lines on maps. Regional Intelligence Units were being established and they needed clever, driven, operationally credible leaders to meet the spectre of organized crime. Pete was seen as the agent of change needed.

Given a role where he was effectively his own boss meant that he could shine quickly and ensure that any credit due to him was not filtered through a chain of command. Pete had proven his professional and personal integrity many times. He had earned the universal trust he enjoyed.

However, he had a darker side and a perfect storm of temptation brought that to the surface. His job came with a corporate credit card, his work was almost unsupervised and, in his private life, he had befriended a vulnerable old lady.

Eileen Savage was ninety-three. A childless divorcee, she would have been delighted that the senior cop wanted to help her through her twilight years. As dementia gripped, she was happy to appoint Pete her power of attorney, giving him control over her financial affairs.

Whether greed triggered the friendship or whether the opportunities that presented themselves were just too tempting, only he will know.

It was the internal discrepancies that triggered his undoing. Small yet suspicious inconsistencies in the finances of the new unit coupled with a secretive culture prompted wary colleagues to blow the whistle to the Professional Standards Department. His office and home were raided and following a close look at his lifestyle, the true scale of what he'd done emerged.

He had used the cash float and his corporate credit card to buy items including a designer watch and a mini fridge, giving a range of excuses such as the pen was required for a fictitious security operation. He had tapped into the welfare fund, reserved for those with real financial hardship, to pay for his caravanning hobby. Despite knowing full well that Eileen Savage's estate could afford her £96,000 care fees, he hoodwinked the council into funding those.

There were other allegations that were not proven, but those that were ensured his fall was as dramatic as his rise. He was charged, suspended and sent for trial.

Whatever set him on his road to ruin, it had resulted in a whole host of crimes. Despite his denials, the jury recognized the weight of the evidence against him and convicted him of eleven counts of theft and deception. He was subsequently jailed for three years.

His demise left his reputation in tatters. The order to repay £100k was sweeter still to those who had trusted this rising star. No-one forgives a bent copper.

By 2012 I was the Chief Superintendent in charge of Brighton and Hove, and being a Sussex career cop I went back a long way with various heads of the Professional Standards Department (PSD). That never lessened the anxiety when I received a message that one of them wanted to talk to me. It was never good news. Who's done what to whom, would be my first thought. It was never a minor matter – they didn't merit a boss-to-boss chat. Such calls meant that shit was going to happen to someone on my division and it was down to me to manage the fallout.

Throughout most of the first nine novels in the Roy Grace series, our hero is foxed by the near-clairvoyance of fictional Argus crime reporter Kevin Spinella. Seemingly, he had the inside track on each twist and turn of every investigation. He would report details of crimes the police had deliberately withheld, turn up at scenes or search sites at the drop of a hat and repeat chit-chat back to Grace. He had a line into the police.

Grace was convinced that someone was leaking information and no-one was immune from his suspicion. It was not until a bug was found in the software of his own phone that he realized that rather than through a human source, technology was how Spinella picked up his stories. It took the ingenious use of misinformation to trap him at a fishing lake in *Not Dead Yet*, ending his criminal eavesdropping and his grimy career.

Operation Elveden was the Metropolitan Police enquiry into corrupt payments by the press to the police. In 2011, stories of greedy cops and manipulative journalists being caught hit the media. Arrests were made, charges brought and officers imprisoned with sickening regularity. Thankfully no such drama had yet touched Sussex Police.

I happened to be at Headquarters when I got the call.

'Graham, have you got a minute?' enquired Detective Superintendent Ken Taylor, a longstanding friend and colleague and head of PSD. It wasn't really a question, more the entrée to some devastating news.

'Of course, mate, what is it?' I replied, my heart sinking.

'It's a bit hush-hush,' added Ken.

'Are you in your office? I'm at HQ.'

'Yes, come over,' he suggested.

His department's offices were among the most secure in the force, one of the few areas where my access card was impotent. No-one got in unaccompanied unless they worked there.

I patiently waited to be permitted entry and escorted to see my old friend Ken.

'Graham, thanks for coming. This won't take long. Tomorrow morning one of your sergeants is going to be arrested by Op Elveden for accepting corrupt payments.'

'Oh, right,' I mumbled, trying to hide my shock that I had a wrong'un on the division. 'Do you want to tell me who? What have they done and when?'

'Love to answer, Graham, but the Metropolitan Police have asked us to give you no more than that. Just so you know.'

'Well, you can tell them that's worse than bloody useless. I suppose I am being told so I can prepare the division and the public for any fallout but unless I know who it is and what their role is, I can't do anything but guess. What world are they in? Can't you tell me?' I asked, more in hope than anticipation.

I knew he would not reply and it was wrong of me to press him. Someone else was calling the shots and despite my outburst I appreciated the position he found himself in.

'DI Emma Brice will be in your office at eight tomorrow. She will tell you everything,' he said. 'Until then, that's all you can know.'

Overnight, I tried to compile a mental list of likely suspects. I did not get very far. Despite the sergeants under my command having a huge variety of roles and backgrounds, I could not think of any who would sell their soul to the press.

Emma had a fabulously caring yet forthright way of breaking bad news. A consummate professional, she would say what was needed but knew the impact it would have. We sat at my round table, each with a steaming cup of tea. Emma wasted no time in getting to the point.

'Graham, Sergeant James Bowes has been arrested by Op

Elveden on suspicion of receiving corrupt payments from the *Sun*.'

'James Bowes? Are you sure?' I was incredulous. 'I've been trying to work out who it might be since I spoke to Ken. James never entered my head. He's so nice, so quiet, so loyal.'

I was flabbergasted. James was a stalwart of the Neighbourhood Policing Team. He was not your usual copper though. An ex-public schoolboy, he had spurned the draw of the City to join the police. He was in his element in his early years, revelling in the cut and thrust of response policing. His move to the street community team – the officers who dealt with the drunks, drugged and homeless – angered him. However, he soon found that he was starting to make a difference to people's lives, rather than sticking plasters over problems that response work inevitably entailed. His gently assertive manner encouraged some of the city's most desperate people to enter treatment, find hostels and start to turn their life round. He had found new meaning in his job.

Following his promotion he had taken on a sector of the city centre and led a small team of police officers and Police Community Support Officers to clean it up. An electrician in his spare time, he was forever sourcing the latest gadget or gizmo to keep one step ahead of the villains. His highly technical and imaginative funding requests read like reports from the fictional Q, the Mr Fixit of the James Bond films.

'He offered to give them details of a girl who was bitten by a fox,' Emma continued. 'They paid him £500.'

'How strong is the evidence? I mean, how certain are they that he did this?' I probed.

'Well, they paid him by cheque which he put in his bank, so it's pretty cut and dried.'

'So what now?' I asked.

'His house is being searched and he is being taken to a

London police station. I believe he has already offered his resignation.'

'I hope we aren't going to accept it. If he's done what you say he needs sacking, not being able to sneak out with a month's notice and his reputation intact.'

'Yes, that's the plan. The Met are clear that we shouldn't accept it and our Chief Officers agree.'

In that short exchange one of my supposedly finest sergeants had gone from hero to zero. I can forgive a lot of things, see them in context, but leaking information, especially for money, cuts to the heart of all the police stand for. He was finished.

To his credit, his admissions were swift. Taking his sacking with good grace and his early guilty plea must have helped cap his prison sentence at ten months. He was lucky, as selling the fox story was not the only time his greed had usurped his oath of office.

Two more leaks emerged, one involving a child protection visit to a local celebrity and the second regarding a search for dead bodies. Just as no-one suspected Andy 'Weatherman' Gidney of being the corrupt computer investigator in *Looking Good Dead*, who kept evil Carl Venner plied with expertise and confidential information, so no-one had seen Bowes was a mole.

It does pain me to think what he must have gone through in prison. Corrupt police officers are just a shade higher in the pecking order than paedophiles. However, he knew the stakes and got what he deserved.

Most cops have flawless characters and integrity. Most have impeccable morals. When the bad apples are exposed, however, we all feel shame. Every one of us feels let down. We all have to work that little bit harder to regain lost trust. But we do, as the pride we have in the job is indestructible and we can never let those outlaws within prevail.

14: TAKING CHANCES, SAVING LIVES

Drugs hurt everyone. It's a startling statistic that 80 per cent of all property crime in the UK is drug-related.

As Peter James says when quantifying Skunk's drug habit in *Not Dead Enough*, few users are on a £10 per day habit; it's more like £30. So, with 2,500 people in Brighton and Hove whose lives revolve around sticking needles in what's left of their veins and pumping in an unknown cocktail of poisons, that's at least £75,000 (nearly three times the UK average annual wage in 2015) going into the hands of drug dealers and organized crime every day. To get that kind of money most have to steal, and they never get market value for their booty. That, therefore, results in excess of an estimated quarter of a million pounds of goods stolen every day.

Many users will do anything they can to get the gear they so desperately need. They steal, cheat, rob and, if necessary, kill. Skunk is horrible, the scum of the earth. Relentlessly pursued by DC Paul Packer, whose finger he had bitten off in a previous encounter, few will feel sad at his grisly comeuppance, being flame-grilled in Cleo's MG. While his waking each morning 'to the sensation that the world was a hostile cave about to entomb him, sweating and hallucinating scorpions crawling across his face' is unlikely to evoke much sympathy, perhaps there will be at least some understanding of his single-minded determination to do whatever it took to score the drugs he craved.

No-one starts out deciding to become a drug addict. No-one is born evil either, but we are all a product of our upbringing and environment. Who we love. Who loves us. Who we hate. What's right. What's wrong. Nothing can change that. Unless of course, like me, you experience a shocking revelation which makes you question all your values.

I was a detective through and through. Even when I wasn't officially a detective I behaved like one, being inquisitive, tenacious and with a pretty clear notion of right and wrong. Police locked up the bad people to protect the good. The law told us who was bad and who was good. Simple. Thieves, fraudsters, drunks, yobs, druggies, whoever – they were our enemies, they were the ones whose imprisonment we celebrated. Job done. Good Guys 1, Villains 0. People like us were always the virtuous. We had the upbringing, the principles that stopped us stepping over to the dark side.

It was one of those days in the late 1990s when everyone else seemed to be out of the CID office doing exciting things, and I was confined to barracks catching up on a bewildering backlog of paperwork. I hated those days but I couldn't ignore a ringing phone.

'Is Russ there, Graham?' asked the caller from the front desk.

'No, he's out. I think he might be at the hospital seeing the bloke who got stabbed last night.'

'Oh, there's someone down here with a letter from him saying he can collect his property. He was released from prison for burglary this morning and wants his clothes back.'

Oh great, another half hour of my life I won't get back, I thought. Sifting through some mangy bag of clothing and then handing it back to some low-life who won't be in the least bit grateful, and will probably ask about that mysterious £200 that he will allege was in the pocket.

'OK, I'll be down,' I said wearily, having scanned the office without spotting anyone I could delegate to.

Asked to describe him after nearly twenty years, I would have had no chance. I'm sure the reverse was true too. But there was no mistaking him. The first glimpse made those two decades vanish in an instant and his dropped jaw was all the confirmation I didn't need.

'Graham?'

'Sam? Bloody hell, mate. How are you? Listen, I can't stop. I've got to give some con his stuff back, but can you hang about?'

'It's me. I'm that con, Graham. It's me you're here to see,' he chuckled.

Years back, Sam's family and mine had been close. Our parents knew each other before we were born. They lived down the road from us and, like mine, Sam's parents were hard-working and lived for their children. He had two younger brothers and his older sister was good friends with mine.

I don't remember a time in my childhood when Sam wasn't around. Summers, Christmases, weekends, all those memories included Sam and me playing together, getting into scrapes – I can still remember being told off by an irate motorist for throwing grass cuttings at her car from the supposed cover of Sam's picket fence.

A lot changed when I joined the police at eighteen. I moved away from home and immersed myself in a new life. I drifted away from many of my friends, although it was never a conscious decision and I often wished I'd stayed in touch with my roots. So when I didn't see much of Sam I didn't think it was odd. I'd occasionally bump into him when I was back in Shoreham but I just accepted that blokes move on. He would be doing well. He was like me, and we were the good guys. He'd be fine.

'But they said you'd been in prison,' I gabbled.

'In and out for years, Graham. I'm surprised you didn't know.'

The next two hours passed in the blink of an eye. He explained how he had started off doing well, great job, loads of money, parties, popularity, drink. How that began to change through the odd spliff, pills, a little heroin – just to try, mind, more and more addiction, lost jobs, bankruptcy, stealing, eroded trust, broken relationships, risk-taking, burglary, capture, chances, relapses, more crime, prison, helplessness, loneliness; a dark, bottomless spiral.

I was stunned. We had been peas in a pod. Following separate but parallel tracks. At some point, an unseen signal master must have switched the points so our destinations became very different. But deep down we still had lots in common. It hit me that Sam could so easily have been me, and I could have been him.

Drugs do bad things to people. All drugs. They mess with your health and your mind. Heroin did it for Sam. He, like so many others, was trapped in a cycle of addiction and imprisonment.

I've never taken an illicit drug, not even once, but what if I had, what if I got trapped like Sam did? It made me realize that every villain has a story. Equally, as Grace reflected, while watching the film *The Third Man* in *Not Dead Enough*, most villains try to justify what they have done. In their warped minds, it is the world that is wrong, not them.

That day I grew up. I started to see criminals as people who did bad things rather than just as bad people: a subtle but important distinction that helped develop my thinking over the rest of my career.

Something had happened that day to shift my perspectives on good and evil. I didn't predict, however, that it would see me ridiculed in the press, criticized by ministers, yet supported by my more courageous bosses, lecturing internationally and saving many lives.

The chance meeting with Sam had set me on a road of reflection. It had a massive impact on me. I was still a sergeant so fairly junior in the scheme of things but I spent years afterwards soul-searching as to how much difference we actually make criminalizing rather than treating drug users. What was the point? Hell, it was circumstance alone that put me on a rewarding career path and Sam in jail.

I struggled with why do we treat drug addicts as criminals but alcoholics as patients? Sure, people steal and rob to get the money to buy drugs and that needs to be dealt with – even Sam would agree – but if we could get those people off drugs they wouldn't need to do all those things. And they might stop killing themselves too.

Drugs are rife in Brighton and Hove. The city has won many awards in its time but the award for 'Drugs Death Capital of the UK' for the eleventh consecutive year doesn't get presented at some swanky reception at the Dorchester. This grubby title, however, provides much of the backdrop of Brighton and Hove throughout the Grace novels. The presence of drug turf wars and the impact on users is a constant Roy Grace theme, whether overtly described or as part of the back story of his most odious adversaries. It's the undercurrent that, in fact and fiction, runs through everything that is Brighton.

At its worst, the city was losing about one son, daughter, mum or dad a week to the misuse of drugs. That is just the people who died of an overdose, never mind those who have succumbed to blood-borne viruses or taken their own lives as a direct result of drug use. If we'd seen similar numbers of deaths on the road there would have been a national outcry. The common attitude was, because it was drugs and drugs happen to other people, it had to be their fault. So who cares?

Well, I did – a lot. It was a scandal. The treatment services were struggling hard to reverse the trend through needle exchanges, methadone clinics, medically provided opiate programmes, issuing naloxone (a drug which reverses the effects of overdose), but the police were just smashing down doors, some at residential treatment centres, arresting people for possession of drugs and putting them into an ineffective criminal justice system.

A colleague who was at the forefront of taking out the Mr Bigs of the drugs world reflected recently that all he ever achieved was to create career opportunities for the next in line. Locking up the likes of Vlad Cosmescu from *Dead Tomorrow*, who was dealing in drugs, cigarettes, pornography, counterfeit goods and human beings, doesn't mean the crime will stop.

Brighton and Hove had more than its fair share of attention from the big boys of the Regional Crime Squad, National Crime Squad and Serious and Organized Crime Agency, investigating our premier criminals. They recognized that much of the wealth in the city was made on the back of a thriving heroin and crack cocaine trade. These top detectives knew the real prize were the assets amassed by these racketeers, who were more afraid of losing their money than their liberty.

The Proceeds of Crime Act provided a very visible form of justice for communities. People were delighted to see the wealth and opulence so lavishly showcased by their apparently un-employed neighbour being whisked away on the back of a police car-transporter or advertised by a 'House For Sale' sign as the removal truck trundled away shortly after the prison van.

In 2005 I was promoted to DCI to head Brighton and Hove CID. Personal tragedy had struck the year before when my father died of cancer. I missed him terribly and we had forged an even stronger bond since he had saved our lives in the car crash.

His loss rocked me to the core but I was so proud when the Chief Constable awarded him a posthumous Certificate of Meritorious Service. An award for Special Constables was then commissioned in his name and a display was established in Brighton's Old Police Cells Museum that marks his life and con-tribution to policing. My uniform is now displayed there next to his. Back together where we belong.

However, Dad was a strong, no-nonsense, proud man and he would have been thrilled that I had reached such a senior level at the place and in the job we both loved.

I did not go into this new job with any particular agenda other than to do the very best I could to make the city safer and for it to feel safer too. However, I had risen to a level where I could do something about our unjust drugs strategy. Sometimes you have to reach a certain rank to get your voice heard.

The flow of drugs into the city from places such as Liverpool, South London and Wolverhampton appeared unstoppable. We weren't bad at taking out the dealers. The problem was, no-one in the police was doing anything to stem the users' insatiable appetite for the stuff that was killing them. So as we locked up the latest gang of pushers more rocked up to meet the unrelenting demand.

Leadership guru Dr Stephen Covey once said, 'Management is efficiency in climbing the ladder of success; leadership determines whether the ladder is leaning against the right wall.' We needed to find a different wall.

It's hard to prove a negative, such as how many people didn't die or weren't robbed, so it was always easier for the police's effectiveness to be measured on the outputs, the things they did that were easy to count: seizures, arrests, warrants. I decided this was going to change. I wanted to talk about saving lives and getting people help rather than how much of this and what weight of that we happened to find, or how many doors we kicked in.

It was a risk. My career could come to a crashing halt. However, I had once been inspired by Chief Inspector Stuart Harrison. Stuart, a maverick with a mission, espoused the belief that 'forgiveness is easier to obtain than permission'. This stuck in my thoughts as I tried something different.

We were going to find a new way of fighting this unwinnable war on drugs. Our old tactics weren't working; they never really had. I became like a stuck record going round saying 'users belong in treatment, dealers belong in prison'. I knew we could slow the demand, get people well again, lock up dealers and cut crime.

Thankfully, I had two right-hand men whose character and vision were critical to what I wanted to do.

My kids used to say when my phone rang at home, 'Is that Paul again?' DI Paul Furnell pops up in *Dead Tomorrow* as the switched-on intelligence manager that he is. Now a Detective Superintendent, he is one of those sickening people: tall, good-looking, intelligent, likeable yet very persistent. He'd call day and night.

The Brighton Divisional Intelligence Unit, which he ran, was not so much the engine room of the division, more its furnace. The energy generated in their expansive open-plan office was white hot. Nothing could ever wait until tomorrow, jobsworths were excluded, everyone was fired up to catch the bad guys and catch them now. In the middle of it was Paul acting as ringmaster, whipping the team into frenzies of activity. The downsides were that he regarded his team's overtime budget as being a monthly rather than annual allowance and if he had something he wanted to do, he would badger me into submission. A pain in the proverbial but he got stuff done and I needed that.

Sergeant Richard Siggs – Siggsy – was a giant with a big heart. A county rugby coach and former public order trainer, he wasn't the first person you would think of as suitable to cajole drug users and down-and-outs into treatment and shelter. However, he had already won the national Tilley Award for his work with the street-homeless. His colossal physique together with his gentle nature had a tremendously persuasive effect on people who needed convincing that they should seek help. Tough love, he called it. One reformed drug user, Sean, once told me, 'If you have Siggsy behind you telling you to go into treatment, you kind of have to go, don't you!'

The street market works in the city exactly as explained in

Dead Man's Footsteps, as Grace follows a 'migration' of users towards their dealer, Niall Fisher, observing their attempts at furtive behaviour.

These migrations are fascinating to watch. A dealer will arrive at a particular place. Word would get out that they were there and dozens of users would emerge from alleyways, squats and the like, briskly descending on the pusher. Following swift, almost imperceptible exchanges of cash and drugs, all would evaporate into the ether, leaving no trace of the trade in death that had just occurred.

So I got Paul to take over the enforcement role of what became Operation Reduction, relentlessly targeting such dealers, catching them in the act, getting them banged up and denying them time to set down roots.

Siggsy, together with the inspirational Director of Crime Reduction Initiatives, Mike Pattinson, developed a partnership that identified the most criminally active drug addicts. Cops and drugs workers patrolling the streets together hunted down those who needed treatment and from whom the city needed a rest. They were given a stark choice: enter the Op Reduction treatment programme that we had created and remain there or be targeted by the police and locked up. A carrot and stick approach but, with Siggsy and his team providing the 'or else' factor, in four years over 500 users went into treatment who wouldn't have otherwise. Meanwhile, during the same period, Paul's teams arrested around 600 dealers all of whom, faced with the weight of evidence against them, pleaded guilty.

The users were what we branded 'revolving door prisoners'. We first meet one such convict, Darren Spicer, the fictional prison-dwelling burglar, in *Dead Like You*. A high achiever at school but his chances blighted by the effects of his father breaking his back falling through a roof, his abusive mother and a spell in an approved school, he inadvertently books himself a one-way trip to the hopeless oblivion that drug addiction brings.

A victim of circumstance, like Sam, his whole life becomes a cycle of prison, craving and offending. Branson once tells him that they haven't bothered to change his bed sheets in Lewes Prison during one of his brief episodes of liberty. They probably hadn't. The name might be fictitious but the story is spot-on.

The users Siggsy and Mike were targeting were given special treatment to help them break this futile cycle. Their possession and use of drugs was not subject to criminal sanction provided they went to, and stayed in, treatment. Yes, I had to defend falling arrest rates; yes, the numbers of drug seizures fell (although the volume increased thanks to Paul's focus on the bigger fish); but we cut crime, saved money and saved lives. Not bad going – and I slept soundly at night.

Some sections of the press questioned whether this top cop had gone soft. A government minister made specific mention that the government did not support my views on decriminalization. Thankfully I convinced my bosses that this approach would, in the long run, be more effective and humane than our traditional approaches. As time went on, my critics started to see sense in what I was doing. Brighton was hailed for all the right reasons.

In early 2008 a strong batch of black heroin was hitting the streets. So called as it turned that colour when prepared for injection, it was 70 per cent pure; its lethal strength was wiping people out. Addicts are typically used to purities of around 30 per cent or less, the remaining mixture being cut with compounds such as citric acid, caffeine and sometimes brick dust. Often these adulterants kill as much as the drug itself. The death toll had suddenly doubled and, as the coroner put it, taking heroin had become like Russian roulette; users had no idea what they were taking.

Op Reduction made tackling whoever was behind this its number one priority. Through a variety of overt and covert methods, Paul and his team soon identified a gang from Liverpool who had infiltrated the drug market in Hove. Using locally known and trusted street dealers, the Mr Bigs quickly had a supply network established.

Planning the arrest of these peddlers in death was agonizing. As the users were dropping like flies, the temptation was to hit the dealers hard and fast. That would have been foolish. Swift arrests do not always lead to swift justice. We would probably have been able to nail only the lower ranks of the street dealers and there would be plenty to fill their shoes. We had to hold our nerve despite the risk of more deaths.

The evidence against the main dealers had to be unassailable. We had long since abandoned the hope of a convenient 'cough' in an interview, where the accused fills in all the gaps. This used to happen in the old days when villains considered their arrest a fair cop. Those days had long gone and police had to battle for every piece of the jigsaw. We now assumed the accused would keep silent and employ a range of tactics to block our discovery of more evidence. Without a fully built case, all an early arrest would achieve was a few hours' inconvenience to the suspect and the police showing their hand.

However, one sunny May lunchtime, expert detective work and careful planning culminated in an explosive action drama erupting close to the tranquil Hove Lawns.

The evidence was finally in place, the conspiracy to supply drugs all but proved. Paul was bouncing with anticipation, ready to strike. Unbeknown to the targets, who were no doubt cursing the painfully stop-start seafront traffic, their plans for the day were about to be rudely disrupted.

It's easy for unmarked police cars to hide in plain sight; there's nothing like a heavy traffic jam to act as camouflage. The network of streets around the coast road allow cop cars to invisibly race into position, surreptitiously surrounding the pre-ordained location where the arrests would take place.

The targets were showing no sign of sensing anything wrong. It had to stay that way. The crawling traffic gave the firearms commanders the upper hand; the strike had become a 'when', not 'if'.

The timing had to be right, the safety of everyone paramount, the element of surprise total. The threat of force must be overwhelming. A firefight was not an option. The targets had to know resistance was futile; they could not attempt to flee.

Through carefully rehearsed procedures, everyone knew what had to be done. The operation was handed over from the Silver to the Bronze commander, the sign that the strike was moments away. Bronze's fine judgement was now critical. Not too soon, not too late. Once he gave the order, it was the point of no return. Training took over. Everyone was poised, psyched up to swoop.

'Strike,' came the crisp command.

A cacophony of shouts, racing engines and the sight of scruffily dressed men donning chequered baseball caps and thrusting machine guns and pistols at them, stunned the occupants of the stationary saloon. Even if the villains did manage to muster some courage and try to break through the blockade of police cars, they had no hope.

'Armed police! Get out of the car. Put your hands on your head.' Bystanders fruitlessly looked round for the TV cameras or a gaudily dressed director bellowing 'Cut' through his megaphone.

All they saw was crestfallen drug dealers spread-eagled on the tarmac, awaiting their trip to the cells, guns pointed at their heads and their wrists bound together with cable ties. A quick search revealed £1,000 in cash stuffed in one dealer's pockets.

A few short months later, the evidence overwhelming, justice was dispensed at Lewes Crown Court. Following their guilty pleas to conspiracy to supply heroin Liverpudlians John Lee and Karl Freeman were jailed for ten and nine years respectively.

Their minions Darren Hogarth and George Wood each received two-and-a-half-year sentences for supplying heroin and crack cocaine.

A good outcome, if ever there can be one, given how many deaths these four were directly responsible for.

There are still drugs in Brighton. People still deal, people still die.

About a year before I retired, I took part in a BBC TV documentary with comedian Russell Brand, who was exploring the merits of an abstinence-based approach to drug rehabilitation. He was fascinated by the work we were doing in the city and the impact it had. Managing the hundreds of autograph hunters who besieged us as he interviewed me walking around some of the hotspots was a challenge in itself, but we got our message across clearly – users need help, pushers need jail.

In 2012, given Peter James' passion for Brighton and Hove, his concern for the people who live in and visit the city – particularly the vulnerable – and his determination to use his profile for the good of others, he volunteered to chair a Commission to examine whether the city was doing enough to reduce the impact of drugs on its people. As the city's Police Commander I acted as an advisor.

Peter's leadership and vision, supported by the international drugs expert Mike Trace, enabled twenty recommendations to be put before the City Council and other services which, if adopted, would enable the city to start to reduce the number of lives that drugs wrecked, and stem the misery drugs cause.

An unforeseen by-product of the Commission's recommendations was my being asked by the BBC to make another documentary after I'd retired. This one was to examine the Drugs Consumption Rooms operating in Frankfurt. These are supervised places where users can take their own heroin, safe in the knowledge that the equipment is clean and medics are there should things go wrong. I was asked to consider whether they would be a solution in Brighton. The horrific sights I saw of people struggling to find a working vein in their ulcerated bodies will stay with me forever. Grace visits this same Consumption Room in *You Are Dead* in his search for Sandy.

Frankfurt's problems were far greater than ours and for them these Consumption Rooms have been a godsend. In the twenty years since they were established, the yearly drugs death rate has plummeted from 147 to 30. Things aren't so bad in Brighton and providing the principles of Operation Reduction are sustained, these controversial facilities will not be needed.

Through all the hard work, the city has now lost its drugs death top spot. Crime is right down and dealers don't stay free for long any more. The struggle goes on and I doubt it will ever be over, but if we continue to treat addiction as an illness and remain ruthless towards the dealers we will save lives. And that must be good.

15: LIVE OR DIE – YOU DECIDE

The classic 1950s image of the British bobby is that, portrayed in *Dixon of Dock Green*, of a portly, ruddy-faced, cheery fellow who helps the elderly across the road and clips the ears of miscreant children. Not many postcards depict the other side. Not many souvenirs show elite muscle-bound police marksmen bursting from unmarked cars and shooting gunmen dead in a rapid fire-fight.

I'm glad UK police officers aren't routinely armed. It would change the dynamic of British policing forever and would drive a wedge between the service and the communities. The small but highly mobile and flexible Tactical Firearms Unit is charged with bringing the most critically dangerous situations to a safe conclusion. That is all we need in my opinion.

It's worth noting that in 2013–14 there were around 125,000 police officers in the UK yet only approximately 6,000 of those were authorized to carry guns. Furthermore, shots were discharged by police in only two of the 14,864 firearms operations that year. In contrast, according to the Brazilian Forum for Public Safety, between 2009 and 2013 that country's police killed 11,197 people. That, to me, demonstrates the status quo is more than satisfactory for the time being.

In 2009 I'd risen to what, in my eyes, was the dream job. I was Brighton and Hove's top cop. Its Divisional Commander, the Chief Superintendent of Police.

It had not been an easy climb and neither should it have been. Running the policing of a city as diverse and complex as this required experience, tenacity, patience and grit. I had been a police officer for twenty-six years serving at every rank in Brighton and Hove. I drew on every moment of that to equip me for this privilege. Crucially I had spent eighteen months as the Deputy Divisional Commander and a year as a Detective Superintendent.

The pressure was relentless but during my four-year tenure I relied on a brilliant team of senior colleagues and an exceptionally brave and dedicated 650-strong army of men and women who risked life and limb for the safety of others.

A photograph of my inspiration, my dad, resplendent in his Special Constabulary uniform, stood adjacent to my computer screen, watching my every move with his enigmatic smile softening his chiselled features. During my toughest and loneliest moments of command I would hear him silently implore, 'Come on, Graham. Pull yourself together. People are relying on you and you have a duty to get through this.'

Beside Dad were pictures of Julie and the children, by now eleven and growing into charming, intelligent and loving kids. It's a cliché but they were my rock, my raison d'être. The four of them kept me grounded, reminding me that there was a life outside the job and that was very important. Julie always showed unerring support for me. The fact that, despite my overwhelming workload, I tried to make time for all of the children's special events meant that unlike some of my colleagues I managed to remain central to the lives of my family. This created a bond from which, now they are grown up, Julie and I still reap the benefits.

Two years on, the policing challenges in February 2011 were as routine as they ever got. Although the city was enjoying a drop in the number of house burglaries, people were having their phones and wallets stolen at a greater rate than before and our neighbourhood policing teams were getting to grips with that.

However, we soon became worried about a spate of armed robberies of small post offices happening in Hove and just north in nearby Burgess Hill. All the descriptions of the perpetrator were very similar. Thankfully no-one had been hurt but there had been seven in all and they showed no sign of abating.

A few years previously, I witnessed the life-changing effect that being caught up in two armed robberies in a couple of weeks had on a colleague's wife. Her breakdown and inability to return to work underlined to me the heartless disregard robbers have for their victims. They just see them as an irritating barrier between their greed and the loot.

This run of crimes was certainly unusual enough to capture the attention of the public, the police and those who feared they might become victims. They are rarer now than in years gone by as the risks of being caught have escalated in direct proportion to the advances in technology and forensics.

Those who still choose to put themselves in jeopardy by committing this old-fashioned crime tend to be desperate, drug-addicted and living on the margins of society. Over the years, armed robbery had become less of a way of life, more a desperate last-ditch attempt for survival.

Burgess Hill is one of the many commuter towns that have sprung up in the last 150 years alongside the main London to Brighton railway line. It's a popular place to live for those working in the capital or Brighton, which is ten miles away, but who are either disinclined or financially restricted from settling in either.

On a dark Tuesday evening during the frantic run-up to Christmas, a local convenience store close to Wivelsfield railway station, on the outskirts of the town, was crammed with commuters and residents making use of its small sub post office to send last-minute parcels and cards to loved ones.

Out of the blue, in burst a man wearing a beige stocking over his face. Pulling a small handgun from his pocket he bellowed at horror-stricken staff, demanding cash. Pushing one person to the ground, he grabbed the money that a terrified colleague threw at him. Gathering it up, he scurried out, sprinted past the railway station, through a small housing estate and disappeared into the patchwork of fields that lay beyond.

He netted in excess of a thousand pounds and, while no shots were fired, staff and customers were severely traumatized by the ordeal. Thankfully, because of astute and alert witnesses, a very precise picture of the man started to emerge which would be critical in the weeks to come.

Frustratingly, while this description provided a valuable tool to eliminate possible suspects, no amount of investigation or publicity threw up his name. Detectives worked tirelessly to shed light on who this robber was before he struck again.

Following a lull over the Christmas and New Year period there were two further attacks, both in the centre of Burgess Hill and both in areas and premises swamped with CCTV. This was the sign of a desperate man becoming even more reckless – a recipe for disaster.

The first, late one Friday afternoon at a bank close to Burgess Hill's main railway station, yielded nothing. The man burst in disguised this time in dark clothing, a scarf around his face and wearing a black beanie hat, waving his gun around. He stood inches from the counter staff, yelling his demand for cash to terrify them into submission.

Despite his brazenness, the staff had been trained well. The moment his intentions became clear, in a reflex response, they flung themselves to the floor and triggered the metal shield that created an impenetrable barrier between the cashiers and the public area. Bewildered, he was not quite quick enough to react to the security shutter as it flew up. He was just too slow in pulling his hand away before the razor-sharp steel clipped it as it engaged. The DNA yielded by that fleeting graze was the breakthrough that the detectives were waiting for. While the robberies happened in another town, I was putting huge pressure on my investigators to speed up the forensic results and get the man off the streets. However, even with me breathing down their necks, the answer did not come quickly enough.

The following Monday, again just before closing time, the Burgess Hill main post office became his next target. Dressed in identical clothing he again threatened staff and customers with his black handgun, shouting his demands. This time he was luckier and a few hundred pounds were handed over by the petrified postal workers. He fled as quickly as he'd arrived and, despite the area being flooded with cops, he vanished.

Finally, the DNA result came back. We learned that, with a likelihood of one billion to one, our man was Michael Fitzpatrick, a forty-nine-year-old career criminal whose graduation to armed robbery had been typical if not predictable. Out on licence from prison, Fitzpatrick had a string of previous convictions ranging back through his adult life. It started with minor theft, drugs, a bit of violence that escalated to armed robbery and conspiracy to murder. But nothing as brazen and desperate as this. It was from these arrests that we had his DNA. A further arrest would almost certainly mean an immediate recall to prison. Unfortunately, as in the fictional Darren Spicer's case, that is inevitable for far too many habitual offenders.

Looking for such dangerous people is more complex than TV dramas would have you believe. It's not sexy, it's not always exciting, but it is ruthlessly efficient. Gone are the days whereby a maverick DI would meet a snout in the pub, walk round the corner, kick a door in and get his man – if those days ever existed at all.

The key to any police investigation is information. Without this the police are impotent. The hunt today is fuelled by the investigative detectives who focus on building the evidence and the intelligence officers whose sources can be more nebulous. Both work together in a quest to predict the target's next steps.

'Brains' beavering away in darkened rooms pull together the information to guide commanders and operatives alike, advising them where their suspect is likely to be, when, with whom and the danger he – or she – poses. There is no scientific formula but professional judgement is key.

Manhunts where the quarry could be armed are even more complex. The intelligence gathering is similar but the arrest phase must take place with trained and accredited firearms officers and commanders literally calling the shots. I often ran operations such as these and would ultimately be the one accountable for the outcome. However, each and every officer below me would be responsible for their own actions, including firing their gun. A commander could never instruct anyone to shoot, other than in truly exceptional circumstances. That was always down to the officer concerned.

Not Dead Yet gives a taste of how manhunts happen. The close protection operation of Gaia Lafayette and the hunt for her stalker were driven by Grace with separate but interdependent structures in place to allow the whole complex plan to come together.

The planning of the police response is faultlessly described and takes place in the office of the Gold commander, Chief Superintendent Graham Barrington. Observant readers will have worked out the similarity of the name to mine. The office described is exactly as my office looked, down to the reference to the sweet messages penned by Barrington's triplets on the huge whiteboard. My alter-ego's physical description, however, is all too flattering. I am not athletic and fair-haired and I have only ever run one marathon.

I was not directly running the search for Fitzpatrick. As the Divisional Commander, however, I knew that the outcome of this operation would be mine to manage. I was the public face of policing and would come under huge pressure if we had another robbery or worse. That said, I knew all of those who were involved and my trust in them was absolute. Despite them being the best around, though, however good the plan, however good the team, as Grace says, 'with guns around sometimes people get hurt and that's when all hell breaks loose.' This gave rise to a number of sleepless nights over the years.

As with the fictional Chief Superintendent, during the hunt for Fitzpatrick the Gold commander was weighing up all the intelligence, possible sightings and suggestions for places to raid, and making the final call. It was the paucity of information that I found most exhilarating when in command. It is easy to decide to act when there is certainty. However, when the best you have is probability, alongside crazy time and staff constraints, all your synapses go into overdrive drawing on all your professional experience and judgement before giving the green light. In the 'squeaky bum moments' that follow, you hope beyond hope you have it right. It's one of the greatest buzzes of senior command; Grace experiences it in every book and, like me, he thrives on it.

That February morning, as on every day since Fitzpatrick had been identified, there had been a dedicated intelligence cell working to locate him. The team that would carry out the arrest was the crack Tactical Firearms Unit.

Officers were aware our man knew that police were looking for him, and that he was probably still in the area. His desperation was likely to be extreme as this could not end well for him.

Out of the blue, intelligence came in that at lunchtime he would be going to the Sidewinder pub in the Kemp Town area of Brighton. One of the worst places possible to try to arrest an armed suspect is in a pub. The presence of the suspect and other members of the public, whose sobriety and compliance could not be relied upon, together with the availability of ad hoc weapons such as glasses and furniture, render armed raids on pubs suitable only for the direst emergencies.

Therefore the default tactic is to sit and wait. Try to take the suspect outside by surprise with such an overwhelming show of force that resistance becomes futile. Such arrests are, in the vast majority of cases, resolved swiftly, if not quietly. Such was the intention that day.

Just after 1 p.m., an unmarked car containing covert armed officers was crawling around the area hoping to spot Fitzpatrick, hopefully somewhere they could safely overwhelm him, arrest him and neutralize any threat he might pose.

Rock Place runs between the vibrant centre of Kemp Town, the famous gay village, and the seafront. This area is always throbbing with people and traffic. Rock Place, however, seems out of place. It feels like a homely backstreet with a few shops, a pub, a garage and a music school. It's impossible for two cars to pass along its short length.

The police car inched its way towards the bottom of the street when suddenly Fitzpatrick appeared on foot in front of them. Their heart rates accelerating into overdrive, they eased their BMW to a gentle halt and did what they were trained to do.

The doors flew open and, using the car as cover, they burst out and shouted their challenge at Fitzpatrick.

'Stop, armed police!' Their guns aimed directly at him.

Unlike thousands of suspects before, this one hadn't read the script. Crazily he pulled his own pistol out of nowhere and pointed it straight at the officers.

In a split second they had to weigh up the threat. Real gun or not? Threat or no threat? Shoot or don't shoot? As mentioned previously, only a snap decision is possible.

Believing their lives were in imminent danger they fired three shots at Fitzpatrick. Two slammed into him, devastatingly rupturing his internal organs. He crashed to the ground. The gun flew out of his hand. The officers then did something many would consider bizarre but goes to the core of being a cop. They rushed in and, as Grace did with Carl Venner, tried to save the life of their would-be killer.

Having battled to stem his bleeding, they soon handed over to the paramedics who spent a further thirty agonizing minutes trying to get him breathing before rushing him to the nearby Royal Sussex County Hospital. Once there, a team of twenty-five doctors and nurses combined their skills in attempting to save him before he was finally pronounced dead. In all, police and medics struggled for an hour and forty-five minutes from the moment he pulled a gun on armed officers before they accepted defeat. Their determination to preserve human life was in stark contrast to his contempt for theirs.

I will never forget the mid-afternoon text from my deputy and good friend Superintendent Steve Whitton. 'We found Fitz-patrick. We've shot him and it's not looking good.' Brief and to the point.

It took my breath away. The Divisional Commander for West Sussex, Steve Voice, had recently overseen the aftermath of a fatal police shooting in the village of Fernhurst on the Sussex–Hampshire border. From his experience, he penned a guide to our role following such an event. It became my bible.

Managing the impact on officers and the community was a commitment that continued from the moment of the shooting right through and beyond the inquest. Initially, issuing any public statement was the domain of the Independent Police Complaints Commission who rightly investigate when people are killed at the hands of the police.

It was imperative that we were able to include something in those initial press releases to indicate that the man who had been shot was armed and dangerous and that the police had been threatened. The diplomacy of Steve Whitton in getting two small but significant references into the media statement – that the dead man was wanted for armed robberies and that a non-police-issue gun was found near his body – had the effect of practically eliminating any ideas that trigger-happy cops were cruising the streets of Brighton shooting at will, which may otherwise have prevailed.

At the subsequent inquest, it was established that the gun was an airgun. This only become apparent after the gun was closely examined. The armed officers had no chance of knowing this when it was aimed at them. It was also revealed that Fitzpatrick had told a friend he'd rather be dead than go back to prison. The jury returned a lawful killing verdict, and noted that Fitzpatrick had probably died within two minutes of being shot. They found, too, that the officers had been forced to make that split-second decision to protect the lives of the public and themselves. Their conduct was described as exemplary.

Lots of public meetings, briefings to elected and executive officials and MPs, painstaking preparations for the inquest and IPCC report and convening Independent Advisory Groups became a huge part of my job. Apart from a couple of examples of injudicious statements in the media, the impact of this tragedy on the life of Brighton and Hove was minimal.

It's not always that way. The press can take delight in writing thousands of words and many column inches dissecting a decision that an individual cop has had milliseconds to make. Anyone can be wise in hindsight; my former colleagues rarely have that luxury.

16: HELL HATH NO FURY

Thirty-five-year-old Canadian 'action man' seeks professional white single female between thirty and forty for companionship, days out, holidays and possibly more! Must be willing to tolerate 'Walter Mitty' personality, hidden violent background, refusals to accept rejection, obsessive stalking, psychological torture, arson and plots to harm you and your family.

If only people could be this honest. If only Dr Alison Hewitt had had this insight into the new man in her life from the outset. Much the same goes for Red Westwood, besotted with her lover turned would-be killer, Bryce Laurent, in *Want You Dead*. Had she been given a glimpse beneath his phony immaculate veneer then surely she would have chosen a different path. One that did not involve the complete destruction of her and her family's life.

DCI Nev Kemp worked for me as the Head of Crime for Brighton and Hove. He had been a friend for years and I had mentored and supported him into CID and up the promotion ladder. I had recognized his talent and potential and, when I retired, he succeeded me as Divisional Commander at Brighton and Hove.

Nev was a grafter who had a knack of separating the wheat from the chaff. He had a fabulous eye for detail and could scan the dozens of crimes reported each day and pick out those that might come back to bite us.

As the only other senior officer in the city with a CID background, he felt safe using me as a confidant in those decisions that were not always clear-cut. Professionally and personally I was glad to help; command can be a lonely place. I saw myself as Chief Superintendent Jack Skerritt to his Roy Grace.

The arrest of Al Amin Dhalla leapt off the page at him. It seemed a relatively low-level incident, in the scheme of things, but something about it made him worry.

'Graham, I'm not happy about a job that's come in. Can I just run it past you to check my thinking?' he said as he entered my office one morning in March 2011, gently closing the door behind him. 'It's a stalking job but I think it's going to blow up into more than that.'

'Tell me more.' The very term stalking grabbed my full attention. These cases were never easy and too often dismissed as minor irritations.

Early in my career, I had great hopes to be part of a change that would finally protect people from the horrors of obsessive behaviour. As Staff Officer to ACC Maria Wallis, I had been at the centre of devising anti-stalking laws under the Protection from Harassment Act 1997. Unfortunately, as is sometimes the case, the police, through clumsy implementation, watered down the effect this Act was intended to have and countless victims were left unprotected.

You have probably never heard of Aston Abbotts. That would not be surprising; it's not fame that its 500 residents crave. A scan of its website depicts a charming Buckinghamshire village which appears to be struggling with its transition from a nineteenth-century self-supporting agricultural community to an idyllic rural retreat for professional townspeople. Nothing illustrates this better than its boast of being home to 'one pub, one church and one helipad'.

What a joy it must have been for Alison Hewitt to be brought up in such a lovely little village, even with its issues with incomers. Despite the sad death of Alison's father, her mother, a former probation officer, saw that she and her three younger brothers, Mark, Paul and Dave, wanted for nothing. Alison's ambition to read medicine and qualify as a doctor was nurtured by her perfect Middle England upbringing in this quaint spot. Life was safe, life was good.

The horrors that would befall Alison, however, could have come straight from the pages of a Roy Grace novel. The twists, the turns, the chase, the bluffs, the sheer adrenaline that this real-life nightmare entailed prompted many to question: which is stranger, fact or fiction? The eventual publicity that followed this case, including a gripping Channel 4 documentary 'Living with My Stalker', was among the inspirations for Peter to write *Want You Dead*, to highlight the horrors of stalking and to promote the domestic violence charity the White Ribbon Campaign.

It's no secret that the lot of a junior doctor can be tough. Long, unsociable shifts interspersed with hours of being on call, coupled with endless studying, means there is precious little time for romance. Only those who inhabit that frenetic world understand the demands it makes on tomorrow's consultants. Alison was so immersed in her work and her passion for the outdoor life that she simply did not have time for dating.

At thirty-five, however, she wanted to find the man she would spend the rest of her life with. She'd had some false starts and, frankly, craved a short-cut to happiness. Unlike Red's preferred route to find love, she did not fancy the idea of online dating. She wanted more control; less chance of landing a weirdo. A friend recommended the London-based Executive Club dating agency. Since it catered for the more discerning professional, she felt safe. Even if she didn't find Mr Right, at least she would not end up with some nutter who would not take no for an answer.

Al Amin Dhalla had been a member of the agency for a while. As a thirty-five-year-old Canadian accountant who had been in the UK for a number of years, he seemed quite a catch. Other than being perhaps a little too generous with his first date gifts, nothing about him had rung any alarm bells with the agency. He appeared to be a most eligible bachelor. His introduction to Alison could easily have been yet another success story for the Executive Club.

Alison lived in a small, anonymous rented flat just a short walk from the Royal Sussex County Hospital where she worked. Her and Al's companionship, to start with, was unremarkable. Given her punishing schedule, they would spend what spare time she had enjoying trips out in London, romantic walks along the Brighton seafront or just nestling up together in her flat. He seemed genuinely charming and his knowledge of history, castles and films fascinated Alison. They established a routine of him travelling down to the city from his Croydon home to spend their weekends together.

Soon afterwards, as part of her training, Alison started a placement at the Accident and Emergency Department, which meant less predictable shifts often leaving her completely exhausted. This irritated Al, especially as his weekend visits would often be to an empty flat.

His solution was to propose that he move in with her and effectively be her house husband. It was all a bit quick for Alison, so she gently rejected his kind offer. However, she started to notice more and more of his possessions were stacking up in her cramped apartment. Her objections and his reassurances changed nothing; his clutter kept coming and coming.

Eventually he finally admitted that he had let his London flat go and had effectively moved in. Angry but boxed into a corner, Alison felt all she could do was negotiate that he support her with the rent. She implored him not to make big decisions like that again, at least not without a discussion. With an apology, he meekly agreed.

Fourteen years after losing her first husband and the father of her children, Pam – Alison's mother – was soon to marry the man who had brought meaning back into her life: defence contractor David Gray. The whole family were looking forward to him becoming stepfather to Alison and her brothers. The wedding was to be a celebration of a new chapter in her mother's life.

Al insisted that this would be the ideal occasion to introduce him to the family, especially as two of her brothers lived abroad. This was a rare opportunity, as all the Hewitts would be in one place.

As Alison was to be her mother's bridesmaid, Al was paired up with her grandmother, Peggy, so he was not left alone. During the day he was most affable, chatting easily to Peggy and other guests, moving effortlessly among them. He enchanted them with his derring-do past and his multifarious achievements.

To Peggy, he confided in fine detail the tragic death of his parents in a horrific car crash of which he was the only survivor. The verdict from the gathered well-wishers was that Al was charming – if a little intense – and that he had coped well, considering that meeting all the family in one go must have been quite overwhelming.

Peggy thought otherwise, however. His resistance to her gentle yet rapier interrogation caused her to conclude that he was hiding something; he had a big secret. More than once, after the event, she warned Pam, 'This is not the man for Alison.'

Not long after the wedding, Pam treated her four-year-old grandson to a visit to the seaside to see his Auntie Alison. During a meal at a seafront restaurant, Pam gently questioned Al about the tragedy that had so scarred his childhood. Instead of an emotional skate through the events that orphaned him at such a tender age, he painted a gruesomely detailed picture of a raging fire, the stench of petrol and the screams of his dying parents. His clinically detailed, emotionless testimony convinced Pam that Al was lying.

The Accident and Emergency shifts were starting to take their toll and Alison felt she needed some proper time with Al.

They decided on a romantic getaway to the Greek island of Ski-athos. Having selected the date and hotel, Alison got online and made the booking. It was while she was entering the passport details that she noticed something odd. Al was, in fact, five years older than he had maintained and had only been in the UK for two years not the five he had previously said. She immediately asked him for an explanation and he apologized, explaining that he felt that to tell her his true age might have put her off him at the get-go. She accepted this white lie, smelling no rats, and they flew off to Greece.

Sun, sand and sea provided the perfect relief from those punishing shifts. However, on her return from snorkelling one day, another of Dhalla's unwelcome surprises awaited her.

As she dried off she noticed him grinning like a Cheshire cat next to a freshly built sandcastle. For some reason, she mischievously kicked the castle over only to reveal a black box buried in the powdered rubble. Her heart sank as she flipped the lid. The contents glistened.

They had talked about this. He had quizzed her about ring sizes. He had hinted about marriage. She thought she had been firm in her rebuffs and had made it clear. Apparently not.

'Alison, will you marry me?'

Her stomach was in turmoil. What had he not understood? Why was he putting them both through this? Once again she gently but firmly refused his misplaced offer.

His reaction to yet another rejection was pitiful. He behaved like a scolded child so, to appease him, Alison reluctantly agreed to briefly slip the ring on her fourth finger. Of course it fitted, of course it was stunning but there was no way she could keep it.

Sheepishly, he gathered up the box and slipped it away, out of sight but not out of mind. The rest of the day was a series of awkward silences, both of them walking on eggshells. She assumed that Al was wallowing in humiliation. She felt for him. He, on the other hand, like *Want You Dead*'s Bryce when confronted by Red's first rejection, was burning with rage. You don't treat men such as Al and Bryce like that. If you try, you will learn the hard way.

Meanwhile, Peggy's warnings coupled with her own suspicions induced Pam to dig a little further into this enigma. During a call to her son Dave in Australia, he admitted that he had seen no reason to be wary but promised to play around online to see what he could come up with.

To his surprise, Al had been busy. A simple internet search uncovered a breathtakingly arrogant website which purported to catalogue Dhalla's claims to various athletic, military, charitable and educational accomplishments. Titled 'The Memoirs Of Al Dhalla (His Legacy And Contributions To Society)' it read like a *Boy's Own* sketch of a swashbuckling modern-day conquistador. Worryingly too, it paraded several, clearly staged, photographs of Dhalla with various women who he proclaimed were former girlfriends. Of most concern were nearly forty snaps of the woman he described as his fiancée. The woman who had gently rejected his proposal on those silver Greek sands.

Pam became more and more determined to protect her daughter from this man who at best was delusional, at worst predatory. Never had she thought she would need to immerse herself in the murky undercover world of secret surveillance, but never had she feared for her child like she did now.

Having researched extensively, she eventually found a private eye who she felt might fit the bill. After some mutual jousting to test each other's credibility, Pam decided that Elliot was the detective who would be charged with unmasking Dhalla for what he was. She had been mildly surprised that she would never meet him in person, but he appeared thorough and the fact that he had contacts in Canada seemed ideal.

Al's behaviour was becoming increasingly possessive. Despite the clear rejections of his marriage proposals, he persisted in his determination to get Alison down the aisle. Having been confronted by her about the website, he casually fobbed her off. He was by now starting to show a darkly offensive and condescending manner to others when he did not get exactly what he wanted. Alison brushed all this to one side. She had bigger worries, as there was an investigation at work following the death of one of her patients that was causing her great concern.

In October 2010, Alison and Al were invited to join David and Pam on a short break to their villa on the Costa Blanca in Spain. Around this time Elliot had revealed that he was convinced Al was not the orphan he purported to be. He was sure that Dhalla's passport would confirm that.

One afternoon, while Alison and Al were out for a walk, Pam and David seized the moment and after a brief search they found what they were looking for. The pages of Al's blue Canadian passport revealed not only his fictitious age and the lie about how long he had been in the UK, but that the aunt he had talked so often about, Gulshan, was in fact his mother. The whole car crash story had been a sickening sham.

After about half an hour, Alison and Al arrived back at the villa. As they put their stuff back in their room a sixth sense overcame Al. Something told him that all was not how he left it. Darting straight to the bedside cabinet, he became incandescent with rage. Someone had been messing with his papers. Someone had been snooping.

A furious row followed with Dhalla shouting and swearing, alleging all sorts of breaches of trust and declaring his hatred of Alison's parents. He was uncontrollable. Alison had not seen this side of him before. It scared her but still she tried to placate him. After all, she knew of none of her family's suspicions so saw his accusations as bizarre.

Al's anger intensified over that day and into the next. His rage saw him crashing furniture around their small bedroom. Alison persuaded him to take a walk with her to cool off but still he remained incandescent, lashing out at thin air. Even sleep did not pacify him. At 5 a.m. Alison was awoken by him venting his temper again. Efforts to mollify this spoiled child were wasted.

Pam and David decided they needed to confront Al with what they had found. They tried to tell him that they knew he was lying and that they were worried about their daughter. Nothing they said made him see reason.

Inconsolable, the fuming Dhalla grabbed his belongings, stuffed them into a bag, stormed out of the villa, jumped into a taxi and headed for the airport. Seeing that Alison deserved some explanation, Pam and David sat her down and gently told her all. They delicately took her through Peggy's warnings, their suspicions, the findings of the private detective and now, the proof they had that Dhalla was a liar.

While confused and angry, Alison remained blind to the risks that Dhalla posed. She felt there had to be a reasonable explanation but it now dawned on her that Peggy had been right; Al was not the man for her.

Once back in the UK, Alison confronted him with what she had been told. He had already admitted lying about his age and his time in the UK but now he finally confessed that the whole orphan story was also made up. So distraught was he over his troubled and fractured family that to the outside world he had effectively airbrushed them from his life, re-designating his mother as his aunt. He said he had been telling this story since he was a little boy as a way to stop people asking too many questions.

Al knew he had to let Alison in on some more of his secrets if he was ever to make her his bride. To her horror, he revealed that he had a dark and violent past. Depicting himself as the victim, he described how, in self-defence, he'd hospitalized an uncle who was attacking him. He tried to justify the fact he'd grabbed a kitchen knife and used it by saying he had finally found the courage to stand up for himself. However, given his uncle's injuries the court was left with no option than to imprison him.

As time passed, Alison was starting to make concerted efforts to split up with Al but he simply refused to move out of her flat. It was becoming unbearable. She was worn down by his intransigence together with the pressure brought by the investigation at work.

She desperately needed to get away and recharge her batteries. In better times, they had booked a holiday to Canada, so she agreed to keep to those plans and use the break as an opportunity to rest.

Being stalked and intimidated saps so much spirit from victims that they often do things that look odd to those observing from the sidelines and to themselves looking back. Alison described it when she advised me on this chapter as 'dumb in hindsight' but she was burned out and in desperate need to get away from it all – even if it was with Dhalla. While there she met the woman Al had by now admitted was his mother.

Back home, Elliot was revealing to Pam all the dreadful facts he had learned about Dhalla. The man had served at least two prison terms, had a history of violence including, as recently as in 2006, using a knife to assault his uncle. He was banned from possessing weapons in his homeland and had been barred from entering the USA. Pam shared Elliot's worries that the trip to Canada might be a ruse to engineer Alison's kidnapping.

Despite those fears being unfounded, on the couple's return to the UK their relationship was going from bad to worse. Warnings, which had been coming thick and fast from Pam, were starting to come true.

Alison's renewed vigour since the Canadian holiday had given her the strength to try to get Al out of her flat once and for all. Despite this, she was becoming aware that he was reading her emails and texts, as he seemed to know her day-to-day movements.

During a busy Christmas Eve night shift, following yet another attempt to get through to Al that the relationship was over,

Alison returned to find all the festive decorations ripped down and her degree certificate destroyed in the dustbin. He later denied this but Alison is positive in her claims and there seems no reason to doubt her.

Even visits by the police, triggered by Pam, and an enforced eviction by David and Alison's brother Paul did not stop Al's obsessive behaviour. This time it was through the cynical use of silence.

As any stalking victim will confirm, the terror never lets up. The acts themselves are appalling but the anticipation and the fear of what will happen next are equally sinister. He piled on the pressure by doing nothing for a while.

When he broke cover, it was a multi-pronged attack on the reputations and characters of all who had crossed him. A letter to the hospital accusing Alison of murder and theft of drugs was the first twist of the knife. In letters to those he had celebrated with at Pam and David's wedding, he accused the whole family of drug dealing, possession of weapons, domestic violence, using prostitutes and failing to bury Alison's grandfather properly. The accusations were as diverse as they were ludicrous.

On their own, these attempts to turn loyal friends, colleagues and employers against such decent people as the Hewitts would be laughable. However, each poison pen letter hurt. The family tried to remain optimistic, hoping that life would settle down once his rage had burned out. If only.

Guessing that Pam and David had employed a private eye, Al did likewise, securing the local services of Tony Yates. Unlike Elliot's brief, Tony's was not just to find out information. It was to watch Alison twenty-four seven. See where she went, whom she met and what she did. That was pretty standard. When the requests escalated to asking him to get her to confess who she'd had sex with recently and whether David used prostitutes, Yates became suspicious and refused.

Reality had now dawned on Alison and she knew it was time

to involve the police. She had already tried obtaining an injunction but, curiously, this failed as she could not provide a current address for him. Alison had produced a stack of incriminating letters from Al, which were more than enough for us to launch an investigation from. She had suffered so much, as so many do before they go to the police. I am always astounded by what people will go through before they think they can report it. We never really get across well enough that no-one has to put up with violence, abuse and intimidation. The thresholds for police intervention are surprisingly low. Despite what people imagine, there really are no 'more important things' for us to be getting on with.

Thankfully, one of Brighton and Hove's finest and most sensitive detectives, Emily Hoare, now had a grip of this case and would be part of Alison's life for the next critical months, providing her a vital lifeline.

Nev had clearly got his head around this harrowing and haunting case. He had ramped up the police activity and ensured that he would now be kept personally informed at every turn. He brought me up to speed with what we knew now and what we were doing about it.

Frustrated by his world collapsing around him, Al was now trying the more direct approach. Not quite as direct as *Want You Dead*'s Bryce however. There were no incendiary bombs in supermarkets or mysterious Queen of Hearts drawn in the shower room condensation but his tactics were no less petrifying.

Just when Alison had assumed Al would be keeping his distance, one Sunday in March 2011, as she was leaving for work, he appeared bold as brass at her front door.

Ever the optimist, Alison decided to agree to his request to 'just talk' but on the strict condition that the conversation would last only as long as the short walk to the hospital and then that would be the end.

He managed to convince her that he had moved back to London and had pawned the rejected engagement ring. He tried to assure her that he had got the message and just wanted to know where it had all gone wrong. Alison didn't want that conversation; she was determined for him to hear loud and clear that he was ruining her life.

Beneath that facade of acquiescence, however, the embers of Dhalla's wrath had ignited once more. He upped his campaign against Alison and her friends with various out-of-the-blue visits. His ingenuity in finding ways to harass her knew no bounds. Discovering her work pattern to plan when to target her and inviting himself to her friend's wedding 'as a romantic surprise' were just two ways by which he turned the screw.

His scariest act to date, however, was waiting at the end of Alison's driveway for her to get home and, picking his moment, leaping in through her unlocked passenger door. Terrified, she crunched the gearshift into reverse and drove onto the main street, parking next to a coffee shop, as she was confident that he was too smart to become violent in the public gaze.

As if completely oblivious to the effects of his actions, while Alison trembled in the driver's seat, he calmly announced he had tickets to Leeds Castle and would she like to come?

She persuaded him to get out of the car on the promise that she would see him a few days later. As he appeared to have fallen for this, she called the police. Recognizing the urgency of her plight, our response was swift. Unfortunately, despite a thorough search, Dhalla was nowhere to be found – although the officers told Alison they thought they glimpsed him getting onto a bus nearby but were unable to confirm it.

Alison's feigned promise to see him again provided a fabulous opportunity for the diligent officers. While the search for him continued and warnings were added to her address record at the Force Control Room, a plan was hatched.

That Monday, for once, it looked like Dhalla was running

late. The best-laid plans can be blown out of the water by an unreliable target, as happens occasionally. However, soon enough Al rapped on Alison's door. He was expecting a fair-haired professional to open the door – just not that the person would also be six foot tall, wearing police uniform and going by the name of Rick.

After a pathetic protest he was handcuffed, marched away to a waiting car and driven off to the cells. As with many so-called brave inmates of the cells at Brighton Custody Suite, once safely behind the cell door he effed and blinded and, with complete futility, tried to crash his way through the four-inch metal door.

He was eventually released on bail on the condition that he did not contact Alison or enter Sussex. As Nev briefed me, I sensed that he had little optimism, that this would dissuade Dhalla from his relentless campaign of terror.

'So you see, he is heading towards some kind of endgame scenario,' he told me. He was certain that Dhalla was not going to stop until he died or went to prison. From the days when Nev had been my deputy, when I was head of public protection, we both knew these types. Evil personified.

'Go with it, Nev, and don't spare the horses. You are right, he is building up to something. Your job is to stop him. Whatever you require, you've got it. If you need me to open doors to get it, just shout. Keep me informed day and night.'

Not long after, Nev's fears were confirmed. On Mother's Day, a sharp-eyed farmer 120 miles away in Wiltshire reported a man firing weapons in his fields. Erring on the side of caution, armed police were dispatched. It takes a lot to spook firearms officers. They are tough, fit and very well trained. However, when they approached this particular shooter, something made them feel so uneasy that they discreetly lowered their hands to hover over their pistol grips.

Introducing himself as Al Amin Dhalla, his icy stare pierced straight through them. His answers were brief, his whole aura chilling. He explained he was 'just doing some target practice' with his crossbow. Crossbows are deadly weapons and take expert handling if you want to make a clean kill. Bryce honed his accuracy skills by shooting watermelons while preparing to assassinate Grace at his wedding just as Al had been practising with silhouette targets in this remote meadow.

The search of his van told a sinister story. He wouldn't explain the hammer, blowtorch, goggles and high-powered air rifle they found. Nor would he account for why the van had been modified in such a way that someone inside could move from front to back, or a person could be locked there unseen from the outside. There was even a grille fitted through which a weapon could be fired. As for the addresses, including the ferry terminal to Lundy Island, saved as favourites in his satnav, he was saying nothing.

His choice of weapons had been clever. While deadly, none were illegal. Only his trespassing and out-of-date Canadian driving licence gave the officers grounds for arrest, but it did allow the van and his murderous arsenal to be seized. Despite all the background information from Brighton and the excellent case put forward by Wiltshire Police and Crown Prosecution Service, the charges were at the very lowest end of the scale and the magistrates released Dhalla on bail with the condition that he lived at a particular hotel. In many ways their hands were tied. Dhalla, on the other hand, couldn't believe his luck.

Nev strode round to my office with an inevitable update.

'Dhalla has left his bail address. I'm certain the target practice was so he could wreak revenge on the Hewitt and Gray families. The addresses in the satnav show he has an interest in Aston Abbotts. My single most important objective now is to protect Alison and her parents. It's a race against time. We can arrest him for breaching his bail but I wouldn't bet on him being remanded for long on that charge. We've now got at least three forces involved. I don't really know where he is or when he will strike next, but it is a *when*, not an if.'

'OK,' I said. 'Are we still the lead force? I wouldn't want any ambiguity about who is in charge to allow anything to fall between the gaps.'

'Yes. I'm the SIO and I am getting great co-operation from the other forces. Everyone sees the risk.'

'Well done. Make sure it stays that way. Would you like me to brief the ACC, given it's cross border?'

We all know that can be a thankless task, through Grace's experiences with ACCs Vosper, Rigg and the odious Pewe. Thankfully, my bosses were far more approachable.

'Oh yes, if you don't mind, thanks. Tell him too that if it becomes a firearms job here, Superintendent Steve Whitton is Gold and Chief Inspector Jim Bartlett is Silver.' I was most relieved. Steve was the best commander the force had, and my deputy at Brighton, and Jim, as well as being a fine leader, is my stepbrother.

Nev's eagerness was tempered with just the right mix of anxiety. He was leading a battle of wits to predict and prevent Dhalla's next move: a fight to protect three innocent lives from a hunter so driven, so focused, that it seemed he would stop at nothing until he had his prey. The stakes couldn't be higher.

The first step was to break the news to Alison that Dhalla was free once more, robbing her of the sense of security she had enjoyed for just one day. Strict measures were put in place to protect her but no-one knew where Dhalla was or what his next move would be.

Alison had mentally mapped out her flat, estimating where her best chances of survival or escape lay. It was not easy. He had lived there. He knew every nook and cranny. Any hiding place would be futile to a hunter as determined as he. She was terrified. She wondered when and how he would get her.

She opted to spend what would be a sleepless night under

the kitchen table. Nerves wrecked and weeping uncontrollably, she found her heart was racing. How was she going to get through this? She had a life to lead, patients to care for. When would this terror end? At least her parents had decided to get away from it all to the safety of their long-planned holiday on Lundy Island in the middle of the Bristol Channel.

She felt exhausted; she could not continue like this. At times she wished he would find her and something, anything, would happen that would end the nightmare one way or another. She knew her kitchen table shelter would offer little protection or refuge but it might, just might, buy her time.

In the small hours she was awoken from a shallow doze. 'Open up, police, open up!' came an insistent shout, as the flat was lit up by a sweep of blinding torchlight through the thin curtains.

Terrified and struggling to place the voice, she edged towards the door, her fingers about to punch out 999 on the phone that never left her side.

'Alison Hewitt?'

'Yes,' she confirmed, having now placed the voice as that of Rick, her blond six-foot saviour from before.

Relieved, she let them in. She sensed that something had happened that might draw all this to a close.

'Someone's set fire to your mum's house,' came the bomb-shell.

'What?' was all she could manage in reply, a thousand scenarios going through her exhausted mind.

'You need to come with us. Back to the police station. You'll be safe there.'

As she grabbed what she could in the short time the insistent officers allowed, they explained that it was almost certainly arson. The whole perimeter of the house was a ring of fire with the front and back doors ablaze.

Alison slouched, shell-shocked, in the back of the police car during the short drive to Brighton Police Station. She knew that she was as safe as she could ever be right now, but still her instinctive fear that Al would pounce from nowhere was never far from the surface.

Once inside the fortress police station, she spent the next hours learning about events as they arose, and revealing, under the gentle skill of Emily Hoare's questioning, the fine details of her life with Al.

The whole family was at risk, but Paul's nomadic lifestyle and the difficulty even Alison had in contacting him, reassured the police that he was probably safe from Dhalla. Pam and David, on the other hand, were clearly in his sights.

Strict procedures kicked in to ensure the likely targets were protected as far as possible. Potential victims are sometimes served with notices called Osman warnings. These set out the risks, what the victim can do and how they should co-operate with the police to protect themselves. Carly Chase's version is set out in *Dead Man's Grip* and demonstrates the impact such a notice must have. Some accept them. Others, like Red, are more reluctant to change their habits in the interests of survival.

Long-term measures take some time to put in place. Therefore, the default in an emergency such as this is for those at risk to be whisked away to police stations. Hence, Alison being safely ensconced in the largest one in Sussex. The race now was to get Pam and David somewhere safe; even their choice of isolated holiday island seemed to be known to Dhalla. Efforts to contact them on their mobile phones to warn them of the threat came to nothing. Fears were growing that he had already struck.

The stark reality was, though, that up until now, Al could only have been arrested for the minor offence of breaching his bail. The fire changed all that. It was now a case of finding him before someone was killed.

He was so resourceful that he could easily strike again and that could be whenever, wherever and at whomever he chose.

He was calling the shots. This was as intense as Grace's hunt for Dr Crisp in *You Are Dead*.

Thames Valley Police had discovered, to their horror, that a neighbourhood police office near Aston Abbotts had been set alight around the same time as Alison's mother's house. Luckily again, it was empty but given that fires rarely happen in that area, the two blazes within hours of each other just had to be linked. Dhalla was running amok since his release from custody in Wiltshire.

A bleary-eyed DCI Nev Kemp was called in and started co-ordinating the race to catch this madman. The crosshairs of Al's hate were shifting between Alison and her parents. Nev knew they all needed protection and needed it now. Eventually he was told that an officer had finally managed to speak to a hotel receptionist on the Island and Pam and David were safe, for now.

Nev picked up the phone.

Devon and Cornwall Police leapt into action the second Nev finished the call. In scenes more akin to a James Bond movie than Middle England tranquillity, a team of heavily armed officers dressed head to toe in black combat gear were air-dropped through the early morning mist onto Lundy. They sprinted to a waiting David and Pam who, having been alerted earlier, were cowering behind their door. Briefed by a gruff officer they grasped the danger they were in.

Minutes later they were being rushed across the dew-soaked lawn towards the waiting helicopter. Some of the crack police team leapt into the chopper seconds before take off. Others had already secreted themselves around the mainland ferry station as Nev could not be sure Dhalla wouldn't be there waiting for Pam and David.

While this military-style operation was unfolding in the Bristol Channel, Alison was still outlining her life history to Emily and her gentle-giant sergeant, Colin Jaques. They were establishing that Dhalla had free and ready access to all Alison's emails and texts – how else would he have known when and where she would be?

The decision was taken that she and her family would be hidden away in a quaint little hotel along the coast in sleepy Eastbourne. They would check in under false names and no phones or credit cards would be allowed. Their survival depended on no-one knowing who or where they were.

Back at Brighton Police Station, another threat hit Nev like a bolt from the blue. He shared his concern with his second in command, DI Jon Wallace.

'Christ, Jon, you know we've turned the tables on ourselves.'

'Sorry, Nev, not with you,' admitted Jon.

'We've gone from hunters to hunted.'

'How so?'

'I have identified a hire car he is using and it was in Brighton just hours after the fires. He must have seen the police cars we have stationed outside Alison's flat to protect the neighbours. Dhalla has shown that nothing is going to get in his way. He knows we are going to nick him if we see him. He's already torched one police office. If he knows we have got the family with us he is going to be furious. There is every chance he's going to try to get us too.'

In assessing Dhalla, Nev mirrored Grace's reflections of Bryce: *He has to win, there's no other possible option for him. He would kill her and then himself, and see that as a grand act of defiance.* This was what we were up against.

'Shit, you're right. We need to put some protection around the police station and the safe hotel. He's clearly capable of doing us some serious damage too,' deduced Jon.

Nev brought me up to speed on his latest hypothesis. We agreed that the security at the hotel would be his to manage but that I would get someone else to devise a plan for the police station. He had enough on his plate.

By now Pam and David were back in Sussex and the whole family were safely together, protected and miles from Brighton. All terrified, all hopelessly disorientated, all slowly realizing that life would never be the same again, they were effectively imprisoned for their own survival.

Nev had already dispatched a team of detectives armed with photos of Dhalla to the Royal Sussex County Hospital and its sister building, the Princess Royal at nearby Haywards Heath, where Alison was due to start her work placement on the obstetric and gynaecology ward.

Following dozens of the usual blank looks cops are used to receiving when showing a suspect's photos, a sharp-eyed nurse at the Princess Royal did a double take.

'I know that man,' she declared.

'What?' said the startled officer.

'He was here on the ward an hour ago. He said he was a new doctor. He was asking about rotas. He didn't stay long but I thought it was odd. He wouldn't make eye contact when we spoke to him and most doctors these days don't wear white coats.'

This was the breakthrough Nev needed. Finally a sighting, a clue – nowhere near conclusive but a snippet to latch on to.

Immediately the order went out to search the hospital and the grounds and to scour the CCTV. Bryce used CCTV to his advantage by trying to feign a trip to the continent. For Dhalla it would be his undoing. There on screen walking through the hospital car parks, just before dawn, about three hours after the fire in Aston Abbotts, was the menacing stalker. He had drawn suspicion at the time and there was clear footage of security guards challenging him. Not knowing his past, his intentions or that he was now wanted by police, they accepted his story of being unable to sleep and sent him on his way.

Dhalla clearly had a plan and, thinking he had struck a blow at Pam and David, he had made straight for Alison.

'Graham, we think he is hacking into her emails,' Nev declared.

'Why do you think that?'

'Well, there is no other way he would know so much about her movements.'

Playing the part of his coach, I asked, 'So what are you going to do about it?'

'He thinks he is so smart so I'm going to set him a trap.' He took me through his cunning plan.

It was simple yet brilliant. He phoned it through to Emily. She sat down with Alison and carefully briefed her. It would work only if it came from her, in her words. He would smell a rat otherwise. So she typed an email:

Hi Mum,

I hope you are well. I've finished with the police now. I'm back on duty at the Princess Royal tomorrow at 8 a.m.

Speak on your return.
Love Alison

The bait was set, all Nev could do was wait. Sensing that Dhalla would remain holed up nearby, Nev instructed that every hotel and guest house in the towns and villages close to the hospital be visited to try to smoke him out. This drew a blank; we would later discover he had driven to London as soon as the hospital security officers had confronted him.

Just as the other forces had decided before, we realized catching Dhalla was a job for the firearms boys. Steve Whitton and Jim Bartlett devised a plan of their own. Guns and hospitals are not a good mix, as we've seen, but these guys were the best in their field. If they couldn't plan a safe but sure operation to nail him, no-one could.

The following morning, the briefing of the elite Tactical

Firearms Unit had only just started when the call came through to Jim.

'Boss, we've had the hospital security on the phone. Your man is on the plot already. Just turned up in a white coat, wearing a stethoscope and carrying a clipboard.'

'Christ,' Jim shouted to the assembled throng, 'get up there now, he can't get onto a ward.'

The fleet of plain and marked BMWs hurtled towards the hospital, lights and sirens blaring. As if on cue, all the tell-tale sights and sounds of their approach were snuffed out on the outskirts of Haywards Heath in case they spooked the prey. As they glided up to the hospital entrance a pacing security guard met them.

'He's in the toilets just through here,' he whispered, awe-struck that he had a bit part in this unfolding thriller.

Three plain-clothes cops leapt from a grey BMW and followed the guard through. As he indicated where to go, they donned their fluorescent chequered 'Police' baseball caps and burst through the door. It did not take long to confirm they had their man.

'Armed police! Put your hands on your head,' snapped the team leader as all three drew their handguns, pointing them straight at Dhalla's midriff. Amazingly, even in the face of such firepower, he did not take the hint. Rather than a peaceful surrender he launched himself at the officers.

Confronted with an obviously unarmed man, they quickly holstered their weapons and resorted to hand-to-hand combat. After several minutes of ferocious fighting in the confined space, Dhalla was eventually overpowered and his hands and legs swiftly bound. A search revealed he was carrying razor blades in his pockets; he would not say why. Finally they had him. Finally Alison, David and Pam could breathe easy – for now.

Nev knew Dhalla would have a car nearby. Where was it? What would it reveal? Soon they found the vehicle Nev had previously identified parked not far from the hospital. This was Dhalla's operations centre. The search revealed a loaded cross-bow, a large knife, fuel cans, more razor blades and a fuel-soaked envelope addressed to Pam. The satnav had saved on it the addresses of Pam and David's house, Alison's flat, the hotel on Lundy Island, both hospitals and a remote nearby wood.

Dhalla's silence in interview was anticipated. He was arrogance personified. Then again, how exactly do you explain such a wicked and relentless targeting of those you purport to love? No doubt he knew he was going to be caught for what he had done but who could guess what more he was intending to do with the armoury in the van? He was charged and remanded to Lewes Prison to await his trial.

This would span a month and further extended the ordeal for Alison. Having to relive all of her terrors brought everything back. Alison and Pam had the comfort of being screened from Dhalla while they gave their evidence but that could not protect them from days of having every truth doubted, every horrific act minimized and their integrity questioned at every turn. The defence, at one stage, made the mistake of questioning Pam's qualifications to label Dhalla a 'narcissistic psychopath'. She was able to gently remind the court she was a trained social worker and probation officer and had worked in both prisons and psychiatric hospitals.

Dhalla spent five days in the witness box being grilled by Richard Barton, an excellent prosecution barrister, with whom I had worked many years earlier on a murder trial. Despite being on the ropes, Dhalla couldn't resist repeating his farcical accusations of Alison, her family and their friends being guilty of murder and drug dealing. He thought he was so clever with an answer for everything. Barton's skill, however, in presenting to the jury the catalogue of terror he had inflicted left them in no doubt of what they thought of Dhalla. Seven guilty verdicts, including for arson and harassment, brought huge relief to everyone except the man in the dock.

His pleas of remorse staged for the jury were hollow. His sentencing, however, was delayed while police investigated an allegation that he and other inmates had conspired to pay for a hit man. He was never charged with that so the hearing resumed.

Sentencing him to an indeterminate prison sentence Judge Charles Kemp (no relation to Nev) explained that he might never be released, certainly not until he was deemed to no longer present a threat. Even then he would face deportation back to Canada.

Alison now works to raise the awareness of stalking so that others don't have to suffer the ordeals she did. Her book *Stalked*, published by Pan Macmillan, gives an extraordinary insight into how the terror of stalking can silently creep up on even the most astute and intelligent people until it explodes with such force as to rip apart their every sense of wellbeing. Her support and blessing for the inclusion of this story shows her resolve to highlight the evil some can inflict on others in the name of love.

Somehow, knowing what they know, living what they lived with, Alison and her family suspect that rather than this closing the book on their evil stalker, his imprisonment is merely the end of a chapter. As Grace explained regarding Bryce Laurent, 'he might not be in jail forever. He still might get out one day, and Red knows that.' So too does Alison.

All she can do is rebuild her life, learn to trust again and hope.

17: THE BEAUTIFUL GAME

Brighton and Hove Albion Football Club has attracted thousands of long-suffering, die-hard nomadic fans for over a century.

Since 1997, it has had no fewer than four homes. Until that year the club had occupied the Victorian-built Goldstone Ground where 36,000 fans would cram onto its windswept terraces. When that was sold they had to lodge with Gillingham FC 70 miles away in Kent. Two years later they returned to the city to occupy a hurriedly converted athletics stadium in Withdean. It was not until 2011 that they finally settled in the long-awaited American Express Community Stadium built, amid much controversy, at Falmer next to Brighton and Sussex Universities. The Albion's loyal supporters have followed them to each and celebrated and agonized over their highs and lows, including almost winning the coveted FA Cup in 1983 and narrowly avoiding the oblivion of demotion from the Football League in both 1997 and 1998.

Wherever the Albion – nicknamed the Seagulls – called home, Sussex Police were central to the safety of fans and the prevention of hooliganism. Or crushing it should it occur.

Football supporters are tribal by nature. Some express that through sheer naked but peaceful passion, others through violence. The trick is differentiating between the two and stopping the latter ruining the game for the former. Some clubs attract a troublesome reputation, sometimes deserved, but occasionally poor policing can turn noisy fervent fans into a rampaging mob.

When the Albion moved to the Amex Stadium, Sussex Police agreed with the club that we would surprise the fans by jointly adopting an amicable customer service model on match days. Our philosophy was that if we treated people like human beings, chances are they would behave as such.

Gone were the days of routinely herding home and away fans from the railway station to the ground. No more locking the away fans in after the match until the home fans had gone and there was no drinking ban in the stadium.

The Albion warmly welcomed visiting fans on arrival at the stadium. They beamed images of their heroes around the bars adjacent to the away stands and provided local ales, specially shipped in, for their delight before and after the game.

Grace visits the stadium in *Dead Man's Time* to flush out Lucas Daly. The state-of-the-art control room he visits, together with the excellent co-operation he witnesses between club and police, are both factors why disorder has plummeted since the Albion moved to the Amex. The added bonus is, as Grace found to his advantage, the zoning of groups of like-minded people together also allows the positive traits of one group to modify the potentially extreme behaviour of another. For example, the family area is next to the away fans, to remind them that football is a game for all.

This was a deliberate strategy. At their previous ground, the club was able to identify the rowdy fans, those who wanted just to sit and watch and those who preferred a family atmosphere. Unlike clubs in old stadiums, before the first season at the new Amex Stadium the Albion could sell season tickets in specific areas to specific groups. Rather like designing the layout of a new kitchen, they had a blank canvas on which to put sections of fans where they wanted them. Once supporters had their seat allocation, being creatures of habit, they simply re-bought the same ones each year. That, and the CCTV that was so highly calibrated it could read the time on your watch, allowed trouble-makers to be spotted and their movements tracked in an instant.

On match days, our cheery Football Liaison Officer, PC Darren Balkham, would meet and greet the opposition supporters, help them find the city's highlights, advise them on transport and even get snapped in a few selfies. Over the previous week he would have been speaking with and welcoming them through Twitter.

Darren polices Albion games up and down the country week in and week out. He is Brighton and Hove's ambassador in whichever police force area the club happens to be playing. His knowledge and authority on all matters football is second to none and few senior officers are brave or stupid enough to ignore his wisdom.

On one occasion, while I was taking part in filming the documentary with Russell Brand, Darren and I allowed my co-star to single-handedly take on fifty rowdy Birmingham City FC supporters in a chanting competition in front of hundreds of day-trippers by Brighton Pier. Given the language involved, I was relieved the cameras were not rolling at that moment.

While most fans responded to this lighter-touch policing – their websites often commented on what a joy it was to meet Sussex Police – others still wanted to fight.

The rivalry between the Albion and South London club Crystal Palace was as ferocious as it was irrational. A real hatred had built up over the years, the origins of which were mysterious. Some will trace it back to a minor episode of crowd baiting in the 1970s by Albion's then manager, Alan Mullery, but most simply don't know. In a deliberate attempt to infuriate Palace, the Albion even called themselves the Seagulls as a variation of their rival's nickname, the Eagles. Whatever spawned it, the violence it gives rise to is sickening.

By 2011 it had been nearly six years since the two clubs had met. Promotions and relegations had kept them apart and cup competition draws had been kind to Brighton and Hove Police. However, all good things must come to an end and in September battle was set to recommence.

Preparations for this match started way back in June when the fixtures were published, as we knew the simmering loathing between both sets of fans was ready to boil over. Six years is a long time to bear a grudge, but hold on to it they had.

We worked tirelessly with both football clubs, the train and bus companies, the pubs and shops, as well as our colleagues in the Metropolitan and British Transport Police. Plans were written, rehearsed and rewritten. Volumes of 'what-ifs' were worked through. We knew that we would only have one chance to get the policing of this match right and, as the Gold commander, I wasn't going to allow failure on my watch.

Once the day of the match arrived, there were early signs that this was not going to be an ordinary mid-week evening fixture. Most 7.45 p.m. kick-offs force spectators to rush home from work, throw some dinner down their throats and dash to the stadium in the nick of time.

This was eerily different. Groups of fans had started to assemble in pubs across the county from lunchtime. All within a short travelling distance of the city centre, they had arranged to meet up out of town to drink, plot and prepare for war.

This was clearly just the first phase; the tribal gatherings were allowing the warriors to get reacquainted, rousing each other for the long-awaited showdown with the enemy. It was just words at this stage, but we knew exactly what was to come.

Darren and his team of spotters were racing around the towns and villages of Sussex, identifying known troublemakers holed up in these bars, trying to predict their next move. Pre-warned is pre-armed, and with his knowledge of the dynamics of most groups who followed the Seagulls, supported by his Crystal Palace counterparts, we knew Darren would have the best chance of smoking out any conspiracies to start a fight.

As the afternoon wore on, groups from both sets of supporters started to drift towards the city centre. The ground itself is four miles north of downtown Brighton. However, apart from a country inn and a pub famed for being the domain of strictly local drinkers, there aren't many places to have a beer in that neck of the woods.

The streets around the main Brighton railway station, on the other hand, are crammed with bars. It is bewildering how many survive such intense competition, but survive they do and on match days they transform into waiting rooms for thirsty football fans.

Normally supporters are jovial, if a little rowdy, but on this day they were seething with animalistic tension. The normal banter had been replaced by muttering. Darren's presence, usually welcomed by the Albion fans, became despised as drinkers went to great lengths to whisper away from his ears.

Queens Road is the main thoroughfare from the station to the city centre. When it reaches the imposing Clock Tower it becomes West Street, the heart of Brighton's club land.

The Albion fans were in bars along Queens Road. The Crystal Palace fans had congregated in West Street's Weatherspoon's pub, just few hundred yards away. This posed a massive problem for the police.

For the visiting supporters to reach the railway station to embark on the final leg of their journey to the stadium, they would have to pass within feet of the waiting and baying Albion fans. Other routes were available, but it was proving impossible to persuade the crowd to add another fifteen minutes onto their journey when a short walk up the hill would take them quickly to their train.

We knew in the planning stage that we would need to move hordes of fans around the city, but the when and where would always depend on the dynamics on the day. The strength of any plan is in its flexibility.

Had she been a smoker, Chief Inspector Jane Derrick would have used the back of a fag packet to draft her swiftly devised orders. A seasoned marathon runner, she was unlikely to have one, but the cover of her notebook served just as well.

Jane was one of my first choice of commanders on any operation. You would pass her in a crowd but she was one of those officers who just seemed to have got better and better as she rose through the ranks. Having paused her career to bring up her two boys, she returned as an inspector to run the Hove Neighbourhood Policing Team when I was the superintendent.

Her promotion to Chief Inspector came soon after and this quiet, assured and supremely perceptive officer topped the tree of firearms and public order leaders.

She became a good friend; one of her sons helped my son Deaglan in his successful application to read Natural Sciences at Cambridge University, and I mentored her progress to Superintendent.

Jane called her unit commanders around her and showed them the hastily scribbled map of the area, setting out how she wanted to move the visiting fans and where she needed her troops. She stressed that it was essential that no pre-warning be given to the Albion fans.

This grated with Darren, whose reputation hinged on the trust and openness he showed the football community on match days. He understood though that extraordinary circumstances call for extraordinary measures – the home fans would find out soon enough what was happening.

He carried on as normal, popping into the pubs, making an effort to chat to his regulars; just being his usual genial self, setting the tone, trying to keep the mood light. His poker face gave nothing away. If they detected anything different in his manner, they would smell a rat and the result could be carnage.

The first to realize that the opposition were being escorted in their direction were the smokers. Loitering outside the pubs they spotted a mass movement in the reflection of the shop windows down the road. Flickers of the red and blue colours of Crystal Palace flashed in the huge plate glass shop fronts flanking West Street as it became Queens Road. The mirroring effect created an illusion of an army of a thousand men marching to the top of the hill.

Darren was in the Royal Standard when word spread that battle was about to commence. Not the largest of pubs, it is the most southerly of the ones favoured by the Albion fans who were to be at the vanguard of the defence.

As the crowd drew nearer, a line of police officers supported by police horses formed a cordon between the pubs and the road. The human barrier was less likely to withstand a rush than its equine back-up, but it showed our intent.

In the pub the mood started to turn ugly. The fans were fuelling each other's anger. 'They're walking past our pub.' 'What a fucking liberty. We ain't having that.' 'Come on, let's kill 'em.' Darren attempted to get through to them. As if reasoning with a stubborn child, he repeated their names and sought to get them to see sense.

If they heard his words, they ignored them. A fierce, savage force had taken them over. They were ready for a fight.

They swallowed what was left in their beer glasses. Some ordered more and downed the drinks in one gulp. Never was alcohol's illusion of invincibility more needed than now.

As the Palace supporters neared, their battle cries became deafening. This just spurred the Albion fans on even more. All had experienced a rush of adrenaline through their veins. They had waited six years for this.

Once the enemy had passed by the side street that would have provided the last chance of escape, the crowd in the Royal Standard and in pubs closer to the station rushed into the road. The hostility hurled across the police lines was vitriolic.

People who led perfectly respectable, often professional, everyday lives had turned into a howling pack, simply because another football club was in town.

Bottles and glasses intended for the Palace fans rained over the brave officers. The cry of 'Missiles' rose from the police ranks as the officers drew their batons and attempted to push back the crowd. As this happened, the officers escorting the visiting supporters broke into a trot to encourage their charges to hasten past the hostile reception committee.

The wail of sirens rose above the chants as more public order officers raced to support their beleaguered colleagues. Time was against them as the escort was nearing the bigger, fuller and angrier pubs directly outside the railway station. If reinforcements didn't arrive in time, this would be a bloodbath.

With seconds to spare, three police vans screeched to a halt in the carriageway between the Queen's Head pub and the station concourse. Normally packed with buses, taxis and cars, this, one of the city's most important arteries, was swamped by riot police. Quickly throwing themselves in a line across the road, they created a sterile area for the Londoners to pass through to reach their train to Falmer. The anger from both sides was growing and it was imperative to get all the Palace supporters into the railway station, where British Transport Police were waiting, and away.

Outside the station the line of police held, while inside the visitors were guided onto a train that whisked them off to the stadium.

With the Palace fans safely gone, the time had come for the Brighton supporters to be marched up to a separate train and away. This is the thing about football policing at its worst; so much time is spent separating opposing fans only to deliberately bring them back together later on. That said, we have more control at the Amex stadium, not least because it sits in an island flanked by a railway line, a fast road and acres of farmers' fields.

Once everyone had spilled out of their trains onto the tiny platforms at Falmer station, both sets of supporters were escorted on the short walk to the ground and shepherded into their respective enclosures, where the stewards took over. All trained to the highest level, the stewards were able to use their innate abilities to diffuse tensions, setting the fans clear expectations. Not far away, just in case, were pockets of police ready to rush in and help.

This was all so unlike our normal approach to the fans but we had to show we could deal with any threat they presented.

In the scheme of things, the game itself was reasonably uneventful in terms of crowd trouble. There were still venomous chants, threats and oaths to kill yelled between fans but the segregation arrangements were impossible to get around and any attempts to breach them would be swiftly foiled.

As full time approached, the score was one-one. For me, it could not have been better. Both teams had seen their side score, both would come away with a point, but there were no bragging rights to claim.

My mouth has often got me into trouble and as I heard the Silver and Bronze commanders issuing their orders for the post-match deployments, I couldn't help basking in the ideal result.

'One all,' I gloated to anyone who would listen. 'That'll take the wind out of everyone's sails. Ha, only a few minutes to go, I couldn't have planned it better.'

'Guv, Palace have just scored again. They are two-one up,' announced a public order tactical advisor, smirking as he watched me deflate.

'Shit.'

Hurriedly the same information was relayed to all officers. Those in the ground did not need telling. If they could not see the pitch, the crowd noise told them all they needed to know.

This was a game changer in every way, the worst possible outcome. For Crystal Palace to come to Brighton's brand new stadium and nick a victory in the dying moments would inflame the home fans into a frenzy. They would be looking for swift and brutal revenge.

As the officers were reorganized to the pinch points around the stadium and in the city, salt was ground into Brighton's wounds.

'Palace have sealed it. They've got another. They are winning three-one now, guv,' said the same advisor.

With just a minute or two to go, any hopes that Brighton would score twice and restore the status quo were dashed. We were going to have a battle, for sure.

I had already made the decision that we didn't have enough staff to hold back the away supporters until the Brighton fans had cleared, and we had been let down in our request for a special train to take the visitors off straight after the game. That meant that both sets of fans would meet on the concourses that led to Falmer railway station.

During the construction of the stadium, the station was effectively rebuilt. Originally it was intended to cope with just the placid arrival and departure of students frequenting Sussex and Brighton Universities. Its new role, to accommodate up to 26,000 jubilant or angry football supporters, required a fundamental redesign. The designers did as well as they could but certain factors, such as the nature of the track and the proximity to the main A27 road, prevented it from becoming totally fit for purpose.

To mitigate this, a network of sturdy bridges and spacious footpaths guided fans to where they needed to be. Normally this was fine as the good-humoured banter and the sense of occasion the club and police promoted was well established by the end of the game, whatever the result.

Today was different. Gloating South Londoners and vengeful Brightonians were about to have their last chance to settle old scores. The short distance from stadium to station meant that we would be decanting rival fans from the pressure cooker of the ground to the cauldron of the platforms with no cooling-off time in between.

At the end of each game Darren, together with his British Transport Police colleagues, always adopted a position on one of the bridges. From here he had a fabulous vantage point to spot troublemakers, pick up the signs of crush and, crucially, be seen by the crowds.

As they made their noisy way to the trains, the Palace supporters had to walk over that bridge to get to the side of the track allocated to them while the Brighton supporters went under it. Behind these bridges is a footpath that leads to the Moulsecoomb council estate. Many locals use this path to reach their cars that they have illegally left in the surrounding streets.

As the bulge of Palace fans reached the bridge, Darren became aware of missiles being thrown from behind him. The cops on the ground were working miracles in controlling both sets of supporters, but no-one had noticed a hard-core group slip away down the footpath.

Darren spun round and saw around twenty of his 'usual suspects' hurling stones, broken bricks and bottles at the Palace supporters on the bridge. This sparked a ferocious reaction and the Palace crowd turned as one to face their foe.

As they did so, the Brighton fans below also turned and glared upwards. Darren quickly registered that some of the debris being thrown was going over the heads of the targets and landing on the home supporters below. They, in turn, assumed they were coming under attack from the opposition, not realizing that their comrades were over-throwing.

It was obvious to Darren, and to the four officers with him, that this called for urgent action. There was no time to summon reinforcements; there probably weren't any free anyway.

He and the four others battled their way down the ramp through the thicket of angry supporters, and ran off the bridge towards the group hurling the rocks. There was not much five police officers could do but draw their batons, snarl, shout and run like hell towards the mob. This was all or nothing; if the crowd fought back Darren and his mates would be toast.

But their battle cry, their controlled aggression and the cowardice of the antagonists resulted in the group scattering like scared children into the darkness.

When they returned to the station, the train company and police had done their best to evacuate the crowds onto trains heading to Brighton city centre. We, of course, had a welcoming party there for them.

As the fans alighted at the main Brighton railway station, they were poured into yet another cauldron of fury. Thankfully, all the pubs had followed our advice and closed early, meaning that at least they could not further fuel the hatred, but this gave both sides just one focus.

We were prepared for one last confrontation, and we were not to be disappointed. As the trains spilled the fans onto the platforms, the majority had to dash to make their connections but for some the presence of their adversaries proved too tempting.

Despite the proximity of electrified rails and hundreds of tons of rolling stock, the rivals clashed once more. It was only kicking, punching and spitting, but these people, who tomorrow would be back behind their desks – we once famously ejected a City of London hedge fund manager from the Amex for disorderly conduct – became mindless morons again. We quickly crushed this and with tremendous courage separated the fighting fans.

Soon the city returned to normality but I had to contend with the post mortems in the press and from my bosses over the following days. All were reasonably satisfied, despite the idiocy we had to control.

I was blessed with supportive leadership throughout my

command at Brighton and Hove. Having a Chief Constable who was an avid sports fan certainly helped this time round, but all my bosses honoured the trust they had placed in me. Grace's experience is varied but I saw many similarities between his interaction with ACC Rigg when being briefed on an impending arrest in *Dead Like You* and the discussions I was accustomed to. His boss, through the simple use of the word 'we', affirmed to Grace that if things went wrong he would not be hung out to dry alone. Such was the backing I was lucky to receive.

Future matches between the two clubs have remained hate-filled and characterized by tribal stupidity, but it seems the fans burned themselves out that day and the levels of disorder we saw then have not been repeated since.

Much of the credit for that goes to Darren Balkham and his counterparts in London. They worked tirelessly behind the scenes to demonstrate to the fans that their lawless behaviour would not be tolerated and, to a degree, the fans have listened. Time will tell if that remains the case.

18: BATTLE OF RIGHTS

It doesn't take much to trigger a riot. A determined crowd with a subversive element mixed with aggressive policing is an almost guaranteed recipe for disorder.

In some cases, such as the UK riots of 2011 where towns and cities across the country burned and shops and warehouses were looted by rampaging mobs, the police can be caught off-guard by a mob so intent on creating mayhem and so huge in number that, despite everything, they become overwhelmed and the trouble spreads like a plague. In others, anarchy can be sparked by the two sides, police and protestors, refusing or not knowing how to communicate across the divide.

There are dozens of theories why Brighton is one of the most politically active cities in the UK. Some say it's the two universities, others its proximity to London. But whatever it is, as a cop balancing people's rights to protest while preventing looting, arson and chaos is one of the biggest challenges of policing this unique place.

Being a detective, like Roy Grace, for most of my service, I spent much of the 1990s observing the pitched battles between groups such as Reclaim the Streets and the police from a distance. Occasionally picking up an investigation into a group of protestors who had been arrested for violent disorder was about as close as I came to the action. I had actually trained as a public order officer early on, but that came slightly too late for the 1984 miners' strike and my move to CID robbed me of the chance to police the live animal export protests at Shoreham Harbour, ten years later.

However, you make your choices in life and for me the day-to-day buzz I felt catching some seriously bad people eclipsed the occasional adrenaline rush of standing on a riot line. Little did I know that in the twilight of my career I would command hundreds of officers keeping the peace at anti-war protests, student demos and major football matches.

I knew when I was promoted to Superintendent at Brighton some retraining would become necessary. Every year, Sussex – second only to London – would typically have over thirty large protest events, the vast majority being on my patch. Someone needed to take command of those and now, in my shiny new uniform, much of it fell to me.

I was up for it. It was like a rebirth; something new to immerse myself in. The thrill of planning and running a major public order incident is about as good as it gets for senior officers. The ambiguity of intelligence, limited resources, the eyes of the public firmly upon you; it is decision-making at its most critical.

Even now, I miss sitting in my office on a Saturday afternoon, advisors around me, overseeing an unfolding protest that, despite all the preparation, was teetering precariously between rowdy and riot. I loved being forced to make knife-edge choices based on every ounce of my training, experience and the trust in those around me. I knew whatever I ordered, however, would result in backlash from one quarter or another.

Too much force and the protestors and certain politicians would cry foul, too little and business owners, other politicians and residents would accuse me of running scared. The rights of the protestors inevitably conflicted with the rights of everyone else; I had to walk a thread-like tightrope.

These dilemmas were against the backdrop of the widespread criticism the Metropolitan Police experienced following the 2009 G20 protests. Some sections of the press had unhelpfully induced the public to think that public order policing was rooted in a philosophy of stifling free speech.

That is not to say there were not some dreadful things that happened in London over those few days; the death of bystander Ian Tomlinson being the worst. However, most officers aren't looking for a fight – they just want to keep the peace and their mind, body and job intact.

There was acute nervousness at the top of our organization. Roy Grace spends a huge amount of time briefing and reassuring the Chief Constable or his ACCs that he has a strong grip on his investigations. His first encounter with his new boss ACC Peter Rigg, soon after his team picked up the investigation into the rape of Nicola Taylor in *Dead Like You*, presented him with a dilemma I was often faced with: provide them with platitudes or the warts-and-all truth.

As a Gold commander of any incident, you are the person in charge; the buck stops with you. However, the Chief Officers have a right to know what you are doing. I took this responsibility as seriously as Grace does. It could be easier to tell the bosses what you thought they wanted to hear but, like Roy, I never did that. Of course it was necessary to tune into their wavelength and talk about the things that would rightly concern them rather than the minutiae. But sugaring the pill to make things appear better than they were will always come back to haunt you.

By the time I had taken on the role of Divisional Commander at Brighton and Hove in 2009, the conflict between Israel and Palestine was flaring up, austerity was starting to bite and immigration rarely left the front pages. Amid all the cuts, this was a time of growth for public order policing.

Added to this was the rise of alternative politics, nowhere more so than in Brighton and Hove. Not only did part of the city elect the UK's first Green MP, Caroline Lucas – for whom I have the most tremendous respect – but also its first Green-led council. The legitimacy of protest as a form of political engagement was burgeoning.

On a simple public order operation most of the work of the Gold commander is before the event. During the hours of meetings with the Silver commander I would set out exactly what I wanted the police to achieve. Then we would go about choosing the right people for the key Bronze roles, working out how many officers we needed in all the disciplines, consulting with the affected communities and agreeing a detailed yet flexible plan. It's actually more complicated than that but you hope, on the day, that with a fair wind it will all go like clockwork and, other than checking in at regular intervals, you can crack on with other matters.

However, it became very clear late one wintry Wednesday afternoon in 2010 that I was about to truly earn my money. Having planned the policing for what was billed as a peaceful protest through the city centre, I decided that as the operation was running smoothly I could chair the weekly Divisional Command Team meeting.

We were just debating where we would take the next round of savings from when a normally demure inspector burst in and spluttered, 'Er, Mr Bartlett. I've been monitoring the radio. I think you'd better go up to the Silver control room, it's all kicking off out there.'

In a reflex response I crashed my chair back and ran towards the nerve centre, watched by my envious colleagues, who all wanted a piece of the action.

As I dashed up the two flights of stairs, a plethora of possible disasters raced around my mind. Any hope of sliding off early today had been well and truly dashed.

We were policing a protest by students and others, following the recent announcement that university tuition fees were to treble. I knew that many local school children had decided to join the demonstration.

As I reached the Silver Suite, I burst through the doors and glanced at the same bank of CCTV screens that Grace relied so heavily on as he frantically tried to locate Red Westwood in *Want You Dead*. I could see a line of anxious-looking police officers stretched out along the Churchill Square shop fronts facing a hostile crowd.

I sensed a tension in the room, heightened by my presence. Clearly the inspector who had summoned me, in the style of *You Are Dead*'s Andy 'Panicking' Anakin, was not acting under anyone's direction.

Public Order Tactical Advisors are the Regimental Sergeant Majors in any operation. Massively experienced and politely assertive they are invariably larger than life. While they make no decisions themselves, only a fool ignores their guidance. One of the most inspiring of these was PC Jonny Reade, who was working for the Silver commander, Jane Derrick, that day.

As an ex-Army officer, Jonny knew how the rank structure worked. He respected those who made courageous decisions, especially if they sought his counsel beforehand. He knew that promotion does not bring with it absolute knowledge and that the best leaders know whom to consult, and when. His military training gave him mastery in making his succinct advice, delivered beautifully in received pronunciation, sound like orders.

His vast form blocked my path as I tried to venture further in.

'Sir, I am just wondering whether this is the optimum place for you to exercise effective *strategic* command at this very moment?' he eloquently suggested.

Before I could argue, with a broad grin he clarified, 'In other words, would you mind just fucking off for a few moments? Just a few, you understand. Silver and I will pop next door to see you just as soon as we have resolved a few issues.'

Before I could argue he held the door open for me and said, 'Thank you so much, sir, I knew you would understand.'

Now that might seem odd, but Jonny was right. When all hell is breaking loose, it is the job of Silver to sort it out. Gold, the strategic commander, can do more harm than good. He or she can confuse the command structure, their presence can distract Silver's urgent decision-making and they may be tempted to meddle. The place of Gold is at one step removed. In these circumstances Gold must let the dust settle, if only for a moment, and then bring everyone together to reassess the plan.

I quietly resolved to give them just five minutes to sort them-selves out as I waited in the poky anteroom next door. It took no longer than three.

'Right, sorry about that, Graham,' said Jane Derrick as she and Jonny joined me. 'You caught us just as we were reorganiz-ing the troops to deal with some breakaway groups who tried to storm the shops in Churchill Square. I'm concerned too that there are so many kids in the crowds, they are putting them-selves at risk.'

I asked Jane to run through what had happened and whether she had the right resources and specialist tactics available. I grilled her to make sure she still had control and was going to get the result I wanted.

'It's very stretched out there. We are being pulled in all sorts of directions. I've got some knackered Police Support Units (PSUs) and there are hours of work yet to do. Anarchists have infiltrated the march so we need to isolate them and try to per-suade the kids to go home. All that, while we allow the rest of the protestors to continue peacefully as is their right.'

As she said that, there was a sharp rap on the door. 'Ma'am,' said a PC. 'You are needed back in the room. The anarchists are making their way to the police station. Word is they are going to try to storm it.'

'Shit,' we all said in unison. All three of us, Jane, Jonny and I dashed back to the suite.

'Before you say anything, Jonny, I'm coming in so don't waste your breath.' I sensed that this was one of the times when Silver would want me at her shoulder to give her the green light for some of our heavier tactics. 'Right, Jane. Tell me what you need,' I said.

'I want every available officer outside the police station under the direction of an inspector. I want an extra two PSUs from around the force here ASAP,' she replied.

It was a no-brainer to agree to her request, but easier said than done. However, when I saw one of the radio controllers, PC Nick Andrews-Faulkner, get up from his chair I knew the spirit of being all in this together was alive and kicking.

'I've arranged a civilian replacement from next door. I'm going out to protect the building,' he announced as he departed to don his protective uniform.

I could hear the orders being echoed through phone calls, radio messages and loudspeaker announcements, all directing any available cops out onto the street.

Soon, the few remaining officers left in the police station had taken up posts at every entrance and exit. Some were more prepared than others. While there were those in the correct uniform, many of the detectives were ill-equipped for battle, but no less eager for it.

Stiletto heels and woolly jumpers were unlikely to withstand the rigours of combat but the officers were trained – albeit some years ago – and no-one was coming into *their* station uninvited.

We knew we were up against it. Radio operators were snapping Jane's orders out to those on the ground, external windows and doors were locked, CCTV was fixed on the front and rear of the nick. It was unthinkable that anyone should breach our stronghold. It would also wipe out radio control to half of the force.

As a background to the frantic radio transmissions, through

the closed windows I could hear a rumbling crescendo of roaring and chanting.

'Kill, kill, kill the Bill' suggested that these black-clad and masked activists had no interest in the rise in tuition fees. They only wanted to fight the police and destroy the city.

In no time the crowds surged into John Street and started to build outside the police station. The chanting from the baying mob was angry and urgent. Our mishmash of willing staff could not hold out for long; they needed reinforcements.

I had authorized Operation Spearhead, the force mobilization plan, and I knew we had fifty extra officers due with us imminently. They couldn't arrive soon enough.

The atmosphere in the control room was intense. The safety of the public and our officers rested squarely on the decisions we would take. It was much, much tougher out there on the streets, but the responsibility we bore to make the right choices at the right time was massive. Sussex Police does not have its own horses, we have to buy them in, and baton rounds and tear gas have yet to be used on the mainland. We only had what we had: highly trained, variably equipped and phenomenally dedicated officers.

As we tried to convince the desperate staff guarding the station that help was on its way, I heard from the street the distinctive cry of one of my old duty inspectors, Nathan Evans. Now in a training role at HQ, he never let an opportunity to come back to the city for some action pass him by. His distinctive Welsh holler signalled that the cavalry had arrived.

It was hard to work out what orders he was bellowing from three floors up, but the fact that they were followed by the yells of a terrified mob fleeing along John Street meant they were clearly working. He had corralled the willing detectives and controllers, augmented them with fresh troops from the far-flung corners of the county and gelled them into a formidable band who proved too strong for those who presumptuously thought they could overrun us.

In the nick of time we had reasserted our control of the police station. Now we could get back to singling out the trouble-makers and allowing those peacefully protesting to do just that.

After considerable discussion, I agreed with Jane's request that we should employ what was, at that time, the most contro-versial tactic available. We were going to contain the anarchists.

The Metropolitan Police had recently been berated for this 'kettling' but, properly used, it is a very effective non-violent way of suppressing disorder. I knew I would spend the next days justifying this to a scandal-hungry media, but I had a commu-nity and dozens of cops to protect.

With our strengthened numbers, we were able to isolate the anarchists and identify the ringleaders. We ensured that we found out exactly who the hard core were and gauged whether they should be arrested for any previous offences before letting the innocent go, one by one. We might want to talk to them later when we started to trawl the CCTV, so collating their names and addresses before letting them trickle out was essential.

This show of strength marked the beginning of the end of a day that, as well as the attempt to invade the police station, saw shops overrun, Brighton Town Hall put under siege and a Brigh-ton University building occupied. However, due to the effective preventive policing, just five people were arrested. More would follow, but we never let the disorder get to the point that we needed to lock up dozens of thugs as that would have tied up an equivalent number of valuable cops.

Some officers faced the anger and missiles of a minority of violent protestors for over twelve hours, and all showed remark-able resilience and restraint. There are distinct parallels between Grace's fictional world of crime investigation and its factual counterpart across all areas of policing. In *Dead Man's Time*, the hours and commitment he is expected to give to the job cause him to reflect carefully, like I did, on how he will rise to the challenge of fatherhood. Each of the officers I had deployed had families and friends who would be wondering when they would next see them and would be desperately worried for them during the conflict. Few received the accolades they deserved.

In the days that followed, the armchair critics surfaced providing their ill-informed opinions that we had been either too harsh or too soft. Some even asserted that it was our, not their parents', responsibility to scoop up the kids and take them home for their safety.

Damned if you do, damned if you don't.

This was just one of a succession of protests and marches. The opening of a factory in Moulsecoomb that manufactured components for fighter planes provided plenty more.

Activists frequently besieged the EDO MBM factory, often supergluing themselves to the railings in an effort to stop production. Occasionally the protests became more intense, characterized by violent attacks on police and wholesale disruption to the city.

Some would seek out secondary targets, such as multinational businesses, to attack. Forgetting that innocent local people worked for these firms or shopped, ate or banked in them, they would terrify anyone in their quest to overthrow the distant oligarchs who ran them.

In one particularly sickening episode dozens of children were trapped in McDonald's by a baying mob, protected only by a thin line of brave young officers denying the thugs access. The attempt to overturn a parked police van outside just added to the intensely frightening ordeal.

Early in my tenure as Divisional Commander, protestors had managed to break into the factory and cause thousands of pounds of damage. A Hove jury unexpectedly acquitted those responsible. Their defence was that their actions were justified

given that they 'had an honestly held belief' that they were preventing war crimes.

The private view of some supporters of direct action was that
the acquittal should have prompted the protest group to take
the moral high ground and become more measured in their
future activity. It was no secret that business owners, residents
and some politicians were fed up with the seemingly endless
rounds of protests, blockades and marches. For a city that
thrives on tourists, it was not good for trade.

Others, however, had different ideas.

In late 2010 a huge protest was advertised, aimed at noisily
expressing 'universal' disapproval of EDO MBM. On the face of
it, this is exactly what the police were there to facilitate. The
right to peacefully protest is the bedrock of any healthy democ-
racy and, despite what some detractors may say, our job was to
allow that to happen.

We never simply dusted off previous plans when preparing
for a big event such as this. No two protests are ever the same
and to use a previous strategy and tactics would smack of com-
placency. We would of course learn the lessons from before but
I always insisted that, despite the huge extra effort involved,
every deployment be looked at from scratch.

In *Not Dead Yet* my dual role as Divisional Commander and
Gold is expertly narrated. Peter James deliberately puts me – or
rather my alter-ego Chief Superintendent Graham Barrington –
at the centre of running fast-moving critical incidents while still
taking care of the rest of the city's policing. This was very much
as it was, and intentionally so. I worried that to parachute in a
strategic commander for a specific public order event, where
that person may have no other stake in the city's interests,
would risk a disjointed policing style and cause someone else –
me – to pick up the pieces if it all went wrong.

As Gold commander, given previous attempts to attack EDO
MBM, I instructed we seek the Chief Constable's authority to

establish a designated protest zone at the end of Home Farm Road leading to the factory. This was right next to one of the main roads into and out of the city and perfect for the purpose of a visible and vibrant protest.

Word got to us, however, that some hard-core anarchists intended to disrupt our plans. We discovered that a squat had been established in Ivy House, an old cottage nestled in the woods at the back of nearby Wild Park. Dozens of protestors were to spend the night there dossing down, enabling them to give us an early-morning surprise by approaching the factory from the rear.

Of course, we had a plan for that. As the protestors awoke that damp autumnal morning they were met with a ring of police officers encircling their temporary home. Leading this squad was Chief Inspector Jane Derrick. No accident that, once again, such a capable and charismatic leader would be the one chosen to set the policing tone for the day.

As the squatters emerged into the misty dawn chill, each was wearing a full-faced black balaclava – not indicative of people just wanting to make a legitimate political point, in my experience. Prepared for such an eventuality, Jane was authorized to order them to remove the offending masks.

This created the first stand-off of the day. Compliance in their minds would indicate capitulation. Defiance would mean certain arrest. It was likely that some planned to be arrested during the course of the day but not this early, in an isolated wood miles from the public gaze. The only cameras to play up to here were those held by the police evidence gatherers and the one fixed to the police helicopter hovering over their heads.

The Silver commander, Chief Inspector Nev Kemp, and I were in the command suite nervously watching the soundless CCTV pictures being beamed from our eye in the sky. Our bacon rolls going cold, we were transfixed by this stalemate. We could not afford to fail this first test.

I could make out Jane having an animated conversation with the group's self-designated spokesman. Her body language suggested that she was using her charm, her impeccable reasoning and her indefatigable patience to get her point across – 'You are going nowhere with those masks on.'

Numerically, we could have just swept them up and bussed them off to custody but that was not in my plan. We had to negotiate agreement and demonstrate our reasonableness. We would nick them only as a last resort but if we did, we knew it would tie up manpower that would cause us heaps of problems later in the day.

The stand-off lasted for ages. Nev, who is famed for his infectious enthusiasm, yelled, 'Just take them off and we will let you go.'

I grinned. The fact that they were still talking was a positive sign.

I detected a change in Jane's posture and tried to interpret what it meant.

The stalemate seemed to be coming to an end, but in whose favour? Had they crossed a line? Were we going in hard? Had they listened? Had we won the first round?

The spokesman appeared to turn to his followers. The line of officers took a step back. This looked good.

The evidence gatherers' cameras were pointed into the undergrowth and the helicopter climbed a few hundred feet – obviously part of the negotiation: *no cameras*.

We could no longer see what was going on but Jane's radio message said it all: 'All the masks are off and we are escorting them to the protest area.'

'Yes, get in there,' cried Nev.

'Calm down, mate,' I said 'It's going to be a long day. You'll give me a headache if you whoop every time something goes well.' Inside, however, I too was punching the air.

Despite this first victory, we knew that the rest of the day was unlikely to pass as peacefully.

Different cameras at the protest area showed that as time went by the crowd swelled. They were becoming increasingly rowdy and were taxing the resolve of the officers charged with keeping them there. It became clear that they were not going to be satisfied with staying in the pen we had provided for very long. Despite us supplying water and toilets, they wanted to get to the factory or at least test us trying to stop them.

The growing tension was relayed to Nev in the Silver Suite. The recent acquittals had changed much about our policing. We had to be even more careful that none of our officers said or did anything that would suggest we didn't, honestly, welcome and support peaceful protest.

The ground commanders had it all covered while Nev and I got our heads together to run through the contingencies. What if they got to the factory? What if they attacked a member of the public? What if a member of the public attacked them? All these possibilities needed a plan before they had a chance to happen.

Suddenly a call came from the Silver Suite.

'Boss, you are needed. They have burst out of the protest area. They are running amok.'

We dashed back in and saw a mob bolting and rampaging in all directions. Most were making for the woods that skirted the back of the factory, some were trying to head up the road towards the main gate, others were attempting to engage officers to prevent them giving chase.

We knew our inner cordon at the factory should hold but the last thing we wanted was a pitched battle in the rugged copse that bordered not only EDO MBM but also a railway line. We had earlier found paint bombs and baseball bats secreted in the woods, so knew that was part of the protestors' plan.

Nev rattled off a list of instructions: reinforcing vulnerable points, mobilizing units on standby, shifting officers from A to B.

The radio operators faithfully repeated his orders through short sharp commands, all swiftly acknowledged and obeyed.

One of the UK's most respected public order commanders, Superintendent Ian Davies, was the Bronze in charge of the security of the factory. He knew that his own reputation depended on him and his officers holding their ground.

We couldn't see everything on our CCTV screens, but the radio traffic indicated a frenzied effort by the protestors to breach the police fortifications, get through the woods and storm the factory.

It was so frustrating not being out there. Some say that people like me get promoted to avoid the front line – not a bit of it. I would have loved to be on the ground. It's what we all join for. Grace often dabbles in tasks that really belong to the lower ranks purely on the basis that he still loves the job he signed up to. It's why Ian Davies always flatly refused any indoor job on many of these deployments.

After about twenty minutes of running at protestors to disperse them, Ian's units achieved their aim and the would-be invaders scattered out of the woods onto the surrounding streets.

Unfortunately for the local communities, they spilled out not only right in the middle of the main Brighton to Lewes road, but also outside a junior school whose children had just come out to play.

It was terrifying. Teachers had to frantically grab the pupils and take them back inside to safety as the crazed mob rampaged around the area. Thugs were running in and out of traffic, jumping on cars, petrifying the occupants who were unable to escape due to the rabble surrounding them.

Our phones lit up. The public and press were demanding action. Twitter went wild with worried parents and residents desperate for us to do something. As Grace knows, especially when matters are moving fast, such as in the race to catch Bryce

Laurent in *Want You Dead*, you have to feed the media, especially social media. Ignore that basic principle and you risk the vacuum being filled by those hell-bent on promoting misinformation and disaffection. We had to do something, and be seen to do something.

'Graham. I want to nick them all,' announced Nev.

'Right. How are you going to do that and what are your grounds? How are you going to make sure you don't sweep up the innocent with the guilty?'

He laid his thinking out for me. The carnage and fear this minority were causing was simply not acceptable. The public were, rightly, demanding action. We had the grounds to arrest the most disruptive group to prevent a breach of the peace. We had the officers to do it and, with Jane and Ian, we couldn't have asked for two better commanders to make it happen.

We briskly went through the detail and, satisfied that it was justified, necessary, proportionate and achievable, I gave Nev the green light.

I heard him bark his instructions to the radio operators and in no time at all we witnessed a fabulously choreographed manoeuvre play out on our bank of CCTV screens.

Ian and Jane's officers had managed to gracefully encircle the hard core of violent protestors. The mere presence of so many officers containing them in the middle of the normally bustling main road sucked the wind right out of their sails. Like naughty school children, and doubtlessly responding to some commands that we could not hear, we saw them all sit down on the tarmac.

Soon the message confirmed what we wanted to hear.

'Forty-three in custody to prevent a breach of the peace.'

Despite the logistical nightmare this caused, it had just the effect we were aiming for. It isolated the troublemakers from the peaceful protestors. To others it showed that we would put up with disruption only to a point and that to intimidate, harass or try to break into private premises was not going to be tolerated. Those not arrested drifted away, worried they might be next.

This was a defining moment in the policing of protests at Brighton. I knew we could ill afford to continue with a style that set protestors against police. The cost and impact on the community of deploying hundreds of cops to manage what should be a peaceful and lawful activity was unsustainable.

Having heard him speak at a conference, I asked Europe's leading crowd psychologist, Professor Clifford Stott, now of Keele University, to come down and help us adopt his theory of facilitated dialogue to improve how we dealt with protestors.

Essentially this was about establishing meaningful communication with protest groups before and during events, encouraging a genuine openness about their aims and our requirements. I commissioned training for a dozen Police Liaison Officers who would undertake this essential role during each protest. I also set up a small team to work permanently on developing long-term relationships with activists. It was stunningly successful. In a matter of months we practically eliminated all forms of disorder during the dozen or so protests we policed, just by talking, listening and understanding.

Even at the next EDO MBM demonstration, a full twenty months since we had arrested those forty-three, although it was characterized by animosity and antagonism, we experienced no disorder, no arrests, no damage and no injuries.

I managed to use this evidence to persuade Chief Officers and the Police Authority that this new method should be the default style for all public order policing in Sussex. It has grown and thrived since and, through like-minded officers in this and many other forces, is now in place across the UK.

I'd like to think that I have left a number of important legacies since retiring from the police. This mature approach to protest and the more humane drugs strategy are the two I am most proud of. Both required me to think differently and – with a degree of bloody-mindedness – to persevere in getting others to think likewise. Both, I firmly believe, left Brighton and Hove in a better state when I hung up my handcuffs than it was when I had started my wonderful journey, thirty years earlier.

I know that those who follow me will have the same passion and drive to make the city even safer. It gets to you that way.

EPILOGUE

I had said farewell to my last visitor as I checked my watch: 6 p.m., Friday, 1 March 2013. The time that I had been both dreading and working towards since I was eighteen had arrived.

I gently closed the door and took a deep breath. I turned and absorbed the sights that had been my backdrop for the last four years. The office was suddenly less a place to work, more a symbol of where I had come to and what I had achieved.

I reached to my left shoulder and, with a heavy heart, slowly unbuttoned one of the epaulettes that I wore with such pride. The Chief Superintendent insignia it bore represented the fulfilment I felt. How typical that it came off far easier now than when I first struggled to fix my shoulder badges on three decades ago. Taking the right one off I placed both on what, for just a few more minutes, was my desk.

Policing had defined me for all of my adult life. I waited in vain for the lump in my throat to swell and the tears to flow. This was supposed to be emotional. In their place, however, was just an overwhelming sense of pride and of a mission accomplished.

Peter James' good friend Pat Lanigan, a detective in the New York Police Department, once said that being a cop was like having 'a lifetime ticket for a front-row seat to the best show on earth'. I could not have put it better myself. I had seen the best and worst of human nature. I had been there for people at their lowest moments and hopefully made a difference. How could I feel tearful at all that I had experienced?

I loved every minute of my career but have now moved on.

As well as writing and helping Peter with his books, I use the skills and experiences from my extraordinary vocation in other ways, supporting people, organizations and partnerships to go on protecting the good from the bad.

Julie and I can now enjoy some wonderful time together. I have been around far more for Conall, Niamh and Deaglan during the precious years as they enter adulthood. You can't have that part of family life back, so to be there before the children fly the nest has been phenomenal and immensely important.

I was very fortunate to have served with so many fantastically dedicated people and during such a period of change. So much of the technology we take for granted, DNA, the internet, CCTV and mobile telephones were confined to science fiction movies when I started. Conversely, the challenges policing now face through the explosion of drugs, cybercrime and international criminality underpinned by swingeing budget cuts, lower public satisfaction and a twenty-four-hour news media, which seeks to blame first and listen later, all make the job far harder.

As smarter criminals exploit the latest developments, such as through phishing or using the dark web, the police are forever playing catch-up. Within three weeks of Peter James and a couple of his friends setting up Pavilion, one of the UK's first internet service providers in the early 1990s, West Midlands Police were complaining that the Information Superhighway was being turned into a dirt track by paedophiles downloading child abuse images.

Many criminals and ex-criminals I have spoken to, while in the police and during research for this book, say 'I couldn't do your job', citing the abuse and violence cops have to endure and the rules that constrain them. Some of those offenders lived a very comfortable life, ill-gotten but comfortable nonetheless. Many had bigger houses, better cars and more cash in their pockets than I ever would.

The flip side though is that although they turned a blind eye to the misery left in their wake, they never knew when we would come knocking nor when the Proceeds of Crime Act would take it all away. I know which lifestyle I preferred. There is no softer pillow than a clear conscience. I guarantee I sleep better than Messrs Bloomstein, Sherry and Chiggers.

It is hard leaving a life that has defined you for so long. Not being part of something so unique and honourable takes some getting used to. The camaraderie, the unifying sense of purpose and the instinct that we would all lay down our lives for each other create a powerful bond.

I could never imagine Roy Grace, Glenn Branson or their colleagues shedding the values that define them as people when their time comes to leave. Neither have I. As the adage goes, 'You can take the man out of the police but you can never take policing out of the man.' I would still run towards danger rather than away and would prefer to give my time to help someone in need than to make a buck.

I don't regret one day of my service. Nor do I regret retiring from the job that fulfilled me and made my family so proud. I loved policing Roy Grace's Brighton. Now it's someone else's turn.

Acknowledgements

This book is the culmination of thirty years of policing combined with twelve Roy Grace crime novels. However, the experiences we both have could not have compiled such a rich compendium of policing tales without the support of a huge number of people. Some of those mentioned in the book chose to have their names changed and we will use their pseudonyms here too.

Many former colleagues have been so generous with their time and recollections of events and investigations of years gone by. Amongst the retired officers who showed that memory does not always fade with age are the real Roy Grace, Detective Chief Superintendent David Gaylor, Detective Superintendent Russ Whitfield, Detective Chief Inspector George Smith, Detective Inspector Malcolm Bacon, Detective Sergeants Don Welch and Jim Sharpe, Detective Constables Debbie Wood, Dave Swainston, Nigel Kelly, Andy Mays and Dave Cooper and Police Constable Bob Elliott. They provided substantial detail on a number of crimes and showed why each of them was a force to be reckoned with in their day.

The support from the highest level in Sussex Police, from Chief Constable Giles York QPM and Olivia Pinkney QPM, now Chief Constable of Hampshire, has been invaluable, not least in allowing David Tonkin to check the manuscript on their behalf to ensure no secrets were revealed.

Our very good friend Chief Superintendent Nev Kemp, Brighton and Hove's Divisional Commander, has been enormously helpful as has Detective Inspector Bill Warner, who was only too happy for his crazy ways to be laid bare for all to read. DS Julian Deans and PC Darren Balkham, who in their own very different ways make Brighton and Hove so much safer, have provided a rare insight into their unique worlds. Inspector Matt Webb and PC Mark White of the Police Federation have provided fabulous support in researching people and events gone by.

The courage of the victims of crime who helped cannot be underestimated. To ask them to relive traumatic events seemed an intrusion but Dr Alison Hewitt, Glynn Morgan and Fiona Perry were so incredibly helpful and we will be forever in their debt.

On the other side of the law, for some ex-offenders to happily talk to us about their exploits and the consequences of their crimes was as welcome as it was surprising. David Henty, Clifford Wake and Paul Teed were only too happy to provide a perspective that, otherwise, would have been sorely missed.

Like cops, journalists have enduring memories and see the world from a slightly different angle to that of the police and crime writers. The help of Phil Mills, Emily Walker, Michael Beard and Mike Gilson, all either currently at or previously of Brighton's *Argus* newspaper, is hugely appreciated in not only contributing to the stories but also in sourcing some of the photographs from their dusty archives.

Special thanks go to our wonderful agent Carole Blake of Blake Friedman Literary Agency, who always goes the extra mile, and to the incredibly patient and inspirational Ingrid Connell, who provided such magnificent guidance throughout the writing. Much gratitude too is owed to our editor Susan Opie, whose patience and eye for detail are something to behold. Geoff Duffield, of Pan Macmillan, deserves a particular mention as it was he who, when presented with the embryonic plan for this book, gave such fulsome encouragement and support, something he has sustained throughout. Others who have provided excellent critical reflections on various stages of the manuscript include Linda Buckley and Phil Viner.

The fabulous and energetic staff at Midas PR, especially Tony Mulliken, Sophie Ransom and Becky Short, have been brilliant in so fully and enthusiastically promoting this book,

Mostly though, for not only providing constant physical and emotional support and encouragement but also for reading and re-reading draft after draft, huge love and thanks go to our wives Julie and Lara. Julie has been with Graham on the roller-coaster of self-doubt and elation every step of the way. To adapt from a wife whose husband was mainly at work trying to cure the ills of a city he loves, to having him under her feet pulling his hair out over rhythm, syntax and grammar is no mean feat. Thank you both so much as we literally couldn't do this without you.

Graham Bartlett and Peter James

Glossary

ANPR – Automatic Number Plate Recognition. Roadside or mobile cameras which automatically capture the registration number of all cars that pass. It can be used to historically track which cars went past a certain camera and can also trigger alerts for cars which are stolen, have no insurance or have an alert attached to them.

ARV – Armed Response Vehicle.

CCTV – Closed Circuit Television. Can be either publicly owned and monitored (e.g. by the police), or privately installed in people's houses or businesses.

Chief Officer – A police officer of or above the rank of Assistant Chief Constable (in most forces) or Commander (in the Metropolitan or City of London Police).

CID – Criminal Investigation Department. Usually refers to the divisional detectives rather than the specialist squads.

Commanders

Gold (or strategic) Commander – The Gold commander sets the strategy and assumes and retains overall strategic command for the operation or incident.

Silver (or tactical) Commander – The Silver commander commands and coordinates the overall tactical response in compliance with Gold's strategy, and is the tactical commander of the incident.

Bronze (or operational) Commander – The Bronze commander is responsible for the command of a group of resources, and carries out functional or geographical responsibilities to deliver the requirements set by Silver in their tactical plan.

CPS – Crown Prosecution Service. The public agency that conducts criminal prosecutions in England and Wales.

CSI – was SOCO – Crime Scene Investigators (Scenes of Crime Officers). They are the people who attend crime scenes to search for fingerprints, DNA samples etc.

DNA – Deoxyribonucleic Acid. A molecule that encodes the genetic instructions used in the development and functioning of all known living organisms and many viruses. Used in policing to identify the source of bodily samples left at crime scenes. Generally provides a 1:1 billion certainty of the source/person.

DVLA – Driver and Vehicle Licensing Authority. The Government agency that registers motor vehicles and issues driving licences. An important source of intelligence in many enquiries.

Golf 99 – The call sign for the divisional duty inspector who is expected to take ground command of critical incidents, working usually alongside Ops-1 or to the CIM.

HOLMES – Home Office Large Major Enquiry System. The national computer database used on all murders. It provides a repository of all messages, actions, decisions and statements, allowing the analysis of intelligence and the tracking and auditing of the whole enquiry. Can enable enquiries to be linked across force areas where necessary.

Intel Cell – Intelligence cell. A dedicated team of officers and staff who provide the intelligence research and analysis to a major crime or incident.

IPCC – Independent Police Complaints Commission. Body that oversees the police complaints system in England and Wales and sets the standards by which the police should handle complaints. Will determine, in certain cases, whether the investigation should be handled locally, managed/supervised by themselves or independently investigated.

LST – Local Support Team. The standing unit of officers who provide public order, search and low-level surveillance tactics on a division. Can be drawn together to form a PSU (see below).

MIR-1 – Major Incident Room 1. One of the large rooms in the Major Incident Suite where most of the investigation team work and brief.

Misper – Short for 'missing person'.

MO – Modus Operandi (method of operation). The manner by which the offender has committed the offence. Often this can reveal unique features which allow crimes to be linked or suspects to be identified.

Ops-1 – The call sign of the Force Control Duty Inspector, who has oversight and command of all critical incidents in the initial stages.

PCSO – Police Community Support Officer. These are uniformed neighbourhood officers who work in communities but do not have police powers such as arrest, search, use of force etc.

POLSA – Police Search Advisor. A trained and accredited officer who provides advice on where to search for something or someone, and how in any given circumstance. Can be used as the Bronze commander (see above) for the search elements of an enquiry or incident.

PSU – Police Support Unit. A unit of police officers trained and equipped to deal with public order or crowded events. Usually comprises one inspector, three sergeants, eighteen constables together with two medics and three drivers.

RPU – Roads Policing Unit. The new name for the Traffic Division.

RTC – Road Traffic Collision (commonly known as an 'accident' by the public, but this term is not used as it implies no one is at fault when usually someone is).

SIO – Senior Investigating Officer. Usually a Detective Chief Inspector who is in overall charge of the investigation of a major crime such as murder, kidnap or rape.

SOCO – see CSI.

SSU – Specialist Search Unit. The team who provide expert search skills such as searching underwater or in confined places at height, as well as locations where a high degree of search expertise is required, such as large or complex crime scenes.

TFU – Tactical Firearms Unit. The small, permanently armed department of the police that responds to firearms incidents. They often deploy in ARVs (see above), and also have other specialist capabilities.

TPAC – Tactical Pursuit And Containment. Describes a range of methods for managing and terminating police pursuits, including boxing the target vehicle in using police cars and, where necessary, causing it to stop by use of controlled collision.

SLANG AND PHRASES

ABC – Assume Nothing, Believe No-one, Check Everything. The Senior Investigating Officer's mantra for maintaining an open and enquiring mindset in investigations.

Copper's Nose – a police officer's instinct. The sixth sense which often guides an officer's suspicions.

Golden Hour – the first hour after a crime has been committed or reported when the best chances of seizing evidence and/or identifying witnesses exist.

PC Rain – so called as a good downpour has a greater chance of clearing people, including drunks and criminals, off the street than any number of police officers can!

Q Word – short for 'quiet'. Emergency services personnel never say the word 'quiet', as it invariably is a bad omen, causing chaos to reign!

Shit Magnet – Slang for a police officer who seems to attract trouble and around whom disaster invariably reigns.

CHART OF POLICE RANKS*

Police ranks are consistent across all disciplines and the addition of prefixes such as 'detective' (e.g. detective constable) does not affect seniority relative to others of the same rank (e.g. police constable).

Police Constable

Police Sergeant

Inspector

Chief Inspector

Superintendent

Chief Superintendent

Assistant Chief Constable

Deputy Chief Constable

Chief Constable

* Note: these can vary between forces.

Picture Acknowledgements

All photographs are from the author's collection with the exception of the following:

Page 1, bottom, and page 6, bottom: courtesy of Sussex Police.

Page 2, page 3, top left and right, page 4, bottom, page 5, page 6, middle, page 7 and page 8, top: courtesy of The Argus.

Page 6, top: courtesy of The Argus and Sussex Police.

Page 8, bottom: courtesy of Andy Mays – Inspired Images www.inspiredphotoimages.co.uk

THE THRILLING NEW STAGE PLAY FROM
THE NO.1 BESTSELLING AUTHOR
THREE MURDERS
ONE SUSPECT
NO PROOF
PETER JAMES'
NOT DEAD
ENOUGH
Adapted by SHAUN McKENNA Directed by IAN TALBOT
COMING TO A THEATRE
NEAR YOU IN 2017

extracts reading groups
competitions books new
books discounts extracts extracts discounts events
competitions new books reading groups extracts discounts reading groups
books new
events extracts reading groups discounts events
extracts books new titles reading groups
interviews
books events extracts extracts new books
discounts new books events
events new events interviews new books extracts
discounts extracts discounts

www.panmacmillan.com

extracts events reading groups
competitions books extracts new books